GW00871196

# The Story of Malta

by

# Maturin M. Ballou

The Echo Library 2010

2

Published by

The Echo Library

Echo Library
Unit 22
Horcott Industrial Estate
Horcott Rd
Fairford
Glos. GL7 4BX

www.echo-library.com

Please report serious faults in the text to complaints@echo-library.com

ISBN 978-1-40689-627-5

# THE STORY OF MALTA

## By

## MATURIN M. BALLOU

*"This precious stone set in the silver sea"*

BOSTON AND NEW YORK

HOUGHTON, MIFFLIN AND COMPANY

The Riverside Press, Cambridge

1893

Copyright, 1893,

BY MATURIN M. BALLOU.

*All rights reserved.*

*The Riverside Press, Cambridge, Mass., U. S. A.*

Electrotyped and Printed by H. O. Houghton & Company.

## By Maturin M. Ballou.

THE STORY OF MALTA. Crown 8vo, $1.50.

EQUATORIAL AMERICA. Descriptive of a Visit to St. Thomas, Martinique, Barbadoes, and the Principal Capitals of South America. Crown 8vo, $1.50.

AZTEC LAND. Crown 8vo, $1.50.

THE NEW ELDORADO. A Summer Journey to Alaska. Crown 8vo, $1.50.

ALASKA. The New Eldorado. A Summer Journey to Alaska. *Tourist's Edition*, with 4 maps. 16mo, $1.00.

DUE WEST; or, ROUND THE WORLD IN TEN MONTHS. Crown 8vo, $1.50.

DUE SOUTH; or, CUBA PAST AND PRESENT. Crown 8vo, $1.50.

UNDER THE SOUTHERN CROSS; or, TRAVELS IN AUSTRALASIA. Crown 8vo, $1.50.

DUE NORTH; or, GLIMPSES OF SCANDINAVIA AND RUSSIA. Crown 8vo, $ 1.50.

GENIUS IN SUNSHINE AND SHADOW. Crown 8vo, $1.50.

EDGE-TOOLS OF SPEECH. Selected and edited by Mr. BALLOU. 8vo, $3.50.

A TREASURY OF THOUGHT. An Encyclopaedia of Quotations. 8vo, full gilt, $3.50.

PEARLS OF THOUGHT. 16mo, full gilt, $1.25.

NOTABLE THOUGHTS ABOUT WOMEN. Crown 8vo, $1.50.

HOUGHTON, MIFFLIN & COMPANY,
BOSTON AND NEW YORK.

## PREFACE.

Perhaps the strongest recommendation for faithful books of travel lies in the fact that intelligent people consult the best maps while perusing them, and thus familiarize themselves with important facts in geography. Such books are especially advantageous to the young, too many of whom are inclined to neglect this all-important branch of education. Although Malta appears upon the map as a mere speck, on account of its superficial area being comparatively so diminutive, yet the patient reader who is not already familiar with its absorbing story will find herein a new field of historic and romantic interest, exceeding that which pertains to any other of the numerous Mediterranean islands. In all his experience as a traveler, the author has failed to discover any locality of similar dimensions which embraces so thrilling a history, or whose present aspect is more attractive and picturesque. Since the opening of the Suez Canal, it has become the maritime halfway house between Europe and Asia, which imparts to it vast commercial importance, and causes it to be visited by many people who, but for the force of circumstances, would probably never have become conversant with its singularly beautiful surroundings, or its fascinating capital, the unique city of Valletta.

Specialists, students of antiquity, geologists, and lovers of the early development of art, together with many others, visit Malta to avail themselves of its rare old library; to view the mouldering monuments of a commercial people who lived here three thousand years ago; to examine the peculiar geological strata of the island; to study its quaint examples of statuary, tapestry, and paintings; to collect skeletons and bones of extinct races of animals, still to be found in its spacious caves and beneath the surface of the ground. The average tourist has not been attracted hither, and little realizes the pleasurable experiences which await the intelligent and observant visitor.

While preparing these pages for the press, the author has received a letter, written by an experienced traveler, from which he quotes as follows: "The reading of your book entitled 'Due North' promptly sent me to view the glories of the 'Midnight Sun,' at the North Cape. I thank you sincerely for the inspiration." Perhaps these pen-pictures of the Queen of the Mediterranean may influence others in a similar manner.

M. M. B.

# CONTENTS.

Low Wages.—Beggars.—Wind Storms.—Blood Oranges.—The Carob-Tree.—
Maltese Lace.—Sailing along the Shore.

Thoroughfares.—The Military Hospital.—Characteristic Street Scenes.— Emigration.

Malta.—Città Vecchia.—Toy Railway.—About the Vatican at Rome.—An Ancient Cathedral.—Dungeons of the Middle Ages.

of the Chivalric Brotherhood.—Momentary Revival of the Old Spirit.—
Treacherous Surrender.—French Sovereignty.—End of the Order.

Conclusion.—A Picture of Sunrise at Malta.—The Upper Baracca of
Valletta.—A Favorite and Sightly Promenade. —Retrospective Flight of Fancy.—
Conflict between the Soldiers of the Cross and the Crescent.—A Background
Wanting.—Historical and Legendary Malta.—The Secret of Appreciation.—Last
View of the Romantic Group.—Farewell.

CHAPTER I.

Geographical Position of Malta.—A Pivotal Location.—Warden of the Great Inland Sea.—First Sight of the Group.—How to reach the Island.—Early Inhabitants.—Language of the People.—Phoenician Colonists.—Arabian Dynasty.— A Piratical Rendezvous.—Suez Canal.—Two Sorts of Travelers.—Gibraltar.—Harbor of Valletta.—A Place of Arms.—Various Bays of the Group.—Dimensions.— Extensive Commerce of the Port.

The island of Malta has been known by several significant appellations during the centuries in which it has claimed a place upon the pages of history. In our day it is often called the Queen of the Mediterranean, not only because of its commanding position, dominating, as it were, the coasts of Europe, Asia, and Africa, but also as possessing a degree of historical and present picturesqueness unsurpassed by any land between the Columns of Hercules and the coast of Asia Minor. To the north lie Sicily, Sardinia, and Corsica; to the east are Greece, Turkey, and Syria; and to the southwest is the coast of Barbary; thus forming an amphitheatre of nations. Malta is therefore a pivotal location about which vast interests revolve. The loving, patriotic Maltese proudly call this shadeless island in the middle of the sea, *Fior del Mondo,*—"the flower of the world." Yet it must be confessed that the downright ignorance of these natives concerning the rest of the globe is appalling. To the critical reader of history it is as much classic ground as Athens or Rome. Situated twenty-five hundred miles from England, the government fully realizes its importance as an effective base of naval and military operations, and as an essential outpost for keeping open the route to India. In fact, Malta is the strongest link in the chain which connects Great Britain with her possessions in the East.

During the Crimean war, it was made an English sanitarium for the sick and wounded who were invalided in that protracted struggle between the Western powers and Russia. We regarded it, after India, as one of the most important of the English dependencies. It is in no sense a colony, but is much more of a military focus than Gibraltar. Naval men consider Malta to be the warden of that great aqueous expanse, embracing nearly a million square miles, which separates the continent of Europe from the northern coast of Africa, the *Magnum Mare* of the Old World,—a sea whose memorable shores are thickly strewn with bays and cities, each one of which teems with historic and poetic interest. It is not the tranquil and lake-like expanse which it is popularly considered, but is capable of nearly as fierce commotion as the Atlantic. Another property usually but incorrectly attributed to the Mediterranean is that it is tideless, but it actually responds to the same lunar influence that affects the great waters of both hemispheres. The fact of its being so much warmer than the open ocean is probably owing in part to the absence of polar currents. The tide is most noticeable in the Gulf of Venice, where the rise and fall is from three to four feet.

The author, while on a journey round the world, was coming from the East when he first sighted Malta. It was before daylight, early in the spring of the year. A ship's officer pointed out what appeared like a bright star on the horizon, but which soon proved to be the clear, far-reaching fortress-light of St. Elmo, "with strange, unearthly splendor in the glare." It seemed like the eye of a Cyclops peering through the darkness, as though one of Vulcan's workmen, fresh from the fiery furnace beneath Sicilian Ætna, not far away, had come forth to gaze upon the progress of the night.

In seeking to reach Malta from Boston or New York, the island would be approached from the opposite direction. After crossing the Atlantic to England, the most direct route is by the Peninsular and Oriental Steamship Line, by way of Marseilles. These vessels depart every alternate Thursday, and make the passage in eight days, touching at Gibraltar, forming, perhaps, the most economical route. If a land journey is preferred, the steamer can be taken at Naples, where the vessels of this line touch to receive and deliver the regular mails. This charming Italian city can be reached from London by way of Calais, Mont Cenis, and Turin. The island, however, is accessible from England and the continent by many different routes, as the fancy of the traveler may dictate.

So much in the way of introduction it seems proper to state for the information of the general reader.

Malta holds an important place in the records of history as far back as three thousand years ago, during which period the island has been constantly associated with heroic names and startling events, playing a prominent and tragic part in the mighty drama of the past. The transient visitor to the group, however well read, fails to remember its vivid story in detail, and to apply it intelligibly. He is too ardently stimulated by the unique surroundings, the strange mingling of races, the Oriental style of the architecture, the curious site of the capital, and the general glamour of local color impregnating everything, to pause for comparison or analysis. Like one sitting down to a table teeming with choice viands, he is at a loss where to begin to appease his voracious appetite. It is while engaged in quiet afterthought, when reviewing the experiences gained upon the spot, that the fullness of interest is aroused, as he turns to the quaint pages of many an ancient tome, to seek for the story of its earliest inhabitants. We can recall no other country which has experienced so many and such notable changes among its rulers, though it requires but little research to discover the paucity of detailed information concerning its early history, which is absolutely lost in the mist of ages.

Three thousand years—this is not looking backward very far, comparatively speaking. The author has seen objects of Egyptian production, in the Boolak Museum, on the banks of the Nile, which were six thousand years old. The Sphinx, standing in its grim loneliness ten miles from Cairo, is still older, while in the South Sea Islands there are prehistoric ruins which are believed to antedate the Sphinx. The probability is that a degree of antiquity applies to this globe so inconceivably remote that, like stellar distances, the mind can hardly realize the truth. Professor Agassiz talked confidently in his day of a million years having been required to bring about the present conditions of the earth. Since Agassiz's time geologists and scientists generally do not hesitate to add the plural to million, guided by the light of modern progress and discovery.

Such ancient mention of Malta as does exist is crowded with fable, like the early history of Greece and Rome. An example of this is found in the popular legend of its having once been inhabited by a cyclopean tribe, a race of giants, "half human, half divine." These extravagant legends of poetic history impress us as having, perhaps, some foundation in truth. It is not falsehood which tradition seeks to perpetuate. Possibility, if not probability, is required of the wildest romancers. Truth and fable run in nearly parallel lines. Jules Verne, when he wrote some of his seemingly extravagant stories, scarcely thought that he was simply anticipating possible circumstances which would so soon become realities. The reading world hardly believed that his "Round the World in Eighty Days" was strictly within the lines of truth; yet that record has been reduced.

Malta is known to have been the vassal of ten different nationalities. What the character of these various dynasties may have been can only be conjectured. There are no records extant by which we can learn aught in detail concerning them. A few half-ruined monuments, a series of rock tombs, the debris of mouldering temples, or a nearly obliterated underground city, "rich with the spoils of time,"—these are significant suggestions which the student of the past in vain essays to translate into coherency. The most casual visitor is moved to thoughtfulness as he contemplates these half-effaced tokens of a long dead and buried race, who had no Froissart to hand down their story through the lengthening vista of ages. First came the Phoenicians, who were here many centuries before the birth of Christ, and who were the earliest known colonists of Malta. Their sovereignty is believed to have extended through a period of seven hundred years. Greeks, Carthaginians, Romans, Goths, and Arabs succeeded each other in the order in which they are named, followed by German, Spanish, French, and English possessors, the latter having maintained an uninterrupted mastership since the beginning of the present century. To a nation whose naval supremacy is its greatest pride, and which already holds Gibraltar, the key to the Mediterranean, the holding of Malta is of inestimable importance. With these facts in view, it is not surprising that its security is so jealously guarded by England. Perhaps the boastful threat of the first Napoleon, that he would make of the Mediterranean a French lake, has not yet been forgotten. At present it is strictly an English dependency, though surrounded by a score of other nationalities. With the entrance and exit in her hands, besides holding this unequaled central dépôt of arms, no nation could hope successfully to dispute the control of the Mediterranean with Great Britain. That nationality not only dominates the great marine highway of the south of Europe, but also the coast of Asia.

Malta is situated in the middle of the great highway of commerce between the East and the West, and is the most southerly land in Europe, on about the 36th parallel of north latitude, its longitude being 15° east. The neighboring nations have often and fiercely contested for the sovereignty of Malta, until its soil has been irrigated by the life-tide of human beings. How strange the history it presents to us, what ages of melodramatic vicissitudes, emphasized by the discord of warring cannon and of dying men! How many and how varied the changes it has known in a period of thrice ten hundred years! Mutability is written on all things human, while Time, the remorseless iconoclast, performs the bidding of Destiny.

It would naturally be expected that the language of a people who have had such a peculiar experience as the Maltese should be a conglomerate, formed from various Asiatic and European tongues. It seems to be a mixture of Italian and Arabic, mingled with the patois which is common in the Grecian Archipelago; but English being the current official language, it prevails among the educated classes, and is also in general use for business purposes, especially in the retail shops of Valletta, the capital. The language of Dante, Petrarch, and Ariosto is still unknown to the common people, though generally understood and spoken in society. The masses adhere tenaciously to their native dialect, even after they have emigrated to other countries. In Gibraltar they pick up just enough of Spanish to make their wants known, as they do in other Mediterranean ports to which chance has brought them.

As is often the case in Eastern countries and oceanic islands, Malta is used both for the name of the island and that of the capital. The one collective term answers for the entire group; so with the beautiful island of Ceylon; people do not usually speak of Colombo, its capital, but of Ceylon, as designating the whole island. Martinique is sufficiently distinctive as regards that picturesque West Indian island; St. Pierre and Fort de France, the commercial and political capitals, are rarely mentioned. Thus Valletta has little significance to the world at large, while Malta is familiar enough.

The Phoenicians, the Greeks, and the Romans, each left tangible evidences of their sovereignty here. The ubiquitous Phoenicians, who are considered to have been the earliest of the commercial tribes, were by no means entirely free from the charge of piracy, which seems to have been almost universal upon this central sea in the earlier and middle ages. Strange, that sea-robbery should have been one of the active agencies in the world's advancement! It is said that all progress since the beginning has been from scaffold to scaffold. In our day no lapse from honorable commercial methods is so abhorrent to civilized nations, and no crimes are more severely punished. Next to the Turks and Algerines, the Greeks were the most reprehensible in this respect,—a people whose love of "freedom" has become a proverb; a country which has enjoyed more of American sympathy and material aid than any other, but whose sons in former times never failed to adopt a corsair life when opportunity offered.

There are very few monuments relating to the occupancy of these islands by the Arabs, who were settled here for more than two centuries. The most durable memorial of that people is their language, a tongue unsurpassed in poetic beauty of expression. After the lapse of ten centuries it is still spoken among the natives, and is held to be remarkably pure, especially in Gozo, the sister isle of Malta. Though it is customary to say that the natives speak Arabic, still it can hardly be a pure tongue; and yet the newly arrived Arabs can understand the Maltese, proving that the basis of the two languages must be identical. An educated resident took occasion to prove to the author that here and there one could select words from the current speech of the common people, the derivation of which was clearly Phoenician. Residents of the capital who are engaged in commerce, and many others of intelligence, speak English, French, and Italian fluently, and most of them speak the native tongue as well. The facility for acquiring foreign languages is a national trait. Cultured Maltese are surpassed only in this respect by educated Russians.

Italian is the official tongue of the law courts, though English is gradually superseding it. Why the former language should be persisted in, it would be difficult to say, though it is the key to all those common in the Levant. The Maltese are not Italians, and never were. Not to put too fine a point upon the matter, they are Arabs in their manners, customs, and language. When the Knights of St. John were sovereign here, nearly four hundred years ago, there was a certain degree of consistency in the adoption of Italian as the current or court language. The intimate relations of the order with the Pope and with Rome were a predisposing influence which could not but have its effect, besides which there was the close proximity of the mainland of Italy; but to continue it as the recognized language of the courts to-day is to sustain an anomaly.

More is known of the Arab dynasty than of any of its predecessors. As soon as this people had gained possession of Malta, they promptly exterminated the Greeks, putting all the male inhabitants to the sword, while making slaves of their wives and children. They were careful to conciliate the native population, even permitting them to worship after the dictates of their own religious convictions, which is a very rare concession among Mohammedans, where they have the power to do otherwise. The Arabs chiefly prized this group of islands for the safe harbors which it afforded in the pursuit of their one occupation, namely, that of undisguised piracy. Their constant raids upon the coast of Italy caused many expeditions to be fitted out from that country for the purpose of driving them away from their stronghold; but as we have said, the Arabs maintained their sovereignty here for over two hundred years. Strong defensive works were erected by them on the present site of Fort St. Angelo, at the entrance of the harbor of Valletta, on the island of Gozo, and at the old capital of the group, Città Vecchia, also known as Civitá Notabile,—"Illustrious City," which appellation, in the days of its glory, was probably not inappropriate. This old city, near the middle of the island, was a fortified metropolis centuries before the Arabs came, its defensive walls being contracted by them so that they might be the more easily manned and defended. To visit Città Vecchia to-day is like the realization of a mediaeval dream.

A glance at the map will show the reader that the strategic importance of these Maltese islands is almost unequaled. Lying in the middle of the vast and famous inland sea,—happily designated as the cradle of civilization,—within a brief sail of three continents, sixty miles from the shore of Sicily, one hundred and ninety from the mainland of Italy, two hundred from the nearest point of Africa, and equidistant from

Constantinople and Marseilles, Valletta has naturally become a popular port of call, as well as an important coaling station for many lines of steamships. This is particularly the case with those bound to or from England and India by way of the Suez Canal and the Red Sea. The opening of that famous and all-important waterway insured the lasting commercial prosperity of the Maltese group. From that day to the present its material growth has been steadily progressing and its population increasing. It is well known how much the Suez Canal promotes the commerce of Europe and Asia, but comparatively few people realize that we have in America a similar means of transportation which is the avenue of a much larger marine traffic. We refer to the Sault Ste. Marie Canal, which connects the State of Michigan with the Canadian Province of Ontario. The aggregate of the tonnage which annually passes through the American artificial river is shown by government statistics to far exceed that of the great canal which connects the Red Sea and the Mediterranean.

Malta is the halfway station, as it were, of the P. & O. line between London and Bombay; but there is other regular communication between the group and England, as well as mail steamships running to Marseilles, Alexandria, Belgium, Tripoli, and Tunis. Occasionally a single passenger or a small party of tourists stop at Valletta until the next packet touches here, enabling them to resume their journey east or west; but it is rather surprising how few visitors to Malta remain long enough to see one half of its many objects of interest, while others, who might easily do so, will not even take the trouble to land. One can sail half round the globe without finding a locality from which such a store of historic information and pleasurable memories can be brought away, or whose present aspect is more inviting. People who have no poetic sense or delicate appreciation will not find these qualities ready furnished for them, either at home or abroad. The dull, prosaic individual whose ideas run only in a practical groove, who lives purely in the commonplace, will be impressed by travel much after the fashion of the backwoodsman from Maine, when he saw Niagara Falls for the first time.

"Great Scott!" said he, gazing approvingly upon the moving aqueous body, "what a waste of water-power!"

A somewhat similar scene, of which the author was a witness, is well remembered.

"Are you going on shore, madam, while we take in coal?" asked the captain of a P. & O. steamship, addressing one of his lady passengers, who was en route from India to England.

"Can I get me a dear little Maltese dog there for a pet?" asked the lady in response.

"It is doubtful," was the answer. "The animals you refer to are now very scarce in these islands."

"Then I think I'll remain on board," rejoined madam. "There's nothing on the island worth seeing, I believe."

"Some persons come thousands of miles solely to visit the place," was the captain's quiet reply. "Its history is very curious."

"Are there any palaces?"

"There are over half a hundred edifices so called, though they have nearly all been diverted from their original purpose by the present government."

"They have nice old lace here, I am told. But one can get the same thing in London, you know."

"Oh, yes, and perhaps you will be able to find a 'puppy' to your liking, in London," said the sarcastic captain.

"I think I'll be content with reading about the place," was the final response of the obtuse passenger.

As to Gibraltar, that gray old solitary rock lying about a thousand miles to the westward of the Maltese group, and looming to a height of fourteen hundred feet, it is a far less attractive place, though among passengers generally there seems to be a different opinion. Here travelers usually manage to make a break in their sea voyage, and to remain a couple of days or more to examine the dreary old fortress and garrison town. We say it is far less attractive than Malta: as regards its past or present, it bears no comparison to this group. With the exception of the old Moorish castle which overlooks the town, there is not a single edifice in Gibraltar with any pretension to architectural merit or antiquarian interest.

The Maltese dog, about which the lady passenger inquired, is a sort of spaniel with long, silky, slate-colored hair, which hangs down from its head and body, touching the ground. It has in the past been much esteemed by royal families as a lapdog, and is of a very ancient breed, being conspicuous upon old Roman monuments. It is spoken of by the historian Strabo, but it seems to have almost entirely disappeared in our time, as the captain remarked. We saw an indifferent specimen offered for sale in Valletta, for which ten pounds sterling was demanded.

The port of Valletta contains two marine docks, capable of receiving ships of the largest tonnage, and is resorted to by both naval and commercial shipping for needed repairs, while it is also the headquarters of the British Mediterranean war fleet. The aggregate tonnage of vessels entering and clearing is double that of Gibraltar. As regards social life, and the usual associations of a commercial capital, Valletta is far and away in advance of the City of the Rock. One comes quickly to this conclusion upon comparing the commonplace Water-port Street of Gibraltar with the unique Strada Reale—"King Street"—of Valletta. The former is like a dull, narrow lane in an English seaport town, while the latter, full of life and color, resembles a picturesque boulevard in an Italian or French capital. Each is, however, above all else a place of arms; everything is and has ever been made subservient to this idea.

Malta is more distant from the mainland than any other Mediterranean island. It is less than twenty miles in length, not quite so large as the umbrageous Isle of Wight, on the coast of England, though it has nearly three times as many inhabitants. One often hears that garden of England compared with Malta, but wherefore, it is impossible to understand. It would be difficult to imagine a greater contrast than these two isolated places present. One, embowered in grand old trees and the rural accessories of a land which nature has delighted to clothe in verdure; the other, a solitary rock, a convulsive upheaval of the sea, reclaimed only by patient toil from utter sterility.

The various natural causes which have operated to reduce Malta to its present size and shape have been very thoroughly discussed by scientists, a majority of whom agree that it was once attached to the continent of Europe or of Africa. Our own humble opinion is that it was probably the connecting link between them both, some time in the long, long ages which have passed,—a deduction which will seem more reasonable to the patient reader as we progress in our narrative.

The island is of an irregular oval form, having a superficial area of about one hundred square miles. The Malta of to-day is only a diminutive, sea-girt, limestone rock, cropping out of the watery depths to a height, at its culminating point, of between seven and eight hundred feet, partly covered with a thin though fertile soil. But its associations are of a character closely bordering upon romance, and intensely interesting for their antiquity and novelty. The highest point of the island is at Casal Dingli, on the south side, where, to be precise, the serrated ridge of the cliffs reaches an elevation of seven hundred and fifty feet above sea level. There is, however, no such average height maintained in any part of the group. The southern shore is of such a bold, inaccessible character as to require few, if any, fortifications to protect it from possible invasion by an enemy. It resembles for long reaches the rugged, precipitous coast of Norway, presenting a line of abrupt, repelling rocks, rising perpendicularly from out of the sea to an average height of two or three hundred feet. The face of these abrupt cliffs is accessible only to sea-birds and creeping reptiles.

The opposite or northern side of the island is quite different; being more shelving, and available for landing purposes. It presents numerous sheltered coves and good harbors for light draught vessels, together with a great variety of pleasing features peculiar to seaside landscape. At the southeast end of Malta is the spacious bay and port of Marsa Scirocco. There is here a good depth of water, and the harbor is divided, somewhat like that of Valletta, by a promontory or tongue of land. There is a large fishing village at the head of the bay. Here the Turks landed an invading army, May 18, 1565, to begin the famous and sanguinary siege of that date. On June 10, 1798, the French under General Bonaparte disembarked their troops in the same bay. Northeast of this place, and half way to Valletta on the coast line, is the small inlet of Marsa Scala, which is only a shallow bay. The small Sicilian traders are accustomed to come hither in their light draught boats rather than to land at Valletta. Still following the northern shore beyond the admirable double harbor of the capital, we have the lesser bays of St. Julian, St. George, and Maddalena, besides the larger ones of St. Paul and Melleha.

Crossing the narrow Straits of Freghi, we find on the north coast of Gozo the bays of Ramla and Marsa-el-Forno, while on the south side are those of Scilendi and Duejra. In this enumeration we have all the bays and harbors of any importance in the whole Maltese group. Landing on the southern side of either the larger or the lesser island is for the most part impracticable, precipitous cliffs rising sheer from the water's edge in Gozo, as we have described in Malta proper. On these cliffs incessant breakers chafe and foam upon the black, barren rocks even in calm weather. Standing on this lonely shore, there is a fascination in listening to the solemn moan of the restless sea, in whose bosom there is so much of sadness, of direful secrets, and of unspent power. The trend of these islands, which form a very compact group, is nearly in a straight line from southeast to northwest. A bird's-eye view of the north side of the island of Malta affords glimpses of the blue sea penetrating the barren and yellow land for short distances, like Norwegian fjords, and supplying the absence of rivers and lakes as regards scenic effect, objects which the eye seeks for in vain throughout this rocky group.

Few islands, or, indeed, we may say few reaches of seacoast on the mainland, of similar dimensions, can show so many good and available harbors as are found on the north shore of Malta. Though the commercial necessities of the group have not yet caused them to be specially improved for shipping purposes, yet they will always be available. The admirable twin harbors of the capital have so far afforded all necessary facilities, but should the group improve as rapidly in business and population for the next few years as it has done during the last decade, another convenient harbor on the north coast will naturally become developed into a commercial dépôt, while the construction of a new and modern city will be sure to follow.

It is doubtful if there are many persons, even among those who are engaged in commerce, who realize the large amount of business which the government statistics already credit to the Maltese group, a commerce which is annually on the increase. The returns for the year 1891 show that the imports and exports of Valletta are almost exactly the same in the aggregate values, each considerably exceeding twenty-two million pounds sterling.

The presentation of an important statistical fact will emphasize this statement. Over six hundred thousand tons of coal are annually imported for use and for exportation. The arrival and departure of ten large steamships is a fair daily average, supplemented by one or two sea-going private yachts. There are few days in the year that the echoes are not ruthlessly awakened by the interchange of salutes with newly arrived vessels of war. Altogether, the two harbors of the capital present a constantly varying scene of great maritime activity, while the town itself is a picture of gay and varied life, rivaling in this respect many a continental metropolis far more pretentious, and having thrice its population.

As the present possessors of the island of Malta, its story has doubtless a greater degree of interest for the English than for any other people. But as regards its relation to the history of the past, its importance is universal. When it was a Phoenician colony, so long ago, it was a powerful factor in the political calculations of the Christian powers; but above all other associations, the island will always be famous as the place where the glory of the chivalrous Knights of St. John reached its zenith, and where it also came to its ignominious end. Of this period the pages of history furnish a fair amount of truthful detail, but conjecture alone can fill the blank which precedes the arrival of this remarkable order at Malta.

CHAPTER II.

Island of Hyperia.—Where St. Paul was Wrecked.—An Historical Bay.—Rock-Cut Tombs.—Curious and Unique Antiquities.—Sovereignty of the Knights of St. John.—An Anomalous Brotherhood.—Sailor-Monks.—Ancient Galleys.—A Famous Barbary Corsair.—Antique Norwegian Vessel.—Navy of the Knights.—Barbaric Warfare.—About the Maltese Nobility.—Romantic History.—"Arabian Nights."—Valletta the Beautiful.

Lovers of classic fable will remember that one of the islands of this group was named Hyperia by Homer, and was the supposed residence of the mystic nymph Calypso, where she entertained—not to say detained—the shipwrecked Ulysses by her siren fascinations, when he was on his way home from Troy. Her grotto, entirely shorn of its poetic adornment, is exhibited to the curious stranger at Gozo. It was while under the Phoenician dynasty that Calypso is supposed to have kept Ulysses prisoner for seven years. Such ingenious allegories impart a certain local and romantic interest, though they rather obscure than illumine history. Homer threw a glow of poetic fancy over the localities which he depicted, while Scott—to present a contrasting instance—gives us photographic delineations of the times and places to which he introduces us. In "Kenilworth," for instance, the novelist teaches the average reader more about the days of Queen Elizabeth than a labored history of her reign would do, presenting it also in such a form as to fix it firmly upon the mind.

It would seem that fable, like history, is bound to repeat itself, since thousands of years subsequent to Ulysses' shipwreck here, another disaster of this sort, but of far greater import, took place upon the group.

According to Biblical record, St. Paul, when a prisoner, on his way from Jerusalem to Rome to plead his case before the Emperor Nero, about sixty years after the beginning of the Christian era, was wrecked in a rocky bay of Malta which still bears his name,—*La Baia di San Paolo.* It is situated seven or eight miles northwest from Valletta, and forms a broad inlet, the entrance to which is nearly two miles wide, running inland about three miles. It has some twenty fathoms of water at the entrance, gradually shoaling towards its upper extremity. Seaward, and near the mouth of the bay, is a small island. The shore is dominated by the Tower of St. Paul, a square stone structure erected February 10, 1610. The day indicated is the supposed anniversary of the wreck. Near the tower is a chapel, in which are some paintings and frescoes, which depict in a crude manner the catastrophe which occurred to the Apostle. A small fishing village exists here to-day, as in the time of the famous wreck. The creek just below the stone church is still the refuge for fishing-boats when the weather is stormy.

A dark, threatening, straggling ledge of rocks rises above the surface of the water some distance from the shore, over which the restless sea breaks in fleecy clouds of spray. Upon this ledge, after being tempest-tossed for fourteen days and nights, the bark which bore St. Paul is supposed to have foundered.

"They ran the ship aground; and the forepart stuck fast, and remained unmovable, but the hinder part was broken with the violence of the waves." On Selmoon Island, just referred to, there is a colossal statue of St. Paul, which was erected by the devout Maltese some fifty years ago. The popular reverence for the Apostle's name in this region is very general, bays, churches, streets, and chapels being designated by it, while in the inland villages may be found wayside shrines, small outdoor altars, and springs of delicious drinking-water, dedicated to this revered name. A grand annual festival takes place on February 10, commemorative of the shipwreck of the Apostle to the Gentiles,—Paul, the poor tent-maker of Tarsus. The church of San Paolo, Valletta, in the street of the same name, is the headquarters of this annual demonstration, which takes the form of processions, illuminations, and church ceremonials. This special style of public display is very dear to the average citizen of Malta.

It was a little over fourteen hundred years after the event of the wreck in St. Paul's Bay, which occurred about A. D. 60, that Malta was deeded by the Emperor Charles V. to the then homeless Knights of St. John, together with Gozo and Tripoli, a fact which will be more fully referred to as we progress with our story of the group.

There has been much ink wasted in controversy as to whether this was really the island and this the bay where St. Paul met with his maritime adventure, but it certainly seems to answer every necessary requirement, and has for several centuries been thus universally designated. The average visitor feels no doubt that he gazes upon the "certain creek with a shore, into the which they were minded, if it were possible, to thrust in the ship" (Acts xxvii. 39). A fresh northeaster was blowing as we viewed the scene, driving the waves in gallant style upon the ledge and shore, while at the same time filling the air with misty spray and rank sea-odors. The long line of milk-white combers, after expending their force upon the shore, rushed swiftly back, drawn by a mysterious undertow towards the deep waters. The noise of the vexed and boisterous element created a continuous roar, as the waves followed each other in endless succession. It was the *grégalé*, the northeasterly blast so much dreaded by the fishermen, and which in the olden time, before navigation was better understood, created such havoc in this midland sea. It would have been difficult to effect a dry landing, even from a well-managed boat, with such a troubled sea running. One naturally remembered "a tempestuous wind called Euroclydon" which the Apostle encountered, while the imagination was busy in depicting the struggle of Paul and his companions to reach the shore on broken timbers of the ship.

The beach of St. Paul's Bay seems to be composed of the very smallest of sea-shells, together with some larger ones, which have been mostly broken and powdered by the endless hammering of the waves. There is a fine sand, or something which represents it, probably composed of the powder from the shells. This place is a favorite resort of the people from Valletta for bathing purposes, but it was not an inviting day when we stood by the shore, and no bathers were seen. It was very natural for one to recall the Biblical words, "He maketh the deep to boil like a pot."

In this neighborhood there are numerous prehistoric rock-hewn tombs, cut by ingenious and skilled hands with effective tools. That these are Phoenician remains, there seems to be little if any doubt. Those aboriginal colonists were the commercial people of their time, who settled much earlier at Rhodes, and other islands of the Levant, than they did at Malta. They planted colonies in Sicily, Sardinia, and Spain. Carthage was founded by them. Malta afforded a convenient stopping-place between Carthage and the mother country, and was naturally prized on that account, having such ample harbors of refuge, and it doubtless afforded the means of repairing any damages which resulted from storms at sea.

Out of the rock-hewn tombs, of which we were speaking, interesting relics bearing Phoenician characters have been taken from time to time, such as vases and mural urns, together with articles of domestic use made from burnt clay, some of which are preserved in the Museum at Valletta. Other curiosities from the same source are to be seen in the private collections of English officials, and of wealthy Maltese. Years of research would not exhaust the interest which the student of the past must feel in these antiquities. We know of no more fruitful theme or more promising field, for the historian and the archaeologist, than is here presented. It is not an untried one, but it is very nearly inexhaustible, in pursuing which little expense and no hardship is necessarily encountered. Every facility is freely accorded, both by the resident population and by the government.

Some of the best examples of Phoenician inscriptions now to be seen in the British Museum were brought to light at Bighi, in these islands, where this ancient people worshiped Juno in a stately temple which stood on the spot now occupied by the moat of Fort St. Angelo. There are few parts of the world so varied in antiquarian interests as the islands of this group. Professor Sayce, the eminent Orientalist of Oxford, England, tells us that Malta contains Phoenician antiquities of a kind found nowhere else, and he pronounces the sanctuaries of the Giant's Tower, in Gozo, together with its companion ruin in the larger island, absolutely unique. These islands undoubtedly occupied an important position in the history of those remote days. The few Maltese who have written about this period dwell with great emphasis upon the glory of Malta while under Phoenician rule, though they are quite unable to give us any reliable details of the long ages in which this people held sovereignty here.

Within a few years some remains were unearthed which were attributed to the Goths, but of all the people who have been mentioned, they probably left fewer evidences of their presence in Malta than did any other race. After becoming masters of Italy and Sicily, they came hither about A. D. 506, and held possession of the group for nearly forty years, until they were expelled by the army of Justinian under Belisarius.

The most romantic period of the ever-changing history of this group of islands, subjected first and last to the control of so many different nationalities, is undoubtedly that embraced in the two centuries and a half of the eventful sovereignty of the Knights of St. John,—Knights Hospitallers, as they were very properly called at first, the most famous order of mediaeval chivalry, whose name is more familiar to us as Knights of Malta. The first convent of the founders at Jerusalem was dedicated to St. John; hence the original name of the order. It was the earliest systematized charity of the sort concerning which we have any authentic record. If the true history of this organization could be written, it would overshadow the most vivid romance. It began in Palestine during the darkness of the tenth century, when the Saracens were masters of Jerusalem, and it extends to the verge of the eighteenth. It is but the outline of important events, which live through the ages to reach us. The individual is sunk in the mass, and yet real history is but enlarged biography. The truth of this is shown in the life of La Vallette, as handed down through three centuries. His biography gives us a better history of the order of which he was Grand Master than do writers who attempt it by treating the brotherhood as a whole. Had the moral character of the Knights of St. John been equal to their dauntless courage, the order would have formed a worthy example for all time; but their record shows them and their deeds to have been of mingled good and evil, the latter quality oftenest predominating. In the period when their material prosperity was at its height, they were equally celebrated for wealth, pomp, and vice. While they were boastful and claimed to be invincible, unlike most braggarts, they were undeniably brave. Nor was this by any means the only anomaly in the character of this singular and famous fraternity. Their career exemplified vice and self-abnegation, hospitality and piracy, the devoted care of the sick and the slaughter of their fellow-men, in about equal proportions. These clerical warriors presented a unique phase of human nature, the outgrowth of a period which, while demanding much sternness of character to cope with its exigencies, was also peculiarly amenable to the influence of religious superstition. The brotherhood owed a large degree of its influence to the cloak of sanctity which it so boldly assumed, but the humble spirit of which it so unhesitatingly and persistently outraged.

The attempt to unite two professions so remote in principles was like trying to make oil and water mingle.

The Grand Master, whose authority was absolute, was elected by the Knights from their own body, and held the office for life. In the choice of this individual, the order seemed to be almost always influenced by more than common wisdom, their election being guided by the best influences and wisest judgment. They realized the proper qualities which should characterize one placed in this responsible position, and chose accordingly. They did not seek to elect such a leader as should favor this or that "language," this or that section of the fraternity, but one who was endowed with sufficient courage and conscientious piety to rule over them with impartiality. That there was an element of weakness ever present among them, emanating from the division into languages, is very true, and it was this influence which the Grand Master had always to guard against. National rivalry was inevitable, no matter how much the fraternity endeavored, as a body, to avoid it.

The Knights of St. John made the island of Malta the bulwark of Christendom against the advance of the pale, but bloodstained standard of the Turks. Even after settling here, which proved to be their final home, a bitter and murderous conflict was carried on by them with the Ottoman power, both on sea and land, but especially in their galleons, until at last, after triumphantly sustaining an unprecedented siege, during which they actually killed the enemy in the trenches, three times their own number, the Knights, with ranks seriously thinned, were left in undisputed possession of these islands. Victory not only crowned their sanguinary warfare with the Turks, but they also rid the Mediterranean, at least for a considerable period, of a much-dreaded scourge, which had so long hampered the commerce of these waters, namely, the rapacious Greek, Turkish, and Algerine pirates. In the armory of the Grand Palace at Valletta, there may be seen to-day, among other trophies taken from the enemy by the Knights, the sword of the renowned pirate chief, known as Admiral Dragut, who was also Pasha of Tripoli. The owner of the sword was fatally wounded in the siege of Malta, before the walls of St. Elmo, in 1565.

This daring man, entirely wanting in the attribute of mercy, and known as the most reckless and successful corsair of his day, yet preserved some chivalrous instincts which were exhibited on occasion. A gallant saying, which is often attributed to others, was first uttered by him, if we may believe contemporary authority. It was at the time when the Turkish forces, with whom Dragut had joined in the attempt to take Malta, after struggling for months in the vain endeavor to capture the fort of St. Elmo, were engaged in the last decisive assault. The pirate, now advanced in years, lay sorely wounded and dying, when he asked the surgeon, who was by his side, "How goes the battle?" "Our soldiers have taken the fort and massacred its defenders," was the reply. "Allah be praised!" gasped the sinking corsair, "then I die content." These were his last words. Dragut was very humbly born, beginning his profession as a common seaman, at the lowest round of the ladder, that is, as cabin boy. His fortune was a strangely varied one, now a galley slave, now a soldier in the Sultan's service, now a pilot on the sea, and now a daring pirate, working his way upward by patient determination, until finally he stood as master upon the deck of his own galley, and was the terror of these seas. It was not long before he became admiral of the entire Turkish navy. Dragut had pursued his piratical and warlike career for nearly half a century. He possessed executive qualities which fitted him to act both as an admiral and as a general, a large share of his victories having been achieved upon the land. He had agreed with the Sultan of Turkey to join forces with him in the attack upon Malta, but was delayed for a few days, so the Sultan's commander began the siege without him. Mustafa Pasha made a bad piece of business of it, and did not open his attack with true soldierly skill. When Dragut arrived, important changes were promptly made, and it was while directing these movements that the famous corsair received his death wound.

We have seen that the organization of St. John did not confine itself to warfare upon the land; many of the order were trained seamen, and were always ready to take the aggressive in marine enterprises when occasion offered. The strict vows of the brotherhood compelled the members to wage ceaseless warfare against the infidels.

This was the most clearly defined and determined of their purposes, in the prosecution of which they adhered tenaciously to the last. In these sea fights their well-known courage, superior weapons, and persistency nearly always insured success. Their galleys, well equipped for that period, were held in readiness for service, moored in the land-locked creeks of Grand Harbor. These were efficient vessels for the immediate service they were designed to serve. They were over one hundred feet in length and twenty-five wide, being propelled by oars or sails, according to the wind. The sails were not designed for use unless the wind was aft, as the art of tacking and sailing to windward was not then practiced. Fifty oars, that is, twenty-five on a side, was a common arrangement, and there were from three to six galley slaves at each oar, according to the size of the vessel. These men were chained in their places, and if they did not work to the satisfaction of the boatswain, the lash fell without mercy upon their bare backs. A galley was rigged with two masts, upon each of which a large square sail was hoisted. When the oars were in use, these sails were clewed up. Several cannon were fitted to each side, and one was designed to fire from the stern; but when in action, the usual plan was to ram the enemy's craft, and thus disable him, or, by boarding, to effect a capture in a hand-to-hand fight. The half-naked, half-starved slaves often dropped dead at the oars, and were ruthlessly cast into the sea. No more cruel punishment could be inflicted upon a criminal than to condemn him to the life of an oarsman in the galleys.

There is probably no more striking and significant example of the material progress of the times than that afforded by contrasting the iron-clad warship of to-day with a fighting caravel of the period of which we are speaking.

Contrary to what might reasonably be supposed, the people who lived upon the shores of the Mediterranean did not build vessels which were at all comparable in general excellence with those constructed by the Northmen at the same period. The galleons used by the Greeks, Turks, and Algerines, as well as by the Knights of St. John, were awkward and unwieldy; their hulls represented no true lines of nautical beauty or usefulness. They were not seaworthy, as the term is usually applied. When the weather was severe, the vessel was always anchored under the lee of the nearest land, or was put into some sheltered bay. These vessels carried far too much top hamper, and exposed too much surface to the wind, to be safe when a storm raged. Their free board was enormous, compared with their draught. The author has seen at Christiania, in Sweden, the hull of an ancient war craft which was dug out of the clayey soil of the country, where it had been preserved for centuries, that antedated these galleons used by the Knights at Rhodes and at Malta, it having been built at least nine hundred years ago. Its lines and construction combined three important qualities, storage capacity, buoyancy, and speed, and it was intended to lie low in the water, thus presenting but small surface to a storm on the ocean. Not one of these characteristics could be claimed for the galleys of this inland sea. The latter were crude, top-heavy, with high-curved poop and stern, and designed only for fair weather service, while the northern-made craft could ride out the fiercest storm in safety when properly managed, and were built for open ocean navigation. In fact, this model, still to be seen at the Museum in Christiania, is such as bore the Northmen across the Atlantic to our shores, centuries before the time of Columbus, whose discoveries we commemorate. The naval branch of the Order of St. John was originated soon after their expulsion from Jerusalem, and was rapidly developed while they occupied the island of Rhodes, but it did not reach its highest efficiency until after their settlement at Malta, where the situation of the island and its extraordinary harbor facilities particularly favored maritime enterprise. There they built many armed galleys, though all the material which entered into their construction was necessarily imported. There was no available wood to be found upon the island, except that which was brought from the mainland of Italy. A people entirely surrounded by water naturally came to be good boat and ship builders, and the galleons produced during the sovereignty of the Knights showed great improvement, and were famous for their staunch character compared with those of their neighbors. These vessels, however, would be considered nothing less than marine monstrosities in our day.

The galleys of the Knights did not remain long idle. When a restless spirit moved their owners, they promptly set sail for the coast of Barbary, where, surprising some unprotected settlement, they burned the place to the ground, enslaving those whose lives they spared. If there were any high officials among their prisoners, or persons of special importance, such were held for ransom. If the payment demanded for their release did not come promptly, they too became common slaves and worked with the rest at the trying galley oars. This service, if they were not in good health and strength, soon put an end to their lives. Such were the deeds of professed Christians, who, in their ignorant and bigoted zeal, actually seem to have thought themselves to be serving God by robbing, destroying, and enslaving those whom they called infidels. In the light which comes to us through the long ages, we can see another and baser motive which must have actuated these monkish freebooters, namely, the desire for plunder and to kill, "an appetite which grows by what it feeds upon." Though they tempered their piratical career with deeds of chivalry and the outward forms of religious devotion, they were none the less blood-seeking corsairs. The red flag would have been more appropriate at the masthead of their vessels than the eight-pointed cross of St. John. The spirit which had originally given birth to the order—then well named Hospitallers—had long since been lost sight of. In Jerusalem, Turk and Pilgrim alike shared their hospitality, and their model was that of the Good Samaritan. Alas, for the degeneracy that followed!

The conflict as carried on for centuries by both the Christians and the Mohammedans was equally characterized by diabolical cruelty, while tinctured by a spirit of blind fanaticism and religious frenzy. On the part of the Turks this was a genuine instinct, since they could not expect, even in the event of victory, to realize anything by way of remunerative plunder. In regard to the Knights, everything goes to show, as we have already declared, that religion was used as a convenient cloak to cover up their questionable purposes. The candid student of history will, however, honestly admit that there were many and striking exceptions to this rule. Some of the

Grand Masters were undoubtedly sincere, though they were grossly bigoted. Of this, L'Isle Adam and La Vallette are striking examples.

Each fresh onslaught between the contending Christians and infidels led to increased bitterness and a desire for revenge. The terrible courage and indifference to death evinced by the followers of the crescent were more than matched by the cool, determined bravery of those who fought under the banner of the cross. Let the truth be frankly recorded. If the Turks were guilty of the most barbaric atrocities, and we very well know that they were, the Knights of St. John were not slow to retaliate in kind. History tells us that the latter, at the siege of Malta in 1565, not only decapitated their defenseless prisoners of war upon the ramparts of the forts, in full sight of the enemy, but afterwards fired their ghastly heads from mortars, and projected them by other means into the camp of the besieging army. Alas, for the brutality of warfare, ancient and modern! Who can forget that English officers professing to be Christians, during the unsuccessful attempt of the natives of India to regain their freedom, lashed their living prisoners of war to the cannon's mouth, and applying the match, blew them into eternity? This diabolical act, it should be remembered, was perpetrated not by irresponsible guerrillas, or lawless banditti, but by regular English army officers, in the nineteenth century. Wild African tribes, the Maoris of New Zealand, or the cannibals of Fiji could do no worse, while England poses as representing the highest degree of modern civilization and refinement. All war involves a greater or less lapse into barbarism. It was the first Napoleon who uttered the significant saying, born of his own experience, "The worse the man, the better the soldier!"

But let us endeavor not to diverge too far from the immediate purpose of these pages.

We were speaking of the peculiar order of the Knights of St. John. The natives of Malta furnished no members to the ranks of the brotherhood. They might and did serve effectively as men at arms, and joined in defensive and offensive warfare as common soldiers. A certain exclusiveness was always maintained by the fraternity as to admitting individuals to full membership, it being realized from the outset that an indiscriminate policy in this respect would tend to belittle the order and weaken its influence, as well as to introduce an undesirable element into its ranks. Hundreds of the Maltese were paid auxiliaries of the different "languages" of the order, and others were volunteers in fighting for the sacredness of their homes when the Turks invaded the island. This they did in large numbers during the last memorable siege, but they were in no sense Knights of St. John. The order proper was exclusively composed of Europeans, who, before admission to the first rank of the brotherhood, were obliged to produce indisputable proofs of nobility of birth, to a degree which varied according to the custom of the nationality whence they came.

The Grand Masters created a certain rank of nobility among the Maltese, which was conferred upon individuals for extraordinary considerations, and for valuable services rendered in behalf of the order, but it is difficult to discover the advantage of the titles thus bestowed. The persons thus complimented were not eligible for admission to the brotherhood, nor was any pecuniary compensation attached. Their descendants to-day, though they are quite impoverished, are more tenacious of these empty titles than ever before. The presumption founded thereon is simply ludicrous to an American. The French, during their brief sovereignty of the island, abolished by special edict all titles, but this amounted to nothing, and was soon forgotten. As these meaningless distinctions descend indiscriminately to all male members of the family whose progenitor was thus endowed, the prospect is that titled people will by and by become as plenty here as Maltese oranges, or the "Legion of Honor" in France.

Remembering the marvelous history of the Knights and their often tragic taking off, while we stroll through the palace-lined streets of the capital in the still hours of the night, when the moon throws pale, suggestive shadows across the squares and street corners presided over by effigies of saints, one can easily imagine the ghostly, armor-clad figure of a dead Knight, like Hamlet's father, revisiting its earthly haunts. If these defunct soldier-monks did not leave ghosts behind them, the power of such spirits after death must be effete. Every turn and each surrounding in Valletta, whether in the department of arms or of art, speaks of the vigorous doings of these many-sided knightly friars.

It was the Grand Master Jean de La Vallette, who founded the charming capital of Malta, after his murderous but successful repulse of the infidels in their last attempt to capture the island. Though Vallette did not live long enough to see it reared to its present attractive completeness, still the stamp of his genius, as shown in the grandeur of its architecture, its palaces, churches, hospitals, and fortifications, is his most lasting and appropriate monument. So rapidly did the building of the new city progress after it was begun, that it is said to have been practically completed in six years. To accomplish this, hundreds of able mechanics and skilled artisans were brought from Italy and other parts of Europe. If these stones, whose surfaces three centuries have so wrinkled with age, could but speak, what interesting facts might be revealed by them to illumine this period of the world's history! We have famous telescopes which enable us to search out the characteristics of far-away Mars. Would we could turn one of these giant lenses upon the olden days in Malta, and obtain a tableau of its history with photographic fidelity!

## CHAPTER III.

The Maltese Group.—Comino.—Cave Life.—Verdant Gozo.—Isle of Filfla.—Curious Lizards.—Loss of an Ironclad.—Mysterious Wheel-Tracks.—Earthquakes.—Population.—Military Dépôt.— Youthful Soldiers.—Quarantine.—Arrival of the Knights.—Immorality.—Harbor Defenses.—Land Fortifications.—Charming Photographic View.—The Stars and Stripes Abroad.—The Eight- Pointed Maltese Cross.—Peculiar Sunset Scene.

We speak of Malta in the singular, which is the conventional form; official documents say Malta and its dependencies, it being the name which is also most commonly used to designate the capital; but it should be understood that the Maltese group consists of three considerable islands, namely, Malta, Gozo, and Comino. The latter lies midway in the channel which separates the other two. Comino is nearly circular, measures four miles across its surface, and contains some large and curious caves, also a fort which was built in 1618. There are a few huts in which the poor peasants reside, who labor on the soil, and send fabulous numbers of watermelons to Valletta. It would seem that this circumscribed bit of earth, or, more properly speaking, rock, breaking the surface of the Straits of Freghi, was formerly considered to be of more importance than it is in our day. One ancient author mentions it under another name, that of Hephæstia, which means the island of Vulcan. In the Middle Ages Comino was a very nest of Saracen pirates. Up to the beginning of the present century, the special advantage of the group for the promotion of illegitimate commerce has been its curse. Malta was the synonym of piracy from the earliest times,—a reputation which, as we have seen, the Knights of St. John did nothing to improve. Speaking in plain terms, they were the most pronounced and successful corsairs who ever sailed these waters, and were unmolested by the Western Powers because their piracy was conducted under the pretense of fighting only the infidels, and in behalf of Christianity. In our day we invade Central Africa under pretense of suppressing the slave trade; but in the days of this warlike order, its principal source of income was derived from the capture of Asiatics, whom the Knights sold into slavery, or retained in that condition.

There is said to be ample evidence that the numerous caves of Comino were formerly improved as domestic dwelling-places by the primitive inhabitants. Their partial inaccessibility probably caused them to be used as safe retreats when the group was invaded by a foreign enemy. Where natural caves existed in the early days of our race upon this earth, they were nearly always utilized as shelter for human beings, and doubtless artificial ones were created, it being the readiest mode of obtaining a domestic shelter. The Spanish gipsies of Granada follow this plan even to-day, on the banks of the swift-flowing Darro, not to speak in detail of the numerous cliff-dwellers of Behring Strait, where Asia and America come so nearly together.

There is a cave between Comino and Cominetto, the entrance to which is accomplished by boat, not without considerable difficulty. When once within, however, and the eyes become accustomed to the gloom which pervades the place, the cave is found to open out into proportions of considerable magnitude. At the further extremity nature has formed a beautiful little gravelly beach, on which the lazy waves ebb and flow gracefully and softly. Geologists visit this cavern with much interest, as the sides teem with the remains of marine creatures which lived and died in the waters when these islands were gradually undergoing the process of formation. There are scores of smaller caves on Cominetto, and also on Comino. It was in the cavernous formations of the south side of the main island of the Maltese group that Dr. Adams found the interesting animal remains about which he has written so ably. These tokens of past ages, concerning which we have no other record, exist in nearly all parts of the globe. In the Ozark Mountains, near Galena, Missouri, is a cavern larger than the Mammoth Cave of Kentucky, which has been explored for thirty miles in a nearly straight line. In this Missouri cave, bones of prehistoric animals have also been found.

It may be said truthfully that there are few places which surpass Malta in antiquarian interest.

Gozo is about one fifth the size of the main island which gives the group its name. The circumference of the three islands is a trifle less than one hundred miles. The shores, much worn and still wearing away by the ceaseless action of the waters, give evidence of having been considerably more extended at no distant period of time. Two uninhabited islets, besides Gozo and Malta proper, complete the list of the group; these are Cominetto and Filfla. The first, as its name indicates, nearly joins Comino; the latter, containing the ruins of an ancient stone church, is situated three or four miles from Malta on its southern side. It is a very small islet, being only six hundred yards in circumference. Filfla, from the Arabic word *filfel*, means a peppercorn, and the place is thus called on account of its diminutive size. The name of each inlet, headland, and reef along the coast is Arabic.

Besides the islands which we have cited, there are some small rocks, having sufficient soil upon them to afford a gleam of animal and vegetable life, but which are rarely if ever trodden by the foot of man. Sometimes the hardy fishermen spread their nets from the most available; but this work is generally pursued from boats and at points further from land. There are certain species of shell-fish, including the patella, lobsters, and crabs, which so abound on the circumscribed shore of anvil-shaped Filfla, that fishermen come hither regularly to obtain them. The phosphorescent jelly-fish, that glow-worm of the sea, lies upon the surface near the shore in shoals, with here and there a blue and rose-tinted starfish. The stormy petrel, the manx, and the white sea-gulls build their nests amid the rocks of Filfla. The gathering of coral was formerly a successful business hereabouts, but it is now abandoned as not being sufficiently profitable. Oysters are also found near the shore, and form a considerable source of food supply for the common people; but the Mediterranean oyster does not recommend itself to one accustomed to the superior product in the same line found on the American coast. This bivalve of the narrow sea is often transported in considerable quantities inland to Rome, where it does not always prove harmless to strangers, though the digestive organs of the natives seem quite able to grapple with it. The author was once seriously poisoned by eating "oysters on the shell," at Nazzari's famous restaurant, near the corner of the Via Condotti, in Rome.

As regards this island of Filfla, it gives us a wealth in numbers and an astonishing variety of forms representing marine life, including sea anemones, sea urchins, and so on, together with some small shells almost as lovely as flowers. Men-of-war cruising in these waters use the island as a target, and fragments of shot and shell consequently abound upon its surface. Naturalists tell us of a peculiar species of lizard found on this islet, quite different from anything of the sort to be seen on the larger islands, "beautiful bronze-black creatures, quite tame, and much more agile than their brethren on the mainland." So off the harbor of Bombay, the author has seen on the island of Elephanta remarkable beetles, unlike any of the species to be found elsewhere. They are scarcely larger than one's little-finger nail, but nature has clothed them in harlequin attire, combining golden, steel-blue, and pink. These tiny creatures have prominent eyes, like a King Charles spaniel, which seem to gaze at one with something like human intelligence. The question naturally suggests itself, where can a distinctive species of animal life have been derived and developed after this fashion, in these isolated spots? Is this the outcome of some not understood principle of evolution, beginning as vegetable, and developing into animal life? That the earth produces the former spontaneously we know, and that it may gradually, in the course of ages, become endowed with the latter has been declared possible by scientists. In our museums we see fossil organisms which exhibit in nearly consecutive order the slow evolution of both animals and plants. By this means palaeontologists have been able to connect some of our present mammals, through intermediary forms, with their tertiary ancestors in primitive conditions.

Leaving the field of conjecture to scientists, let us resume the course of our Maltese story.

It is believed that at a comparatively modern date, geologically speaking, the islands of Malta and Gozo were joined together by the island of Comino. Deep wheel-ruts worn in the rocky surface on the opposite shores of the two nearest islands, visible even at some distance under the water, afford what is considered to be unmistakable evidence that the intervening straits have been formed recently, or that the sea was once so shallow here as to be easily fordable by wheeled vehicles. These wheel-tracks are particularly observable at Marfa, whence passengers take boat for Gozo, but they are also found in other places, where the connection is wholly obliterated. On the edge of the shore, to the north of the Bay of Fom-er-Rich, wheel-ruts are to be seen terminating abruptly at the brink of a cliff one hundred feet high, which rises sheer from out of the sea. This shows clearly that some tremendous upheaval, subsidence, or both, must have taken place here within historic times.

Though the Straits of Freghi are now many fathoms deep, navigation is somewhat intricate. A first-class British iron-clad was wrecked here in 1889, by striking upon a sunken rock. In very stormy weather communication between the islands is wholly cut off, but this rarely occurs. The shore in this vicinity is fringed by long, black, straggling ledges, the most dangerous portions of which are exposed only in stormy weather, when the dark, sea-worn rocks raise their heads and stoutly resist the onslaught of the waves, sending aloft transparent masses of white spray. When the sun escapes from the clouds and penetrates this watery ebullition, momentary rainbows bind the moistened atmosphere together with a lovely arch of prismatic hues.

Careful soundings show that the Maltese group stands upon a submarine plateau, which stretches entirely across the Mediterranean from Sicily to Africa, thus dividing the sea into two parts, known to geographers as the eastern and western basins.

Malta, so far as an unscientific person may speak, shows no signs of volcanic action, though there is a powerful agent of this character so near in Sicily. At the present writing Ætna is in a condition of wild physical turmoil, forming new fissures near its summit, out of which the much-dreaded fiery lava is flowing rapidly, while the main crater is by no means idle. Nothing can stem the tide of these rushing rivers of molten rock, which have cut themselves fresh channels for miles, extending to the sea. The last outbreak occurred in the early part of 1865, continuing with more or less force for a period of three months. In 1669, one of these eruptions, besides costing hundreds of human lives, destroyed twenty-two towns and villages, on its mad course to the seaport of Catania, where the lava rushed into the Mediterranean in a stream eighteen hundred feet in width and forty feet in height! This extraordinary statement is in accordance with the local chronicles of the time. It was perhaps the most violent and destructive eruption of which we have any record; many have been slight and harmless. This latter fact accounts for the hardihood of the Sicilians in continuing to plant vineyards and farms within reach of this great subterranean furnace. So the people of Torre del Greco, at the foot of restless Vesuvius, ignore past experience, and all former outbreaks of the mountain which destroyed Pompeii.

In the absence of late and reliable statistics upon the subject, the present population of the Maltese group may be safely assumed as about a hundred and seventy-five thousand, of which number one half centre in and about Valletta. Borgo, Senglea, and Burmulo, on the opposite side of the harbor, eastward from the capital, are populous suburbs of the city, and contain many well-built stone edifices, but none to compare with those of the city proper. These suburbs are the residence of an humbler class of the community than those who live in Valletta. The estimate which is given above as to the population of the group includes the English garrison, which seldom amounts to less than six thousand men. A brigade of infantry is always kept here upon a war footing, known as the "Indian Contingent." The whole number of troops at the present time, in and about the capital, is eight thousand of all arms. In case of another Indian mutiny, which would surely follow an invasion by Russia, England could draw at once from this source. The troops at Malta would be already half way toward their objective point, if ordered to Calcutta or Bombay.

Her Majesty's government also maintains an infantry regiment one thousand strong, whose ranks are filled by natives of the islands, a policy which is also adopted to a large extent in India, and more or less in all English dependencies. Even in Hong Kong, the large body of men who constitute the local police are Sikhs brought from India for this special service. They are tall, dark, fine-looking men, with heavy beards. The Maltese regiment just spoken of is a good-looking body of well-drilled men, though lacking the *esprit de corps* of English-born soldiers. This regiment is officered by Englishmen, and is called the Royal Maltese Fencibles, being mostly employed to man the outlying forts of the group.

We may be permitted a few words upon the subject of the garrison of Malta. One watches with special interest the soldiery of various nationalities. The author has seen the representatives of the English army in Egypt, China, Ceylon, Aden, and in all of the colonies of Great Britain except those of Africa. The men are, on an average, far too youthful for military service. Such boyish applicants would not pass examination for enlistment in our American army as we find enrolled in the English regiments here. Large numbers are under seventeen years. Even Lord Wolseley, in a late published report, admits this glaring defect of the British service. In round numbers, the English army consists of two hundred and ten thousand men of all arms, half of which number is kept at home, that is, in England, while over seventy thousand are stationed in India, and thirty-two thousand in various colonies. The empire of India is an expensive plaything, which the people of Great Britain support for the amusement of the Queen and the pride of the nation. The seventy thousand soldiers distributed over that widespread territory are hardly able to keep the natives in subjection. To maintain her grasp upon India, as we all know, has cost England rivers of blood and mountains of treasure, though she has no more legitimate right to possess the land than she has to Norway and Sweden.

Sweeping pestilence and frequent wars have not seemed to interfere materially with the rapid increase of the population of Malta. Visitations of the cholera and the plague have at different times created great havoc with human life in the group. So late as 1813, thousands of the inhabitants fell victims to the much-dreaded plague, brought hither from the East, where the seeds of the scourge seem to be only slumbering when they are not bringing forth fatal fruit. The local records of the devastation of the plague in Malta are terribly forlorn, dreary, and saddening, and characterized by the calmness and dignity of despair. Since that experience, strict quarantine measures have been enforced, especially toward vessels coming from Egypt. Many travelers who have visited this group of islands have been obliged to pass a fortnight or more in the lazaretto before being permitted to land in the capital, while others, rather than submit to the trying discipline of quarantine, have given up their purpose of doing so.

Untraveled readers can hardly realize the discomforts and annoyances caused by quarantine laws, against the necessity of which no intelligent person will attempt to argue. Late experience upon our own coast, especially in New York harbor, proves not only their importance, but also their efficacy, though they sometimes, in individual cases, operate with seemingly unnecessary hardship. Sir Walter Scott, in describing his detention at the lazaretto in Malta, tells us of an accident which occurred, illustrating the rigid enforcement of quarantine rules. It seems that a foremast hand on board the ship which had brought him hither fell from the yardarm into the sea. The fellow struggled manfully, being a good swimmer. Several native boats, which were near at hand, promptly steered in another direction, but an English boat's crew, belonging to a ship in the harbor, pulled as swiftly as possible towards the struggling seaman and rescued him from the water. For this act of humanity, the boat's crew was ordered into quarantine for a week. By saving the life of the sailor who had fallen from the ship which was in quarantine, they had run the risk of contamination!

On one occasion, while in South America, it was the author's misfortune to be at Rio Janeiro when the yellow fever was raging there. He was bound southward to Montevideo, but no ship going thither would receive passengers, lest the vessel should be quarantined. Passage was therefore taken northward to Bahia, Brazil, which was not a prohibited port, though yellow fever was found to exist there, also. Thence the Pacific Mail Steamship took us south again to the mouth of the Plate River,—*Rio de la Plata*,—passing, but not entering, the harbor of Rio. Thus one was compelled to travel by sea over two thousand miles for no possible purpose save to avoid being quarantined at Montevideo.

The cholera swept away several thousands of the Maltese in 1837, again in 1853, and once more so late as 1887. It will be observed that there exists a serious drawback in the location of the group. It is so situated, midway between the East and the West, as to be the victim of all such epidemics as are liable to be conveyed through the ordinary channels of commerce.

When the Knights of St. John first landed in Malta there were but twelve thousand inhabitants here. The Knights were soon followed by a considerable number of their former subjects in Rhodes, many of whom had, like themselves, been wanderers since they were driven from that island by the Turks. The order was still popular and wealthy, enjoying a princely revenue from various continental sources, as well as from the rich prizes which they constantly captured from the Ottomans, from roving Greeks, and from Barbary pirates. The proceeds of these captures were expended with a lavish hand among the Maltese people, diffusing plenty and comfort throughout the islands. This material prosperity soon stimulated immigration from various Mediterranean ports, and called home many who had endeavored to improve their fortunes by seeking occupation elsewhere. The natives were treated with great liberality by their monkish rulers. No taxes were demanded of them, while they were in constant receipt of money from the plethoric treasury of the Knights. There was occupation for all, and fair remuneration for the same. Never before, as far as we know, had the sunshine of prosperity so smiled upon these isolated shores. The period to which we refer is regarded as the golden age of Maltese history. The most intelligent of the present inhabitants are never tired of referring to the period when the white cross of St. John floated proudly over the castle of St. Elmo.

It was indeed the golden age, speaking in a worldly sense, but not in a spiritual one; yet the average Maltese not only sympathizes with the profession of these Knights, but even indorses their daily lives, public and private, which would not bear for one moment the conventional test of our modern civilization. It would seem as though the virtue and honor of Maltese wives and daughters counted for nothing, in this wholesale opinion of the period covered by the sovereignty of the order, and that the natives of that day ignored all sense of self-respect in their estimate of the value of pecuniary prosperity as compared with the sacredness of domestic purity. Women were bartered for like merchandise; personal attractions formed the criterion of their market value, while there was not even the pretense on the part of the Knights of keeping their priestly vows as celibates, by which every member of the fraternity of St. John was supposed to be bound. Women came voluntarily and openly from Italy, France, Spain, and England to trade upon their charms, added to whose number were those of their sex captured from the harems of the Mohammedans. Among the native women, little regard was paid to marital ties, and virtue among them was scarcely a recognized idea. We may be sure that the vile example set before them by those to whom they were taught to look up as their superiors was not without its evil influence. Lewdness is as contagious as typhus fever, and vice spreads like oil upon the water. We penetrate uncivilized countries and affiliate with barbaric tribes, who, following some strange instinct of the race, promptly adopt our vices, but are slow to imitate such of the virtues as we assume, if we have them not. It is not pleasant to dwell upon such a theme, but contemporary writers tell us that these islands became the scandal of Europe, and the popular resort of titled libertines, many of whom joined the Knights, who were then at the height of their material prosperity.

Let us draw the curtain upon such matters, which have necessarily been considered, and turn to such as are more attractive. Of these we shall find a teeming abundance from which to choose in this *Fior del Mondo.*

The charmingly picturesque capital, Valletta, surrounded at all times by a quaint Oriental atmosphere, lies on the north shore of the island, at its nearest point to Sicily, upon a promontory extending a considerable distance into the bay. For the sake of completeness, its exact position is given: longitude 14° 31Â′; latitude 35° 53Â′ north. The port consists of two spacious land-locked bays, known as Quarantine Harbor and Grand Harbor. The entrance to both is commanded by the massive white battlements of Fort St. Elmo, supplemented by Fort Ricasoli on the one hand, and Fort Tigné on the other. Each of the three fortifications now bristles with threatening cannon of modern construction,—"the red-mouthed orators of war." The two harbors, forming a double port, are each subdivided into small bays, creeks, and indentures, which are well adapted to naval and commercial purposes, for which they are improved, all being embraced within the elaborate lines of the marine fortifications.

Grand Harbor contains the naval hospital, arsenal, dock-yard, and custom-house, with Fort St. Angelo inside and Fort Ricasoli at the entrance. Quarantine Harbor has at its mouth Fort Tigné, while within is Fort Mangel and Lazaretto Island. The landing designed for the mail steamships is also here. The lazaretto is the most perfect of any arrangement of the kind in Europe. The tongue of land upon which the city stands is a narrow, rocky peninsula, dividing, as we have said, the two harbors, so that Fort Ricasoli at the entrance of Grand Harbor, Fort St. Elmo upon the point of the peninsula, and Fort Tigné at the mouth of Quarantine Harbor are all on a line at the sea front, and are capable of repelling the approach of any ship afloat. A bird's-eye view of the topography of the port of Valletta is at first a little confusing to a stranger, but its plan soon becomes clear, and the object of its arrangement is realized. It is then seen that the natural facilities have been admirably adapted to the general purpose by skilled engineers. We do not hesitate to say that there is not a more complete system of fortifications extant, in any part of the world, than the cordon of defensive structures at Malta. The forts of the harbor, however, form but a portion of the vast system of fortifications which completely surround Valletta. Such a gigantic amount of heavy stone-work as they represent could only be erected where the material was abundant and the labor cheap. The stone excavated in sinking the deep ditches was used in raising the escarps; and as to the necessary labor, that was done by the army of slaves retained on the island by the Knights. When they were not confined at the oars of the galleys, they were compelled to labor in erecting these elaborate defenses. Like the Egyptian builders of the Pyramids, the order was obliged to feed these workmen; but beyond that expense their services cost nothing.

While the Maltese capital bears, appropriately, the name of the Grand Master who originated and promoted its construction, these defensive works, so remarkable and so perfect in their character from a soldier's point of view, should perpetuate the name of Jerome Cassan, the accomplished engineer of the order, who designed them, and under whose able superintendence they were erected. No wonder they call forth the admiration of all military officers who visit the place. Immense sums of money and incalculable toil were lavished upon the undertaking, regardless of any probable necessity for the expenditure. So far as the science of military defense goes, it would seem as though perfection had been reached when Chevalier Cassan finished his original plans; but each new Grand Master of the Knights seems to have thought it to be his duty to increase the number of forts, giving to the addition his own name, by which each section thus constructed is still known. Exposed points on the coast of both Malta and Gozo were fortified from time to time, until there were no unprotected bays or inlets left. For centuries before this was done, piratical invasions were frequently made by small Algerine or Turkish expeditions landing at unfortified points. A score or two of armed men were able to ravage a whole district, and carry off half a hundred families to be sold into slavery. The Turkish and Algerine war fleets were almost entirely manned at the oars by captives thus secured.

When these soldier-priests first took possession of the islands, there was but one fort at Malta, namely, that of St. Angelo, which hardly deserved to be called a fort. To-day, as we have shown, there is no unprotected point on the entire coast line of the group. Modern instruments of warfare have revolutionized the requirements of defensive works, and many of these elaborate structures, it must be admitted, are hardly appropriate to our times. Malta is the equal of Gibraltar in a military point of view, though the fortifications of neither are absolutely impregnable. Of the latter, it may be said that nature prepared the place for man's adaptation; but as regards the former, art alone has produced an unequaled amphitheatre of fortifications. On the land side Valletta is protected by a labyrinth of marvelous ditches and ramparts, many of which are cut out of the solid rock, besides having vast chambers, or caves, of the same substantial character, designed for the safe storage of grain in anticipation of the place being besieged. These rock-hewn caves are so arranged that they can be hermetically sealed. It is said that they will preserve grain in perfect condition for a score of years. A quantity of provisions is always kept stored in these receptacles for the use of the garrison, and to meet any sudden emergency, the same policy being adopted at Gibraltar and Aden. The warfare of our day, however, admits of no protracted sieges. Such a struggle as took place before Sebastopol, not very long ago, could not be sustained between two powers with the present means of destruction possessed by both parties. In the future, conflicts will be short and decisive. If anything relating to warfare can be merciful, the sharpest and shortest process is most so. Lingering contests entail such terrible consequent ills that they bring with them sufferings paramount to those caused by the conflict of arms. "The next saddest thing in war to a defeat is a victory," said Wellington, as he looked sorrowfully upon the field which he had won by a fearful sacrifice of human life at San Sebastian.

The two excellent harbors of Valletta might afford anchorage for six hundred ships of war, as they have bold, well-defined shores, and an average depth of ten fathoms. This was not so originally, but is the result of a thorough system of dredging, which has been faithfully completed.

As we look upon the scene from an elevated point, beneath the afternoon sun, while freely inhaling the lotus-like air of the Mediterranean, everything is serene and lovely. Over the terraced roofs of Valletta rises the square tower of the Grand Palace, gay with many colored signal flags. Across the harbor the eye rests upon Fort Ricasoli, and here stands stout old St. Elmo, while in the distance Fort San Rocco crowns a hilltop. Much nearer is Fort St. Angelo, with its record of a thousand years and more. The numerous domes and towers of the city, though they are not minarets, have much the same Oriental effect upon the eye. Myriads of small boats, painted in bright, fanciful colors after the florid Maltese style, and having canvas coverings sheltering the stern, shoot hither and thither like birds upon the wing. The boatmen stand while rowing, as do the oarsmen of the Venetian gondolas, pushing, not pulling, at the oars. Hundreds of small feluccas line the shore. A group of fishermen in rude but picturesque costumes are landing the product of their industry. Half a dozen ships belonging to the British navy, and as many huge mail steamers, swing lazily at anchor, while little erratic steam launches dart back and forth from ship to shore; a memorable picture, the sea and sky being its appropriate frame. French, German, Italian, and English flags indicate the nationality of the several vessels, but the eye searches in vain for the stars and stripes of our Union. The same absence of the American flag is only too observable throughout nearly all the ports of the Mediterranean and the far East. The home-keeping citizen who reads these lines can hardly realize the patriotic sensation mingled with dire homesickness which thrills the traveler, long absent from his native land, at sight of our beloved national emblem proudly expanding its folds upon a foreign shore.

We look in vain for one other significant flag, that of the eight-pointed cross, which for centuries waved over these battlements as the sacred banner of the Knights of St. John, the token of their religious faith and their resolve to conquer or to die, which led them in the van of battle at Jerusalem, at Acre, and at Rhodes, and under which they slaughtered the besieging enemy by thousands beneath the wall of Malta; the gallant flag which so often flashed defiance before the eyes of sanguinary Turks, treacherous Greeks, and rapacious Algerines upon the sea; the flag, alas! which was lowered in disgrace, in 1798, without the firing of a single shot in its defense, to give place to the tricolor of France, and to acknowledge the mastership of Bonaparte. This was an act of cowardice equaled only by that of the arch-traitor Bazaine, who shamefully surrendered a whole army at Metz which was perfectly capable of winning a signal victory over the Germans, if it had been led against them by a brave general. The world knows how that dastard poltroon was tried and punished for his treason, as well as of his miserable subsequent life and unregretted death in a foreign land.

To return to the Knights of St. John. This act of treachery—the surrender of Valletta to the French—was virtually the end of the famous order; the dying hour, as it were, of a brotherhood which had for hundreds of years defied the whole Ottoman power almost single handed, and whose members, as chivalrous knights, won the respect of Christendom.

One often reads of the great beauty of the sunset as enjoyed upon this group, and we cheerfully bear witness to the fact that this phenomenon of nature is justly eulogized. Writers are apt to grow enthusiastic over Italian sunsets, especially along the Riviera; but the author, who has seen this diurnal exhibition in all parts of the globe, can truly say he has nowhere witnessed it surrounded by more beauty and grandeur of effect than in our own beloved land. Bostonians who possess an appreciative eye for the loveliness of cloud and sky effect, have seen at the closing of day, looking westward over the Charles River, as glorious exhibitions of the sunset hour as any part of the world can boast. As to the beauty of the afterglow, the lingering twilight of New England, "whose mantle is the drapery of dreams," it can be excelled in no land in either hemisphere. In the enthusiasm of the moment, while on the Yellow Sea of China, the author gave precedence, in his published notes, to the remarkable sunsets which characterize that region; but in this soberer moment a calmer conviction is honestly recorded. Still, the quivering flame that seemed to burn like lava on the line where sky and ocean met, the iris hues softly reflected by the vapory tissue of clouds in the opposite expanse, and the gorgeous robes in which the on-coming night was wrapped that December evening upon the Yellow Sea, can never be forgotten by any one who witnessed it.

On the disappearance of the sun beneath the Mediterranean at Malta, as soon as the opal fires have burned out of the sky, light clouds usually fringe the horizon, emitting rapid flashes of lightning which continue for hours, recalling the Aurora Borealis as seen at Bodöe and Tromsöe, in Norway. There is no lasting twilight in this latitude. Night follows close upon the footsteps of the departing day. The brightness of the stars supervenes so quickly after the curtain falls upon the scene, and the mellow evening atmosphere is so clear, that the twilight is hardly missed by the watchful observer, as the Spirit of the night, upon dewy sandals, begins her course of the circling hours.

CHAPTER IV.

The Soil of Malta.—Imports and Exports.—Absence of Trees.—Equable Climate.—Three Crops Annually.—Use of Fertilizers.—Ignorant and Pious Peasantry.—Food of the People.—Maltese Women.—Oriental Customs.—Roman Catholic Influence.—Improvisation.—Early Marriages.—A Resort for the Pope.—Low Wages.—Beggars.—Wind Storms.—Blood Oranges.—The Carob-Tree.—Maltese Lace.—Sailing along the Shore.

It has already been mentioned that a large portion of the island of Malta is covered with a thin, rich soil, some of which, it is said, was brought from Sicily at infinite cost and labor. If this is so, of which we have reasonable doubts, it was done only to a very limited extent. Vessels sailing hence with merchandise for the mainland or Sicily, having no return cargo, may have occasionally brought back as ballast quantities of earth, but that there was ever any systematic importation of soil is not probable. Much of the surface of the island is still only bare, calcareous stone, exposed to the fierce winds, rains, and scorching sunshine. A process of disintegration is constantly going on which gradually reduces this surface rock to friable matter, and as soon as a space becomes favorable in its conditions by such means it is promptly improved by the natives for agricultural purposes. The extraordinary success which crowns the husbandman's efforts is the triumph of industry over natural obstacles. All soil is but broken and decomposed rock, pulverized by various agencies acting during long periods of time, counting centuries as days. The molten lava poured from the fiery mouth of Vesuvius has, in the course of ages, become the soil of thriving vineyards at Resina and Castellamare. The Bahama Islands, composed originally of coral and limestone, have, during the lapse of centuries, become such fertile soil at the surface as to nourish the royal palm, the orange, and the banana, together with the stout-limbed ceiba and the most delicate fruits of the tropics. It should be remembered, also, that vegetation does not depend alone upon the soil for its life and fruitfulness. Like human beings, it borrows vitality from the rain and atmospheric air.

This Maltese soil must be of a very prolific nature, and contain hidden properties which stimulate plant life beyond comparison, to furnish the means of support for so large a number of inhabitants in so circumscribed a space. It is true that cattle, sheep, and grain are regularly imported for the consumption of the garrison and the people, as the island does not yield sufficient meat and breadstuff for the support of the population; but other products which are raised here and exported go far towards balancing the deficiency, by the grain and other needed supplies which they purchase in return. Two articles, salt and soda, are produced upon the island and exported in considerable quantities, the annual income from which reaches a large aggregate sum. The early potatoes which are grown in several districts of these islands are of a very choice character, commanding a special market in England, and realizing good prices. So the Atlantic cities on the American coast depend upon Bermuda for their early supply of the same article. Where the ground is not cultivated, wild-growing masses of the prickly pear often form a feature of the landscape, while the almost entire absence of trees in the larger island, outside of the city, creates an arid appearance. The charming color and grateful shade which are afforded by groves is almost entirely wanting. Neither art nor nature can produce an effective landscape without their aid. Where the land is carefully improved, it is not unusual to realize three crops annually from the same ground, by a timely succession of seeds. It is the common practice to follow the harvesting of a grain crop by immediately planting the same field with cotton. This last article has long been an established product of Malta, where it is believed to be indigenous. The islands produce two kinds of cotton, one of which is pure white, the other of a yellowish brown, both having a staple combining length and silkiness in a peculiar degree. It will thus be seen that the capacity of the soil and climate is very comprehensive, and it is interesting to know that there are over sixty thousand acres of land under cultivation in Malta at the present writing.

The climate is so equable and mild that there is no sterile period of the year, no unproductive month in the twelve. Every division of the season has its special vegetation and its fragrant flowers, thus rendering the reign of floral beauty ceaseless. March and April, however, are the months which present the most luxuriant phase of vegetation in this latitude. Though Malta lies much farther south than Naples, the heat of summer is not so intense there as it is in southern Italy. The plants which are so liberally displayed in the balconies of the dwellings require no shelter all the year round. Thus at all times striking bits of color line the second stories of the houses upon the Strada Reale. It will depend somewhat upon the stranger's fancy whether he is attracted by these beautiful flowers, so vivid in color, or by the graceful forms, the lovely olive-hued faces, and appealing eyes, which are half hidden behind them, like screened batteries. One cannot closely observe the use of the Maltese hood, presumedly the insignia of modesty, without becoming convinced that it serves in no small degree the same purpose as the Spanish fan in the hands of an accomplished Andalusian woman.

The obtaining of three crops annually from the same field is not only remarkable in itself, but is also significant of the prevailing industry of the Maltese, as well as of the fertility of the soil and the propitiousness of the climate for agricultural enterprise. It is observed that in sheltered places, where the soil is quite neglected by the hand of man, nature exhibits often a wanton luxuriance of vegetable growth almost tropical. Another obvious reason for this marked fertility of the cultivated soil should be mentioned, namely, that the natives understand and fully appreciate the great value of manure, which no artificial fertilizer can equal in permanent results. Like the Chinese, the people here achieve excellent returns in agriculture by deserving them. The most unwilling soil will succumb to such persevering and intelligent treatment. The careful collection and application of domestic refuse to the land is systematically pursued by the farmers, which process is conducive to cleanliness and health as well as to good husbandry, thus serving a twofold purpose.

Were the same liberal use of easily obtained enrichment, together with a system of irrigation (also well understood in Malta), to be applied to our constantly abandoned farms in New England, we should hear much less grumbling as regards their sterility, while the returns which would be realized in the shape of an ample harvest would liberally compensate for all cost of time and labor. There is no zone where nature will do everything for man; his work upon the farm is only begun with the planting of the seed. The fact is, many of our farmers work on the principle of the Kodak man,— "You touch the button, and we do the rest." Sitting down in indolence and despair, such men wonder that their utterly neglected lands do not yield better crops, talking the while about rich fields and virgin soil which are supposed to exist somewhere, far away in Utopia.

Until the author visited Malta, he thought that the British island of Barbadoes, the farthest windward of the West Indian group, was the most densely populated spot on the globe, but here we find human beings numbering over thirteen hundred to the productive square mile. One intelligent statistician places the population at fourteen hundred, but the first estimate is quite extraordinary enough. As a matter of comparison, it may be mentioned that the population of England averages three hundred souls to a similar space. The steady increase of the people in numbers speaks well for the average health of Malta, on whose dry soil and in whose usually pure air children thrive and adults live to an extreme old age. The residents have a saying that invalids are obliged to go away to Nice or Mentone, on the mainland, to die, since no one shuffles off this mortal coil by natural means in Malta. There is certainly nothing in the local conditions or in the geographical position to generate any sort of malady. No vegetable matter is permitted to decompose, nor are objectionable substances allowed to remain aboveground. Malta no doubt has its drawbacks, but its climate, as a rule, is very healthy. "Malta healthy?" responded a local physician to our inquiry. "Why, we professionals are simply starved out for want of practice." "How about the plague and the cholera?" we asked. "Ah, an occasional visit of that sort occurs, to be sure, at wide intervals, otherwise our occupation would be gone." He added, "All the world is liable to such visitations; but as to the general healthfulness of this island, no one can justly find fault." Such is probably the truth. English physicians continue to send certain classes of their patients hither regularly.

The men one meets outside of the city, in and about the villages, engaged upon the land, or otherwise, form a hardy, swarthy, and capable race,—industrious, ignorant, and very pious. These men, on an average, are not quite so tall as those of North America, but they are strong, broad-shouldered, frugal, and honest, with a decided Moorish cast of countenance, whose usual expression is a compound of apathy and dejection. That the Maltese are a temperate people is very plain. Drunkenness is scarcely ever to be met with even in the humbler portions of the capital, or along the shores of the harbor, where seamen congregate, and where every facility for indulgence is easily procurable. It is but fair to say that sobriety of habit is the rule among the common classes of the people. In the rural districts great simplicity of life prevails. Vegetable diet is almost universal, varied by an occasional meal of fish. Meat is much more costly, and is seldom indulged in by ordinary people, in town or country. Fish, which abounds along the shore, is both cheap and nourishing. Shell-fish, especially, are a favorite food in Malta. We say meat is costly; it is only so, as compared with the means of the common people, and the amount of money they realize in the form of wages. Beef sells in the market here at about the same price as is charged in our Atlantic cities. Considerable mutton is raised in the group, but the beef which is used for food purposes is nearly all brought from over the sea, the larger portion coming from the Barbary coast. As regards the cost of living at Malta, that depends so much upon individual requirements that no general rule applies, but it is certainly considerably less expensive than at either Nice or Cannes.

A certain inclination for seclusion is observable among the Maltese women in all parts of the group. They are rarely, if ever, seen abroad with their husbands. Their predilection for indoor life is pronounced, and when hastening to morning mass through the streets of Valletta, the shielding black hood is always in requisition, unrelieved by a touch of bright or cheerful color. The general effect is nun-like and funereal. There is an axiom current here to the effect that "A woman should never appear abroad but twice,—on the day of her marriage, and that of her funeral." This sentiment emphasises in a degree the fact of the Eastern origin of the people. No such absolute seclusion as this saying implies is, however, observed here. Though the faldetta is universally worn, still, as we have already intimated, many women use it in so coquettish a manner that they not only expose their pretty faces, but they also manage to see all that goes on about them. The average woman is very much the same, whether in Cairo, on the Strada Reale, Malta, or on the Champs Elysées,— whether in the atmosphere of the Mediterranean, or on the banks of the Seine. The semi-Oriental custom of the sex, as observed in these islands, is doubtless a relic of their association with and descent from the Mohammedans. As they neither use nor understand a word of any language except Maltese Arabic, it is of course impossible for a stranger to hold conversation with them. One would have to speak, not Turkish, but Maltese Arabic, to do so.

The land in Malta is universally terraced on the side-hills. This method serves a double purpose: that of beautifying the landscape, while it secures the soil in its proper place, as one sees it in Switzerland or on the Rhine. Being of a spongy nature, the soil retains the moisture for a long time, thus insuring fertility. Though there are long periods during which no rain falls, little trouble is realized from drought. The ownership of the land is about equally divided between the English government, the church, and two or three thousand farming proprietors. The Roman Catholic institution is the same leech upon the common people here that it proves to be on the mainland and in European countries, keeping the ignorant, superstitious class in indigence by taxing its individual members up to the last point of endurance, and beclouding their humble mental capacity. How else could a swarming tribe of useless non-producers like the priesthood be supported in well-fed, sensual idleness, and the costly ornamentation and ceremonies of the church be maintained? There is said to be a priest for every thirty families in the group, men who are intensely bigoted and ridiculously ignorant outside of their professional routine, but who are the apt tools of more able personages who hold higher positions in the church. They are ever ready to show their credulous parishioners pieces of the true cross and other sham relics "to whet their almost blunted appetite." Yet it may be doubted if these cunning Maltese agents of the Romish church could go any further in this direction than was lately done by a priest of the same denomination in the city of New York, who pretended to exhibit for worship a bone from the body of St. Anne, mother of the Virgin Mary, which anxious hundreds of deluded people were "permitted" to kneel down and kiss!

Do not let us talk any more about idol worship among the Fiji tribes or the people of "Darkest Africa," while we have in our midst such barefaced trickery under the veil of religion.

The humble owners of the land in Malta, as we have tried to show, are naturally a thrifty, hard-working people, neither rich nor poor. The reader would be surprised to see how much of seeming plenty, comfort, and contentment exists among these sturdy natives under such adverse circumstances. Notwithstanding their uncultured condition, the lowly country people have a genius for poetry; indeed, all Eastern tribes who speak the Arabic tongue are thus endowed. This talent finds expression in a sort of improvisation, by which means two persons will hold earnest converse with each other, asserting and denying in something very like epic poetry. They chant their words in a wild, Maltese sing-song, which appear exactly to accord one with the other, though the music seems to be equally improvised with the ideas of the singer. However unconventional the words and the music may be, there is still a certain rude harmony in both, evidently animated now and then by gorgeous gleams of fancy.

These Maltese are a prolific race, marry quite young, rear large families, and are very fond of their children. Brides only thirteen years of age are common among the working classes. It is a touching sight to watch these childlike mothers with a crude instinct gently fondling their tiny babes,—dolls, we were about to write. It recalled far-away Japan, where the daily life of the humbler classes presents similar domestic tableaux. Japan is a land of babies, where the annual crop is marvelously sure. In both instances, these youthful mothers, as may naturally be supposed, grow old in appearance at a comparatively early age. It requires no prophet to declare that premature maternity entails premature old age.

We do not intend to convey the idea that ignorance and its natural consequences do not prevail among the Maltese peasantry, when we say that there is much of seeming comfort and contentment to be found among them. As an average class, these children of the soil exhibit only too clearly their want of culture and intelligence. The priests oppose all efforts to improve them by schools. Education is virtually tabooed by the church, it being held that devotion to the Roman Catholic religion is all that is necessary for their spiritual or earthly welfare. Said a famous English general: "Thinking bayonets are dangerous. What we require in a soldier is a machine that knows just enough to obey orders." So it is with the followers of the Roman Catholic faith; people who can read and reason for themselves are "dangerous," so far as putting trust in that bigoted creed is concerned. What the church requires is machines which will obey orders, and yield up their hard-earned wages to support the priesthood and the regal Romish palace of the Pope at Rome. Any unprejudiced observant traveler in Spain, Italy, Mexico, or South America will bear witness to the truth of this statement. Not one twentieth of the inhabitants of this Maltese group can read and write. In populous, overcrowded China, eight tenths of the inhabitants can read and write, and yet the Western nations look upon them as semi-barbarians.

Can any one indicate another people on the globe, eight tenths of whom can read and write? Education is not only compulsory, but it is the only stepping-stone to high preferment in the civil service of the government. Our venal politicians would do well to profit by the example of China.

It will be remembered in this connection that since the suppression of the Pope's temporal power in Italy Malta has been looked upon as a possible future residence for the head of the Romish church. An influential section of the councils of the Vatican has favored the idea, and it would seem to be well suited for the purpose. Were this to occur, Malta would eventually become the Mecca of Catholicism. We may not expect to see such a change brought about in our day; if it should ever happen, it would add but one more to the strange vicissitudes in the history of Malta.

The wages paid to ordinary laborers in these islands are insignificant in amount, though there has been an improvement in this respect during the last decade. Boatmen in the harbor demand but nine-pence, English money, for rowing a person to or from a ship lying a quarter of a mile from the landing. Equally moderate terms prevail for pleasure excursions, according to the service and the time occupied. Women employed in field labor receive twenty-five cents per day, and men one third more. The P. & O. Steamship Company pay to colliers half a dollar a day; the same men get forty cents per day at the wharves. Blacksmiths, carpenters, stonemasons, boat-builders, and sail-makers rarely earn more than seventy-five cents per day. The drivers of the street vehicles in Valletta are quite reasonable in their demands, and a shilling will pay one's fare to any part of the city. The little one-horse vehicles called *carrozzellas* are well adapted to their purpose.

The same economic conditions are found here as prevail in India and China. The multiplicity of seekers for employment keeps the prices which are paid for services at a minimum rate. So, in over-populated Barbadoes, a plantation hand can earn but twenty-five cents for a day's work continued through ten hours. To be sure, that sum will more than feed him; and as to clothes and shelter, these are of secondary consideration in the tropics, where only conventional ideas require the native race to wear clothes of any sort. Idlers swarm about the landings and in the open squares of Valletta, who, it would seem, might be better employed upon the soil inland. An organized effort of capital and official influence to this end would accomplish the object, and render many a square mile of the now sterile ground not only beautiful to the eye, but also exuberantly productive. All over the civilized world the most useless and idle portion of the people leave comparatively comfortable homes in the country, where at least good food and shelter can nearly always be earned, to crowd into cities, attracted thither by the glamour of vice and fast life which always prevails more or less in populous centres.

The arrival of a P. & O. steamship in the harbor of Malta, with a goodly number of passengers bound either east or west, is a harvest time for the beggars, who know very well how to challenge the generosity of strangers. They have made a careful study of the business; they have elevated it, as De Quincey would say, to the dignity of a fine art. The "Nix Mangare Stairs" of Valletta are the congregating place of an army of mendicants of every species, men, women, and children, who exhibit all manner of deformities, both real and artificial, as well as every grade of dirt and squalor. In landing and making one's way up to the main thoroughfare of the city, it is necessary to run the gauntlet of this horde of poverty-stricken people. At the base of these "nothing to eat stairs," the longshoremen and fishermen also congregate. It was just here that Midshipman Easy and his companion procured the boat in which they escaped after the "triangular duel." The evil odors permeating the atmosphere in the vicinity are what might be expected from a people reveling in garlic and eschewing soap. The daily food of the class one sees in this section of the city is a slice of black bread and a raw onion. The traveler's disgust and sympathy are both wrought upon to an extreme degree, while amid all the clamor and whining appeals the practiced eye pauses for a moment to note the picturesqueness of mingled colors and of ragged humanity. The same recalls to mind the broad stone steps leading up to the Capo di Monti from the Piazza di Spagna, in Rome, where the artists' models assemble, clothed in a "congress" of colors.

When it is remembered that the violence of the winds which sometimes blow over these islands is such that in any other part of the world they would be called hurricanes, the successful results achieved by the Maltese gardeners and agriculturists appear more surprising. In order to furnish protection from these fierce winds, high and solid stone walls surround every grain, vegetable, and fruit field, all of which are purposely made small in area. These yellow walls, wearisome, monotonous, and unlovely to the eye, are often ten feet in height, not only sheltering, but also hiding vegetation, so that when the island is first observed from on shipboard, while a few miles away, it appears like a huge stone quarry. Nothing could possibly seem more uninviting. Under these circumstances, scarcely a tree or shrub of any sort is visible, with the exception of an occasional slim and solemn-looking cypress, or a straggling old olive-tree raising its isolated and twisted head above the arid rocks. Some of these walls are redeemed from utter dreariness by the pendulous cactus which hangs from their tops, fringed with yellow bloom. It is a strange though common plant, consisting of a succession of bulbous formations, quite flat and an inch or more thick, which serve the double purpose of stalk and leaves. The incurious traveler is thus impressed, by these screening walls, with an incorrect idea of the true nature of the island.

A passenger once said, in our hearing, replying to a friendly query: "No, I did not land at Malta, and had no desire to do so. It is nothing but a bare rock, with a few dwelling-houses inside of big lines of fortifications. I saw quite enough of its barrenness from the deck of our ship to disenchant me."

How mistaken was this superficial estimate! One would think that the most prosaic passenger would wish to know more of the builders, and the monuments they have left behind them, in the stately city beneath whose stupendous ramparts the ship lies anchored. Let us chaperon the reader, so that he shall entertain no such unwarranted impression of this Queen of the Mediterranean.

Malta is particularly beautiful when seen from the Valletta side. At first, while distance intervenes, the city, softly limned against the azure sky, seems like some phantom mirage; but soon the picture, rapidly growing in distinctness, becomes clear in detail. The grim, defiant, and almost endless fortifications, the many-domed and terraced city, the grand and lofty stone warehouses, the great war-ships surrounded by lesser commercial craft, all gayly decorated with national emblems, combine to form a picture long to be remembered, while the island is girt by a sapphire sea of purest blue, reaching far away to the horizon,—such a blue as is sometimes reflected in the eyes of very young children, or seen in wood-violets just opening their petals to the light. One should approach the place with a kindly purpose, and not harshly repel the happy suggestions of the moment. If we would find picturesqueness and beauty anywhere, we must bring with us a reasonable degree of appreciation. It is the softened soul which receives delightful and enduring impressions. One pities the man who can travel from Dan to Beersheba and say, "All is barren," while we sympathize and rejoice exceedingly with him who finds "sermons in stones and good in everything."

A close inspection of Malta will undeceive any one as to its being a sterile spot. Grapes, melons, figs, oranges,—almost equal to those of Bahia, in Brazil,—lemons, peaches, apples, and pears, besides many other kinds of fruits and berries, are raised here in abundance. Gardening is brought to a high state of perfection; the closest observation reveals no weeds. It is plain that the husbandmen are familiar with toil and endurance. The small but prolific vineyards are charming to look upon, though it must be admitted that the Maltese grapes are not of the best sort for wine-making. The wine in common use here is imported from Sicily and southern Italy. Comparatively little fermented liquor of any sort is consumed by the natives. Grapes are usually eaten in their natural condition, when sufficiently ripe, but they are not so plentiful as to form a portion of the food supply of the populace at certain seasons, as is the case in Switzerland and the south of France. The blood orange is grown in the vicinity of Valletta in great perfection, being propagated by grafting a slip of the ordinary fruit tree upon a pomegranate stem. The color of the pulp of the fruit thus produced inclines to that of the adopted tree; hence its expressive name. This luscious orange, even in Malta, where it abounds, sells for a higher price than the ordinary fruit. In Florida we have large and productive orange groves, but they are the result of infinite care and intelligent methods. Here in Malta the orange seems to grow after its own sweet will, requiring but very little attention from the period of the fragrant blossoms to that of the ripe and golden fruit. The Mediterranean orange is not so large as the Florida product, but it is of finer quality and rich in flavor, with a thin skin and an abundance of juice. One other indigenous fruit should be mentioned. It is called St. John's fig, because it is at its perfection on the anniversary of the fête of that apostle as celebrated by the Romish church. Other species of figs are grown upon these islands, but none equal to this. The mingling of sexes is so important and so clearly defined a factor in regard to the fruitfulness of the tree that the cultivators of the fig-trees in Malta heed it as strictly as they would in the breeding of favorite animals.

The staple product of the group is perhaps cotton, which is exported in limited quantities, sufficient being retained and manufactured here for the use of the common people. The Maltese are believed to have been famous for the production of certain lines of textile fabrics, even in the ancient days of Phoenician sovereignty. History tells us that the Sicilian prætor, Verres, sent hither for women's garments,—certain fine articles of female wear, with which to deck the favorites of his court; and doubtless there was even then produced here something similar to that which is so favorably known as Maltese lace, and which is still so profitable a product of this people. Diodorus Siculus said in his day, "The inhabitants are very rich, inasmuch as they exercise many trades, and in particular they manufacture cloths remarkable for their softness and fineness." Lace is also now made by the Greek women, not a little of which finds its way to the counters of Valletta merchants, where it is sold to strangers as being of native manufacture.

Here and there small plots of sugar-cane and tobacco may be seen under fairly successful cultivation, but we suspect that both are of modern introduction, for certainly they are not indigenous. The appearance of these small fields of the Indian weed and the saccharine plant, to one familiar with their growth in Cuba and Louisiana, is like a broad caricature. Cigars, chewing tobacco, and snuff are produced here, but almost entirely from stock which has been imported in the raw state for this purpose. Considerable quantities are exported in the manufactured form, though the local consumption is large, the English garrison being liberal purchasers, while tobacco in some form is the usual indulgence of the longshoremen.

One occasionally sees in Malta a peculiar tree called the carob, with thick, dark green foliage. It is a species of locust, growing to an average height of ten feet, but spreading along the earth three times that size in width. If its extended branches reëntered the soil it would be like the Asiatic banyan-tree. The carob is said to be as long-lived as the olive-tree, and bears a nourishing bean, which is cooked and eaten by the common people. It is considered particularly excellent for fattening domestic animals. Sheep and goats eat the bean in a green state from the branches of the carob, which has given rise to the saying that in Malta animals climb the trees to procure their food. This tree is green all the year round like our spruce and pine, and flourishes in the most rocky soil, requiring but little depth of earth to sustain and feed it. It seems to have no difficulty in finding or in making fissures, into which to send its expanding roots. It will be remembered that the friable rock of which the group is formed, until it has been exposed for some time to atmospheric influences, is almost as soft as common clay. If there are palm-trees on these islands, outside of the botanical gardens at Floriana, we did not chance to see them, but we have known writers to speak of the palm as growing in Malta. The climate, though semi-tropical, is hardly adapted to the life of this beautiful tree, which is one of the greatest charms of the tropics and the East.

Nothing in the neighborhood of Valletta affords such enjoyment, or is so suggestive and restful, after a busy day occupied in sight-seeing, as a pull along the coast beyond the harbor's mouth, in a good Maltese boat, propelled by a couple of stout oarsmen, while the languid sea breaks upon the shore in tender caresses. It goes without saying that a moonlight night must be selected for the excursion. One is not likely to forget the picture presented by the grim fortifications, the looming towers and domes, the tall, slim spire of the English church, the mass of flat-roofed dwellings, the clear-cut architectural lines of the principal edifices, or the fascination of the cradlelike motion, the delightful coolness, the great sense of peacefulness and silence. Is not this elysium? How responsive are the dimpled waters to the smile of the gracious moon, which suggests so much more than it reveals! How idle and sensuous is every surrounding! When the passing breeze touches the surface of the waters with a gentle pressure, the color deepens, just as a youthful maiden's cheek might do, electrified by a lover's first kiss. Is it because one realizes the evanescent character of these delights that a feeling of sadness intervenes? Is there not a gladness which makes the heart afraid?

It is impossible to give expression to the golden memories we have cherished of these delightful Maltese associations,—pictures which time cannot efface, images, beautiful and enduring.

CHAPTER V.

The Climate of Malta.—The Furious Grégalé.—Liability to Sunstroke.—The African Sirocco.—Cloudless Days.—A Health Resort.—English Church.—View of Etna.—Volcanic Disturbances.—Will Malta Eventually Disappear?—Native Flora.— Flower-Girls of Valletta.—Absence of Lakes and Rivers.—The Moon-Flower.—Grand Stone Aqueduct.—After the Roman Plan of Building.—Fountains.—Results of Irrigation.

The climate of Malta is a subject of more than ordinary importance. The air and sky are African, though its life and associations are strongly European. The winter temperature—December and January—very rarely falls below 50° Fahr., and though hail-storms do sometimes visit the islands, at rare intervals, snow is unknown. The season when such unwelcome visitations occur is very short. An entire day devoid of sunshine, even in the winter months, is unusual. It is not without interest to know that the longest day in this region is fifteen hours less eight minutes. In summer the thermometer rises to 85°, and even 95°, in the shade, while the direct rays of the sun are then almost unbearable by human beings, and especially by unacclimated foreigners. *Coups de soleil* are not uncommon in the ranks of the soldiery. Those familiar with the life of Grand Master La Vallette will remember that he died from sunstroke received here in 1557. A brief exposure to the sun's heat cost the life of the hardy old soldier who had survived so many dangerous wounds received on the battlefield. It is a saying in Malta that only newly arrived tourists and mad dogs expose themselves to the blaze of the midday summer sun. Even the natives are cautious in this respect.

The temperature drops rapidly when the fierce wind known as the grégalé prevails, blowing from the northeast across the Ionian Sea directly into the Grand Harbor of Valletta. When this wind occurs, the blue of the sky turns to a dull leaden hue; clouds troop up from the east in close phalanxes; the birds fly low, uttering ominous cries; and all nature seems to be in the throes of distress. An evil wind,— sometimes it is of such force as to drive the largest vessels from their moorings, while it makes sad havoc among the lesser craft. On such occasions, everything afloat which can be so handled is hauled up on the shore, which is the usual mode of securing small vessels all along the shores of the Mediterranean to-day, just as it has been for centuries. The natives who navigate these waters have quite a reputation as efficient mariners; but they do not compare favorably with either American or European sailors in this respect. They are not seamen of the long voyage, who have learned to contend successfully with the ocean when in its wildest moods. Their instinct is to run at once for a safe harbor when a storm threatens. So with the mariners of the Red Sea, between Aden and Suez, who will not venture out of port if the hot winds of that region blow too hard to permit a candle to burn on the forecastle of their vessels. Asiatics, as a rule, are poor seamen.

A pampero at Montevideo or a norther at Vera Cruz is not much more disagreeable and destructive than is the grégalé at Malta (the "Euroclydon" of the Scriptures). Nor is one other dreaded visitor much less objectionable; that is, a strong wind rising on the Egyptian coast, which, sweeping hitherward, wraps an unwelcome mantle of cold gray mist about the Maltese group.

This bit of terra firma is so isolated and exposed on all sides that when any severe weather prevails in "the great middle sea," it must encounter its entire force. In summer the heat is often aggravated by the sirocco, a humid, wilting, scorching wind which blows from the southeast across the African desert, sometimes charged with a fine, penetrating dust, for which it is difficult satisfactorily to account. This wind, on leaving Africa, is quite dry; but when it reaches Malta, having traversed a long expanse of sea, it becomes heavily charged with vapor, without losing the heat which it borrowed in passing over the African desert. It subjects those whom it encounters to something very like a steam bath. Yet regardless of all drawbacks, whose importance we are by no means inclined to exaggerate, the average winter weather is considered by many Europeans to be delightful and wholesome, attracting scores of English invalids and others annually, who are in search of a temporary home abroad to avoid the dreary London season of fog and gloom. After giving the subject considerable attention, together with careful inquiries of local authorities, the author came to the conclusion that Malta was not a very desirable resort for consumptives; nor should it be forgotten that a low form of typhoid fever is common much of the year in Valletta. The dreaded African wind just described prevails in September and October, often blowing for three or four consecutive days. It must be a sound constitution which can successfully withstand its enervating influence. An invalid quickly loses appetite, courage, and even physical capacity to walk any distance, when the sirocco prevails.

The winds of the Mediterranean are so regular in their occurrence as to be easily and correctly anticipated at their proper seasons. This was understood, and attracted special notice, even in ancient times. "The wind goeth toward the south, and turneth about unto the north; it whirleth about continually, and the wind returneth again according to his circuits" (Ecclesiastes i. 6).

The seasons are divided here into five winter and five summer months, spring and autumn being each one month in duration. Winter begins in the middle of November; summer, in the middle of May. The winds are rather cool in winter unless they blow from the southwest. When they come from other quarters, they pass over snow-clad mountains, the Atlas range, those of Corsica or Sardinia, and the hoary brow of Ætna. The chief advantage of this island group as a winter resort for those in delicate health is the large proportion of sunny, cloudless days, while the main drawback is the occasional fierceness of the winds. This sums up the matter in brief.

A book has been lately issued from the press, written by one who traveled eastward, entitled "Seeking the Sun." It is to be hoped that the author was successful in his search. If not, let him visit Malta, not forgetting to take with him a white umbrella. It is useless to look for a land without climatic objections. The difference between Malta and the famous Riviera on the opposite coast of the mainland is, upon the whole, very slight. At Nice and Mentone, in fact all along that favorite coast bordering the Mediterranean, the mistral is the bane of the health-seeker; while in this group the grégalé is the twin evil. This minute mention is made for the sake of completeness. On the whole, the Maltese climate is equable and mild. It is not so dry, atmospherically, as Algiers, Tangier, or Egypt; but it is quite as warm. As is generally the case throughout the Mediterranean basin, the difference in temperature between night and day is scarcely two degrees. Uniformity in this respect is a great desideratum, and it is certainly to be found here. The author has realized a difference of thirty-three degrees Fahrenheit within twenty-four hours in Cairo, Egypt, and also in St. Augustine, Florida.

Malta was first rendered popular among English health-seekers by the visit, for this purpose, of Dowager Queen Adelaide, widow of William IV., who passed the winter of 1836 on the island, with decided advantage to her physical condition.

The Dowager Queen evinced her gratitude for restored health by erecting here an Episcopal place of worship, known as the Church of St. Paul, situated on the Piazza Gelsi. It is a plain edifice, both inside and out, but of chaste and elegant Grecian design. The old palace of the German branch of the Knights of St. John was torn down to afford a site for this church, the construction of which drew upon the generous donor's purse to the extent of one hundred thousand dollars. Its tall, pointed spire is quite conspicuous, in a general view of the town, the architecture being so in contrast with its surroundings. There was a bitter but useless opposition made by the arrogant Roman Catholic priesthood of Malta against its construction. The priesthood, however, soon found that they had to deal with a power that could crush their influence in the group altogether, if it chose to do so, and were forced to eat humble pie, after exposing their spirit of bigotry. This church has a fine set of bells, and contains a valuable theological library. The Dowager Queen also established an infant school or kindergarten, with an English lady teacher, which proved to be a decided success, and a revelation to this isolated community as regarded the education of children. It proved to be a spur to mental culture in older persons, who saw, with surprise, children five or six years of age able to read and to answer simple questions in arithmetic, as well as exhibiting ripening intelligence concerning everything about them. This admirable example was not without its due effect upon the government. There are to-day ten infant schools and seventy-six primary schools in the city of Valletta. The visit of the Queen Dowager lasted three months, during which time she endeared herself very much to the Maltese by her kindness and consideration.

The excellent and melodious organ used in St. Paul's Church was removed from the cathedral in the quaint old city of Chester, England, where it had long served its purpose, being replaced there by a very superior modern instrument.

The atmosphere of this region is so clear that the grand, solitary, sulphurous cone of Mount Ætna can be sometimes seen, though it is situated a hundred and thirty miles away, in Sicily. The coast, stretching east and west from Cape Passaro, which is the nearest point to the Maltese islands, is also occasionally visible. The mountain, when seen against the northern sky, assumes the shape of an irregular cone with a widespread base. Some not clearly understood law of refraction must aid the human vision to discern these objects at such great distances beyond the horizon. The most favorable time of the day to seek a view of far-away Ætna is at sunrise or near sunset. The reader familiar with the White Mountains of New Hampshire has doubtless seen Portland harbor, in the State of Maine, from the top of Mount Washington, though this is a distance of about eighty miles. In this case, the object which is sighted at such long range is at sea level, while Ætna is over ten thousand feet above the surface of the Mediterranean Sea. Sailors describe the view of far-distant objects as promoted by "atmospheric looming," which perhaps applies in this instance, when one not only sees the low-lying coast of Italy, but it appears to be hardly more than twenty or thirty miles away.

The idea of this group of islands being in some way connected, beneath the bed of the sea, with the volcano just named is no longer entertained. The Maltese islands have often experienced severe shocks of earthquake, but, so far as is known, never at the time when Ætna was in eruption. Sir Walter Scott, in his journal, mentions having experienced a shock while he was on a visit to the island, of which the inhabitants seemed to take little, if any, notice, showing that it was not a very uncommon occurrence. On the Pacific side of South America, say at Valparaiso, it must be a very decided demonstration of this sort to cause remark. The most destructive earthquake in Malta of which we can find any record was in 1693, when the shocks were quite severe, and continued at brief intervals for three successive days, producing great consternation and injury. No loss of life is mentioned as having occurred, but the dwelling-houses and fortifications of Valletta suffered considerably, and one or two churches were nearly destroyed in the city. At Città Vecchia, in the middle of the larger island, the dome, towers, and in fact the entire walls of the cathedral were leveled with the ground by a succession of violent shocks.

There is a remarkable tradition, which has been handed down from generation to generation for centuries past, that the time will come when Malta and its dependencies will be swallowed up by the sea, and that where it is now so securely anchored the Mediterranean will be navigable for ships of any size. When we recall the fact that, within the memory of many of us, an island suddenly appeared off the shore of Malta, between here and the coast of Sicily, so large as to be formally taken possession of by Great Britain (called Graham's Island), but which has since totally disappeared, so that the sea is as deep over the spot where it stood as it is anywhere in the vicinity, the possibility of the prediction relating to Malta does not seem to be so very unreasonable. The only marvel is that the probability of such an event should have been predicted so long ago, and that we should have seen in the present century an exemplification of just such an occurrence in the appearance and disappearance of the island just spoken of, so very near Malta.

The Mediterranean constitutes the greatest marine highway in the world, a fact which particularly impresses one who has traversed nearly all the lonely seas and oceans known to navigators. It is seldom that some sail or island is not in sight from the deck beneath one's feet, while mammoth steamships are constantly met speeding to or from European or Asiatic ports, leaving in their wake two marked features, one of dark wreathing smoke, reaching skyward, and the other of bright, mingled colors upon the frothy sea. Over the seething waters thus churned into a Milky Way, in the wake of the steamships, hover flocks of broad-winged, snow-plumed gulls, watching for bits of marine food, or for scraps thrown from the ships' galleys, while filling the air with their rude, contentious cries.

The native flora of Malta is of a character similar to that of Sicily and northern Africa. The same semi-tropical species prevail, with but few exceptions, and where there is sufficient soil to permit, there is the same wild exuberance of vegetation. It was early in March when the author first landed at Valletta, a most propitious date for a first impression. The trees were in full bloom within the sheltering walls of the city, the lovely blossoms of the fruit trees being especially conspicuous, while every available nook and corner was beautified by a display of fragrant flowers in great variety. Among these were heliotrope, pinks, tulips, hyacinths, pansies, roses, and daffodils, "that come before the swallow dares." Many balconies of the dwelling-houses were wreathed with creeping vines, among which a cluster of scarlet bloom caught the eye here and there, relieved by pale blue and pink fuchsias. Choice bouquets were selling on the streets for a few pennies each, the pretty Maltese girls displaying exquisite taste in the arrangement of colors relieved by backgrounds of maidenhair ferns. Mingled with these charming flowers some very beautiful orchids were seen, though we were told that they were not in their prime so early in the year. To one fresh from a long sea voyage, it seemed as though a floral carnival was in full tide,—a revel of roses. This queen of flowers, together with violets, both of which grow here in profusion, was famous even in Cicero's time, when luxurious Romans reclined upon pillows stuffed with the odorous leaves. The Mediterranean sun and light appear to intensify the native color of every blossom and every flower. Was it a passing fancy only, or do these children of Flora sacrifice in a degree their normal fragrance in order to assume this extraordinary vividness of complexion? One is reminded of the gaudy birds of the tropics. Those of most vivid and brilliant plumage have not the exquisite sweetness of song which characterizes our more soberly clad favorites of the colder north. No zone monopolizes perfection; compensation is sure to peep out somewhere. If a certain charm or endowment be wanting, there is sure to be some equivalent furnished.

One floral gem is especially remembered which was shown to us in a private garden near the Porta Reale, and which was indeed a novelty. It is called in Malta the moon-flower, and its hour of bloom is at eventide. It never sees the sun, folding its leaves at the first gleam of the dawn. The flower is ermine white, like the snowy japonica, and is nearly as scentless as that regal flower. So the lily-like night-blooming cereus of the Bahamas opens its petals at sunset, and closes them at the break of day.

There are no rivers, natural lakes, or running streams worthy of the name on these islands, but there are numerous excellent never-failing springs, whose overflow is improved for irrigating purposes, and whose regular supply has been carefully utilized for a period of over two centuries by means of a system of waterworks of a very substantial character. This important work was begun in 1610, and finished in 1615. The winter rains are fairly abundant in the months of December, January, and February. The water from this source is saved for domestic use by means of ample stone cisterns, nearly every dwelling-house being thus provided. The grand aqueduct which furnishes the city with drinking-water is over nine miles long, finding its chief fountain-head at Diaz Chandal, not far from Città Vecchia. In order to insure a full supply, several springs were united by means of subterranean conduits, so that the combined water flows towards the capital in one large channel. As far as Casal Attard the aqueduct is under ground; from this point it rises and disappears according to the undulations of the surface of the island. These springs are never affected by drought, and as to the quality of the water, we can bear testimony to its purity and excellence. In its course, the water passes over a line of many hundred substantial stone arches, picturesque to look upon, but entirely superfluous. It is built after the old Roman style, being raised to a level across the valleys and depressions. These people did not know that water will always rise to the height of its source. The Romans showed the same want of knowledge regarding this, the simplest law of hydraulics; *vide* the graceful, half-ruined arches which cross the Campagna to the very gates of the "Eternal City." The principal outlet of this Maltese aqueduct is a conspicuous and ornamental fountain in the square of St. George, fronting the old palace of the Grand Masters. From here the water is distributed by conduits, which extend to various parts of the town and fortifications. There are over fifty public fountains in Valletta. Some of these at times exhibit novel pictures, when the people in characteristic groups gather about them for their supplies.

Such a system of waterworks, built in the old style as described, must have cost an extravagant sum of money, but the Knights of St. John did not lack for ample means to perfect any undertaking which might conduce to their health or comfort, and, it may be added also, which would contribute to their luxurious mode of living.

In the course of time, this first aqueduct proving to be inadequate to the demand, a second one was added. The new iron supply pipes were laid after the modern style,—that is, under ground; and as Valletta is situated at a lower level than the springs from which the water is derived, the arrangement works admirably. It is still necessary, as we have said, to preserve all the rainwater possible, for domestic use. In a climate like that of Malta, the consumption of water is much larger per capita than is usually the case in more temperate regions. The amount used for irrigating purposes alone is very large; the prevailing fertility is to be attributed nearly as much to ample moisture as to the free use of domestic refuse for enrichment of the soil. The average annual rainfall is a little less than twenty-three inches, which would be entirely insufficient to sustain vegetation without artificial irrigation.

It was thought that the dry, cracked soil of the pampas of Australia was nearer to positive sterility than that of any known region; but when water was flowed liberally over experimental portions, and the seed, was planted without the application of any other fertilizer, in due time "the soil laughed with a harvest." In China and Japan, the patient husbandmen water their gardens, however extensive they may be, entirely by hand, except the rice-fields, which, being planted in low and marshy soil, are artificially flooded twice or three times each season. These Asiatics have found that serving each individual plant in just proportions produces grand results at harvest time.

Before describing Valletta, the unique and fascinating capital of Malta, in detail, we will ask the reader to accompany us to the adjacent island of Gozo. In coming from the west it is seen before Malta proper, and in point of historic remains is quite as interesting, while in natural verdure it far excels the larger and more populous island, from which it was doubtless detached by some great convulsion of nature in prehistoric times.

To reach Gozo from Valletta, a boat taken at Quarantine Harbor will land the visitor at the shallow bay of Migiarro, on the southeastern extremity of the island, amid a fleet of fishing-boats, hauled high and dry upon the shelving strand. The boats are called *speronari*, and are as buoyant and fleet as a sea-bird flying before the wind. They are pointed at both ends, the prow terminating at a height of two feet above the level of the thwarts. They have retained their peculiar shape for centuries. It is always interesting to pause here for a few moments, to take note of the abundance and excellence of the fish brought in by the boatmen just arrived from their early morning excursion offshore. The variety and redundancy of aquatic life in this latitude is something marvelous.

## CHAPTER VI.

Homer's Fabled Siren.—Singular Topographical Formation in Gozo.—Beautiful Island Groves.—Fertile Grain-Fields.—Flowering Hedges.—Aromatic Honey.—Herds of Goats.—A Favorite Domestic Product.—Milk Supply.—Prolific Sheep.—A Maltese Market.—Quail Shooting.—Rabbato, Capital of Gozo.—The Old Citadel.—Lace Manufacture.—Prehistoric Ruins.—The Giant's Tower.—Attractive Summer Resort.—Pagan Worship.

Gozo, the fabled isle of Calypso, the Gaulos of the Greeks, the Gaulum of the Romans, and the Ghaudex of the Arabs, with its rock-bound, cave-indented shores, is oval in shape, and has the same general characteristics as Malta, but is much more fertile. The undulating surface of the island gives a casual observer the idea of its being a hilly country, yet at only one place does it reach a height of over three hundred feet above sea-level. This is at Dibiegi, where a hill rises to an elevation of about seven hundred feet. When approached from the sea, Gozo appears to lie much lower than Malta proper, and this is really so. Through the early morning haze, both look like huge marine monsters sleeping upon the surface of the waters. The hills we have referred to are singularly conical, but are uniformly flattened at their tops by the disintegrating process of the elements, causing them to present the appearance of a myriad little volcanoes, though they are very innocent of any such dreaded association. In the Hot Lake District of New Zealand, near Ohinemutu, the author has seen a precisely similar appearance, but in the latter instance the effect was undoubtedly produced by volcanic action. The boiling springs, geysers, and hot lakes of this New Zealand district are almost identical in character with our Yellowstone Park phenomena. Both must be the result of smouldering fires far below the surface of the earth. In the New Zealand district an active volcano is near at hand, which often rages with destructive force.

Gozo is beautified with occasional groves of trees, which is an adornment almost entirely wanting in the larger island. These groves, however, are by no means numerous. The one great deficiency of the group is the absence of arboreal vegetation, and yet an abundance of trees could be made to grow and flourish here with very little effort. There are marl beds which might be utilized for the purpose, situated in various parts of the islands, besides which, the rocky formation of the group, as we have shown, is of a porous nature, full of fissures and crevices, easily admitting the roots of vegetation. There is a tradition that Malta was once covered with trees, and that they were gradually sacrificed to meet the demand for fuel and for other purposes. The cultivation of shade trees about the villages would add an element of beauty, and would afford needed shade, besides promoting a more liberal rainfall, which is so very limited here. Some of the Grand Masters have done much by their personal efforts to induce the planting of fruit and ornamental trees in and about the city. Several of the squares are thus beautified, the trees forming an agreeable shade where in midsummer the glare is almost intolerable in exposed places.

A modern survey shows the circumference of Gozo to be a trifle less than twenty-five miles. It has been famous from time immemorial for the large amount and the delicious quality of the honey which its inhabitants send to market. The thriving fields of red-flowering clover, which is called *sulla* by the natives, and which grows to an average height of three and a half feet, together with an abundance of wild thyme and purple blooming vetch, afford rich food for the industrious bees and the gaudy butterflies, "Yellow bees, so mad for love of early-blooming flowers." The peculiar clover of which we speak is indigenous, and a well-grown field, each upright stem surmounted by a large crimson flower, looks more like cultivated roses than simple clover blossoms. When the breeze sweeps gently over these fields, the eye is delighted by broad waves of rich color rising and falling in the warm sunshine, while an indescribable, ripe, harvest smell permeates the atmosphere. The geranium grows to a mammoth size on this island, and tall, dense, and secure hedges of it are not uncommon. In full bloom these form a most striking feature of the landscape, as peculiar as the agave hedges of Mexico. The former, when wearing their full-dress of scarlet, seem like a fiery cordon drawn about the spacious area thus inclosed. The latter, with their pale blue-green sword-like leaves, are as repellent as a line of fixed bayonets, and absolutely impervious to man or beast. The byways of the northwestern part of Gozo are delightful, verdant, and pastoral, while the air is redolent of clover, violets, and hedge roses.

One of the ancient titles of this island was Melita, a name which is believed to be derived from the excellent honey which it has always produced. We can honestly testify to the delightful aromatic flavor of this delicate article. Truly, it is a land flowing with milk and honey,—Melita, "Isle of Honey,"—its choice goat's milk being also a staple commodity. As for butterflies, to which we have incidentally referred, graceful, leisurely, aerial creatures, nowhere outside of southern India can finer specimens of this beautiful and delicate insect be found. An enthusiastic German naturalist in Valletta told the author that he had secured a rich collection in Gozo, and that he was then on his way to the little island of Filfla to reap a harvest in another line, namely, among the curious lizard family, which thrive upon its few square rods of rocky soil.

Who ever traveled in out-of-the-way places abroad, without meeting some quaint German naturalist, wearing a green woolen cap with an impossible leather visor, a sort of Dominie Samson, in search of ugly centipedes, stinging ants, extraordinary spiders, or other hideous bugs? These "Innocents Abroad" are all alike, wearing gold-bowed spectacles, and having a chronic disregard for clean linen. One can easily forgive the butterfly enthusiast, these delightful, innocuous insects, exquisite in their frailty and variety of colors, are so like animated flowers; but pray spare us from poisonous bugs, with innumerable crooked legs.

One has not far to go, after landing upon Gozo, before small flocks of well-conditioned, silky-haired goats begin to appear, intelligent-looking animals, with large, gazelle-like eyes and transparent ears. They are generally tended by a barefooted lad or a young girl having the slenderest amount of covering in the shape of clothes. These boys and girls, nine or ten years of age, are often strikingly handsome, the latter betraying a perfection of youthful promise as to form, distinctly seen through their scanty rags. The boys have the blackest of black eyes, and the brownest of brown skins, such as one sees among the Moors who come into Tangier with the caravans arriving from Fez. These sheep tenders would answer admirably as models for an artist, often unconsciously assuming artistic poses, forming grand pictures, and reminding one of the subjects which Murillo delighted in. The quiet self-possession of these children of nature is both impressive and significant. They are utterly untaught, but how graceful in every movement! It would be as impossible for one of them to be awkward as for a young kitten. Every attitude is statuesque and full of repose. They have borrowed somewhat of the grandeur of their birthplace, bounded by wide, untamed waters and limitless sky. As is often noticed among European peasants thus employed, the girls are always supplied, though never so young, with some knitting or crochet work which keeps their fingers fully employed. In the populous centres, men may loaf in the laziest fashion, and remain quite unemployed, unless it be in the arduous occupation of smoking rank tobacco, but the women seem to be instinctively busy at all times.

We are reminded in this connection of another article of production for which Gozo enjoys a certain and favorable reputation, namely, goat's cheese, a delicate dairy compound, which should be eaten while it is quite fresh. It is so well appreciated by the people of Valletta that little, if any, of the article is ever exported, though choice packages sometimes find their way to the larder of the P. & O. steamers, much to the satisfaction of traveling gourmands. The goats raised upon this island are of a breed which, it would appear, is specially adapted to the local necessities, having singularly well-developed udders, which reach nearly to the ground, and yielding milk profusely, while subsisting upon the most common and inexpensive nourishment. Small herds of these animals are driven by their owners about the streets of the capital, and milked at the doors of the consumers, just as one witnesses to-day in Paris and other continental cities. There is no chance for adulteration when served after this fashion; and we all know that milk challenges our credulity more seriously than nearly any other article of domestic use, where water is so very cheap and accessible.

Cows would require too much pasturage to be profitably kept on these islands, whereas the hardy goats, as we have said, are cheaply fed and easily managed. Sheep, which are kept here in considerable numbers, are quite prolific, often having four lambs at a birth, and rarely less than two. The cows and oxen which are imported are designed almost entirely for food, though some few are employed for domestic or farming purposes. Cattle come almost wholly from the Barbary States. These animals fatten quickly upon the rich clover, which is so cheap and abundant here, thus making excellent beef. Asses and mules are the chief means in use for transportation, and as a rule they are very fine ones. We were told that Malta-bred animals of this class were in special request throughout southern Italy. The native owner has an Arab's fondness for his horse or mule, feeds him abundantly, and cares for him kindly. Animals thus reared naturally present a better appearance, show finer instincts, and bring better prices. Those of Gozo are remarkable for their size and docility.

The gardens of this island supply the citizens of Valletta with nearly all the vegetables which are required for daily use, together with fowls, turkeys, and geese. Large quantities of green fodder come from the same source for the sustenance of the animals kept for use in the town.

An interesting sight may be enjoyed by going into the principal market of the capital of Malta, in the rear of the Grand Palace, at early morning, where one can watch the various products, fodder, fruits, and vegetables arriving from Gozo. The quantity and excellent condition of the supply gives promise of good fare at the average tables of the citizens. Various game birds are seen, also brought from the sister isle, especially quails. This bird not only breeds freely in the Maltese group, but comes hither at times from Algeria in large flocks, driven thence by the close pursuit of the local sportsmen. The Tunisians make a wholesale slaughter of the quails annually in the month of May, shipping the game thus secured to France, it being a favorite bird with the Parisian gourmands. In the mean time the people of Algeria complain of a fearful increase of the all-devouring locusts, indigenous there, which, when young, form the food supply of the quails. So all extremes outrage some clearly-defined law of nature, and entail prompt punishment. Doubtless the securing of a reasonable number of these birds would do no harm; but when the pursuit is carried to the verge of extermination, some penalty must follow.

During the open season, as it is called, the officers of the British garrison— desperately at a loss, it would seem, to find amusement—resort to Gozo for quail shooting. There is also a certain season of the year when a variety of ducks, plover, snipe, and other aquatic birds may be taken. Only about a score of species of the feathered tribe make their permanent home in the group; but there are hundreds seen resting here from time to time, on their migratory course to other climes. In stormy weather, dead birds are found at the base of the big lighthouse on Gozo, attracted and half-dazed by the staring eye of fire piercing the darkness of the night. When flying at great speed, they are dashed fatally against the stout glass which shelters the lantern. Similar occurrences are known in Massachusetts Bay, at the lighthouse on Minot's Ledge, where the keeper is enabled to replenish his larder with game birds after a hard blow at night. This lighthouse at Guirdan, Gozo, dominates Cape Demetri, looming far heavenward when observed from the sea, above which it stands four hundred feet, at once gladdening and guiding the seamen in the nightwatches.

An attempt was made to introduce hares into Gozo for sporting purposes; but the residents of the island, with the dire experience of Australia and New Zealand before them, protested against it, and fortunately succeeded in averting the dreaded scourge. As is well known, the rabbit pest in the two countries named has assumed such proportions as to defy the combined efforts of the settlers to get rid of them. Every green leaf and tender root which comes in their way is destroyed to appease the hunger of these rabbits; and vegetation is as effectually obliterated from the land as would be the case if visited by millions of locusts.

Let us review, for a moment, the geographical and topographical character of this island.

Gozo is situated off the northeast end of Malta, from which it is separated by a deep channel, less than four miles wide, known as the Straits of Freghi. The principal town and capital is Rabbato, a sleepy, Old-World metropolis, of very little consequence to the outside world. It has been named Victoria by the English. The place contains some five or six thousand inhabitants, besides which there are nine thrifty, though small, villages upon the island. Lace-making is the almost universal occupation of the people of Rabbato and its vicinity. The incessant clicking of the bobbins, driven by deft fingers, greets the ear on all sides. Of course there is a "Calypso" Hotel ready to capture the innocent tourist. It is worthy of note that this special industry of fine lace-making should have prevailed so long in Gozo. For aught that is known, it may have originated here. It is certain that its popularity dates long prior to the Roman colonization in the Maltese group. Common usage does not retain the title given to the capital in compliment to Queen Victoria of England, and in honor of the Jubilee year. It is popularly known, as it certainly should continue to be, by its original name.

Rabbato is situated very near the centre of the island, on one of a group of conical hills. The citadel overlooking the place is partially in ruins, but was once quite a substantial and extensive fortification, being over half a mile in circumference. Whoever selected the spot as a stronghold could hardly have realized that it was commanded by more than one elevation in the immediate vicinity. Where its walls are not raised upon the edge of a precipitous cliff, it is approached by very steep stone steps, which could only be surmounted by an enemy under a concentrated fire from several points. The place has a deep ditch after the style of the Valletta fortifications, but this old stronghold is rapidly crumbling to pieces. It was a mistake to select this spot for the capital, if for no other reason than on account of the absence of a good water supply. At the Bay of Marsa-el-Forno, near at hand, there is not only a good harbor, but excellent drinking-water in abundance, while the fertile soil makes a charmingly verdant neighborhood. There are some delightful summer residences on the shore of this bay, the resort of citizens who come hither from Valletta in the "heated term." Only those foreigners whose official duties compel them to do so brave the summer heat of Malta in the capital. The naval vessels which have wintered here disperse to their several stations at that season, and invalids return to England or elsewhere.

Rabbato was chosen as the capital of Gozo for the same reason, doubtless, that Madrid was made the seat of government for Spain, because it was so nearly the exact centre of the country, while almost every other recommendation is wanting in both instances. The same remark applies to Città Vecchia, the ancient capital of Malta proper. The small city of Rabbato contains a couple of fairly good hotels, a Jesuit college, a cathedral, and two or three convents. Without wishing to discourage the curious traveler from doing so, we would suggest that when he visits the capital of Gozo, he go prepared to repel an army of mosquitoes. The neighborhood is famous for this insect pest. The guide, native and to the manner born, remarked that they never troubled him, but devoted their attention entirely to strangers, which affords no consolation to the afflicted.

The visitor finds in this neighborhood some very interesting Phoenician and Roman remains, but mostly of the former and earlier race of colonists upon the island.

Among the antiquities is one very remarkable ruin known as La Torre de Giganti, "the Giant's Tower," which is probably the remains of a prehistoric sacred temple, whose builders bowed before the image of Baal. The careful study of antiquarians points to the fact of its having been formerly the temple of Astarte, the Phoenician Venus. There are others who attribute this ancient monument to a people who inhabited the group before the nomadic tribes of Tyre and Sidon formed a colony in Malta. This singular edifice, be its original purpose what it may, is constructed of stones laid in a very skillful manner, no mortar being used. The builders must have possessed admirable and efficient tools; there is evidence enough to prove this in the careful finish shown in many places. They must also have used powerful machinery to properly adjust such heavy blocks in place. The great antiquity of the Giant's Tower is undisputed. Its style antedates both the Greek and the Roman examples which have been spared to us, and it is plainly the work of a primitive people. It is situated on an eminence not far from Casal Shaara, and forms a large inclosure with walls of great thickness. In shape it is a circular tower open at the top, not unlike the "Towers of Silence" which form the Parsee edifices near Bombay used for the disposal of the dead. In this tower at Gozo, doubtless, the rites of fire were celebrated; human victims were probably sacrificed here, and their bodies burned. Fire, it will be remembered, was the symbol under which ancient tribes worshiped the sun. The character of this tower is also emphasized by a carved serpent cut in the solid stone, an emblem of religious veneration among the ancient people of the East. Egyptian gods were often represented with the bodies of serpents.

Even in our day, certain sects among the Japanese venerate this reptile as sacred. In Benares, India, bulls, elephants, and monkeys are held to be representatives of divinity. The author has seen in the Temple of Honan, at Canton, China, a pen of "sacred" hogs! In the sincere struggle to find some element as representative of the Great and Good, before which to bow down and worship, for these singular devotional freaks seem to be the outcome of such a purpose, one would think that the wildest fanaticism must surely stop short of such excessive grossness.

Touching this most interesting Gozo tower, which it is not unreasonable to say may have stood here for some three thousand years, it shows that the builders, whoever they were, did their work thoroughly. It is entered by two massive doorways, twenty feet in height and five or six wide. The interior is cut up into various apartments, the use of which can only be conjectured. The diameter of the whole is about ninety feet, a considerable portion being paved with large, hewn stones. The whole is supported by a foundation which no earthquake has yet been able to undermine, though, as we are aware, the island has experienced many shocks.

CHAPTER VII.

A Maltese Fishing Hamlet.—Old Fort Chambray.—A Grotto shorn of Poetic Adornment.—The "Azure Window."—Bay of Scilendi.—Pirates' Caves.—Prehistoric Bones and Skeletons.—The Vast Changes of Land and Sea.—Suez Canal.—Geological Matters.—Native Race of Arabic Descent.—Curious Stone Mortars.—Primitive Artillery.—Maltese Fungus.—Springtime.—Riches of the Harvest.—Origin of the Island of Gozo.

The Bay of Migiarro, which means "the carting place," is the commercial port of Gozo, so to dignify it, and was once considered of sufficient importance to cause the Knights to erect a substantial stone tower or fort for its defense. This is now in ruins, but the place has become a busy and populous settlement, whose interests centre upon the fisheries of this coast. The beach is a fine one, much resorted to for bathing purposes. Close at hand, southward, is the grand cliff of Ras-el-Taffal, a promontory nearly two hundred feet in height, crowned by old Fort Chambray, which was named for the member of the brotherhood of St. John whose liberality built it. He was a very rich Knight from Normandy, and when he died, he left one fifth of his large estate to finish this defensive work. The whole sum was required, and much more besides, to complete the well-designed and elaborate fort. It was begun in 1749, and was many years in course of construction, but it is now gradually crumbling away, not being considered of importance.

Notwithstanding their many ancient monuments, the object which seems to be of the most interest to the inhabitants and to tourists is the Grotto of Calypso. This is a rocky fissure on the northwestern shore of the island, situated about a league from Rabbato, and is the spot where the grotto is supposed to have existed. It is now only a simple limestone cavern, presenting no peculiarities worthy of detail. It has the usual stalactitic incrustations and developments, recalling the much more extensive caves of the same nature which the traveler sees at Matanzas, Cuba. It is quite isolated, but is constantly visited by small parties from Valletta, who drink in romantic ideas from the associations of the place, and refreshment from the clear, sparkling spring which meanders through the cave of the defunct goddess,—

"The fair hair'd nymph with every beauty crown'd."

While on the spot we seek in vain for those "verdant groves of alders and poplars, the odoriferous cypresses," and for "the meadows clothed in the livery of eternal spring," with which Homer poetically endowed the voluptuous abode of the Siren whose name he has immortalized. The view presented from the top of the hill crowning the location of the Grotto of Calypso is well worth mentioning, overlooking the Bay of Melleha and most of the island of Gozo, with Comino and Malta in the distance. The surface of the surrounding sea is at all times sprinkled with busy fishing craft, pleasure yachts, row-boats, and large hulls freighted with a wealth of merchandise.

In the neighborhood of Marsa-el-Forno, there is a stalagmitic cave of a curious and interesting nature, which was discovered so late as 1888. It is mainly situated under a field that lies close to the village church of Sciara. This cave attracts large numbers of visitors to Gozo, and in many respects is quite unique. It is eighty feet in length and sixty wide, and contains a museum of curiosities which are the wonder and admiration of all who behold them. When the cave is lighted by torches or magnesium wire, the effect is extremely beautiful, the thousands of crystalline stalactites suspended from the ceiling reflecting prismatic colors of extraordinary brilliancy. It is indeed a fairy-like grotto, much more worthy as a dwelling for Homer's nymph than the crude and exposed cavern on the shore, already described. To one at all familiar with these caves, which are found in various parts of the world, it is no special marvel. These cavities are formed by the slow process of well-understood chemical action, the active agent being the carbonic acid gas which is held in solution by the rainwater that percolates through the limestone roof of the cave. This acting upon the limestone dissolves and conveys it away in liquid and gaseous forms.

Not far from here is a curious natural stone arch on the shore, called Tierka Zerka, that is, the "Azure Window," through which one may look upon the sea as though it were an artificial opening set with clearest glass. It very naturally recalled a somewhat similar freak of nature which occurs on the island of Torghatten, off the coast of Norway, where one gets a sort of telescopic view, through a stone tunnel five hundred feet long, of the blue sea and the islands in range far beyond it.

The next largest town to Rabbato is Casal Nadar, the only one on the island whose population approximates in number to that of the capital. This place is famous for the fruit which is raised in its neighborhood, and especially for its excellent apples and choice ornamental trees. It has nearly four thousand inhabitants. The cultivation of the land is brought to a much higher standard here than in the larger island, but the dwelling-houses are inferior to those of the villages of Malta proper; and yet in estimating the general thrift of the country population of the two islands, the result is decidedly in favor of Gozo.

A pleasant drive of three or four miles from Rabbato, through a garden-like region where poppies, clad in imperial scarlet, peep out from among the hedges to delight the eye, brings one to the Bay of Scilendi, whose perpendicular cliffs contain many rocky caves, few of which, probably, have been explored within the memory of living residents hereabouts. They are believed to have been, in olden times, the rendezvous of corsairs, where their ill-gotten wealth was stored, where they held their revels, and where their prisoners were confined until they were sold into slavery at Constantinople, or on the Barbary coast. The manifest fertility of the soil lying between here and the capital is owing principally to the irrigating capacity of several invaluable and never-failing springs of pure water with which this region has been exceptionally favored. The tangled masses of kelp and seaweed, which constantly accumulate on the shore, are regularly collected by the thrifty natives and liberally applied to the land as a fertilizer. This material, becoming duly decomposed, imparts its rich chemical properties to the soil, and thus repays the laborer tenfold.

Malta has been pronounced by an act of the English Parliament as belonging to Europe, but the fact that the stratification of the southern part of the island corresponds exactly with that of the coast of Barbary indicates a similar origin. Ptolemy thought it was African, but Pliny gives it to the Italian coast. Geologists of our day not only believe that the Maltese group was once a part of Sicily, but that in the far past it was also joined to Africa. In evidence of this deduction, carefully prepared maps of soundings taken between the islands and the continent on either side of the group are produced, while in the soil of both Sicily and Malta the skeletons of hyenas and other animals indigenous to Africa are frequently to be found, besides other fossil remains indicating a like conclusion. If this supposition be correct, how great must have been the changes which have taken place in the physical geography of southern Europe and Malta! What a general upheaval and subsidence must have agitated this famous sea in the remote past! That important topographical changes have taken place in these waters and in their relative connection with the land during historic times is well known. A little more than two thousand years ago, the Mediterranean and the Red Sea were united. De Lesseps' canal was no new proposition. Nature had already half done the work by means of the Bitter Lakes, and the modern engineer had only to restore a connection which time had destroyed.

Among many other interesting fossil bones, teeth, and complete skeletons unearthed at Gozo by naturalists, those of a pygmy species of elephants were found, which must have stood but about four feet in height; these were manifestly of African origin. The Ceylon elephant is distinctly different, in size and in several other features. The latter is the species universally met with in India, the beautiful island named having yielded a regular supply to this country from time immemorial.

Dr. Andrew Leith Adams, a distinguished English surgeon and naturalist, who resided for a period of several years in Malta, found fossil bones and teeth of hippopotami in various parts of the group. He says in a published account that he "unearthed hundreds of elephant's teeth, together with those of other tropical animals." He also discovered, in caves on the south side of the larger island, vestiges of aquatic birds of a species now extinct, and which in life must have been larger than the swan of our day. The presence of such remains indicates a great change of climatic conditions between the far past and the present time. It is difficult to imagine that Malta was ever the native land of elephants and sea-horses, but Dr. Adams shows, at least to his own satisfaction, that it was once covered with a productive soil and luxuriant vegetation. According to the same authority, it must have had lakes, rivers, and lagoons; trees and shrubs must have flourished in profusion, and it was doubtless part of a land the principal portion of which is now hidden beneath the surging waters of the Mediterranean.

Some of the most remarkable of Dr. Adams' discoveries were made in the neighborhood of the village of Melleha, north of St. Paul's Bay, on the principal island of the group. Here, in the sides of the ravine below the hamlet, are numerous caves of various sizes, both natural and artificial. Some of these are thought to be Phoenician tombs, as lamps and lachrymatories have been found in them. A few of these caves are now occupied by Maltese as dwellings. The village of Melleha has a very ancient church, partly excavated in the solid rock, which is held in great veneration, as it is said to have been consecrated by the Apostle Paul. It contains a very ancient picture of the Virgin, believed to have been painted by St. Luke! Penitential pilgrims come from all parts of the group to kneel and pray in this church, a service which, according to the local priests, carries with it absolution for any amount of sin and wickedness. It is needless to say that a good round fee is also contingent thereon.

The inhabitants of Gozo are, as a rule, thrifty, frugal, and industrious; the gipsy-like dark-haired women, who almost invariably have the charm of large, brilliantly expressive eyes, and even the young children, devote themselves assiduously to making the famous Maltese lace, for which a ready and profitable market always exists in European and American cities, especially for the finer quality and more delicate designs. Thus employed, for many hours of the day, they are often seen in family groups, seated by the doors of their humble dwellings,—small, massive, square stone buildings,—singing quaint old songs and gossiping together. Strangers visiting these districts almost always carry away with them, as souvenirs, specimens of this choice article, which has a reputation all over Christendom. The collection of crown laces belonging to the Queen of Italy contains specimens of Maltese lace reputed to be five centuries old, while photographs of objects found in Egyptian tombs date back the history of this delicate fabric to a thousand years or more before Christ. A choice pattern manufactured from a new material is now being made at Gozo, in small quantities. The basis is a peculiar sort of white silk. The completed fabric of this style is costly, and comes very near to the texture of a spider's web.

The Gozitans speak a language which differs somewhat from that common in Malta proper, and which is generally considered to be a pure native tongue, resembling the Arabic much more closely than does the mixed and confusing dialect of the larger island. The names of places, persons, monuments, household utensils, animals, and articles of food are all Arabic pure and simple. It is curious to realize that this people should have succeeded in keeping aloof from their conquerors so as not only to retain their own language in its purity, but also their personal resemblance to their Mohammedan ancestors. Their complexions are almost as dark as those of the natives of Barbary. Sometimes one detects a tendency to protruding lips and flat noses. When the Knights of St. John took possession of Malta, they found the islanders universally professing the Roman Catholic religion, but yet entirely governed by Arab forms and customs. Their constant intercourse with the Barbary States probably served to confirm them in these inherited proclivities.

At several points on the shore of Gozo where the attempt of an enemy to land might be possible, the Knights during their early sovereignty improvised a sort of ordnance called an earth mortar, after the following process. A hole of the proper dimensions was cut or drilled in the solid rock, at a certain angle trending towards the shore, designed to hold a hundred pounds of gunpowder. The explosive was placed at the bottom, and after a proper fuse was connected therewith, it was covered with a layer of boards to act as a sort of wadding. Upon the boards a ton or more of stones and rocks were placed, which completed the charge. On the approach of an enemy, which would necessarily be by boats, the fuse could be promptly ignited, and a wild discharge of rocks would at once take place, sending the missiles high into the air at an angle which would drop them upon the approaching enemy. These stones, falling with destructive force upon the boats and upon those who were in them, would scatter death and confusion in their ranks. We have never heard of such a device put in practice elsewhere, but should imagine that it would prove efficacious in a rude way to defend an exposed seacoast. A large or even a small stone descending from a considerable height, under such circumstances, would be sure, if it fell in a boat, to go through its bottom, causing it to fill at once, and would be equally fatal if falling upon the heads or bodies of human beings. The rock, which is of the nature already described, admitted of being easily hewn into such shape as was desired, while exposure to the atmosphere soon hardened it to the required consistency and resisting power. A second discharge of such a mortar might possibly involve as much danger to the defenders as to the enemy. It must be remembered that at this period, between three and four hundred years ago, the use of artillery was comparatively in its infancy, and iron mortars, when they were procurable, were of the crudest manufacture.

As forming a contrast to those days, and to the present means of conducting offensive and defensive warfare, it may be appropriate to mention that the author happened to be at Gibraltar not long ago, when a hundred-ton cannon was landed there. With this extraordinary piece of ordnance, it was believed that an effectual shot might be fired across the strait to Africa! As it is at least twenty miles from the Fortress of the Rock to the opposite coast, we took the declaration of the artillerist who expressed this opinion of the power of the gun with considerable allowance.

Hagar Tal Girnal—the "General's Rock"—is the name of a small, outlying, and nearly inaccessible ledge off the shore of Gozo, upon which there still grows in profusion, springing from the crevices of the rock, the curious plant known to botanists as *Fungus Melitensis*, Maltese fungus. This was so highly prized by the Knights of St. John as to be most carefully gathered in its prime, dried in the sun, and preserved as a stancher of blood in case of dangerous wounds, and also for the suppression of internal hemorrhage. Indeed, the fungus was believed to possess a variety of valuable medicinal properties. Small packages of it were sent annually by the Knights as precious gifts to the European potentates, it being equally prized by the recipients, who believed it to be otherwise unattainable. It is certainly a very simple weed, which is in flower about the last of April. When fresh it is of a dark red color, like our sorrel, and is of a spongy softness, but it is no longer held in such high repute either as an internal medicine or as an efficacious dressing for wounds. The famous rock is now seldom, if ever, trodden by the foot of man. It was always difficult of access in rough weather, though it is hardly a hundred yards from the mainland. The nearest village to the General's Rock is Casal Garbo. The people of the neighborhood declare that the famous fungus grows exclusively on this rock, but this assertion is not correct, as we have seen it in bloom on the Mediterranean shore at Leghorn, Tunis, and elsewhere.

The language of the people round about Casal Garbo differs somewhat from that which prevails in the rest of the island, seeming to be more Hebrew than Arabic. It is certainly far from being the latter tongue. This fact has given rise to many suppositions and learned discussions. We were told that the subject was to be carefully investigated by a committee of scientists, linguists, and archaeologists who were specially interested.

One hears about an important alabaster quarry, situated in the northwestern part of Gozo, but the author did not visit it. There are said to be ample evidences of its having been worked in an intelligent manner centuries ago, even before the Roman period, if the indications are rightly interpreted. Among so many nationalities as have at sundry times held possession of this group, it is a very nice distinction to attribute this or that work to any special one.

It has been mentioned that the island of Gozo is much more fertile than Malta proper, though why this should actually be so it would be difficult to explain. There is less rocky surface and more natural soil in the former than in the latter. This is realized at a glance. Certain it is that so far as verdure is concerned, the daisies and the dandelions appear and the grassy lanes of Gozo are aglow with vernal ripeness early in February, while the more drowsy soil of Malta does not awaken until the middle of March. Springtime is the season of the year when the earth sends forth her choicest treasures, even in this semi-tropical, Mediterranean clime,—

"Hanging her infant blossoms on the trees."

The deep purple vetch which enamels the fields of the islands, especially in Gozo, is beautified by the scarlet poppies which Nature sprinkles here and there with dainty fingers, producing vivid gleams of color in strong and pleasing contrast with the surroundings. Sometimes the ripening wheat-fields are made lovely after the same winsome manner.

The rich development and beauty of the tall, stout clover at this early period of the year is particularly noticeable, giving promise of a wealth of harvests calculated to gladden the husbandman's heart, while taxing the industry of the bees from dawn to twilight. We know of but few vegetable products which so richly repay the cultivators as this Maltese clover. Surely writers are not authorized to speak of this group of islands in mid-sea, with all these facts before them, as consisting mainly of a series of bare, weather-beaten rocks. Why mock and mislead us by such misrepresentations? In the wildest and least cultivated districts of Gozo, rosemary and thyme may be seen, showing that regal Nature has her poetic moods even under adverse circumstances, and that she often indulges her fancy in lonely places without regard to the cold appreciation of heedless human eyes, sometimes in her charming caprice outdoing more labored and artistic methods. "You will find something far greater in the woods than you will find in books," says St. Bernard.

Regarding the origin of Gozo, Comino, and Malta, we have seen that authorities differ materially. As if still more completely to mystify us upon the subject, Borzesi, a Maltese writer of considerable ability, has seriously attempted to prove that the group is formed of the summits of mountains belonging to the lost land of Atalantis. Signor Grougnet, of Valletta, had formerly in his possession a stone which was dug up from among some ruins near the old capital of Città Vecchia, in 1826, on which was an inscription describing Atalantis, and another to the effect that the Consul Tiberius Sempronius, in the year of Rome 536, ordered the preservation of this stone. This is either an adroitly conceived canard, or it is a suggestion worthy the attention of students of antiquity.

Bidding farewell for a time to Gozo, let us now recross the Straits of Freghi to Malta proper, there to enjoy the unequaled attractions and delights of beautiful Valletta.

## CHAPTER VIII.

Valletta, Capital of Malta.—A Unique City.—Bright Faces, Flowers, and Sunshine.—Architecture.—L'Isle Adam and La Vallette, Grand Masters.—Mount Sceberris.—Stone Dwelling-Houses.—Streets of the Capital.—A Specialty.—Fancy Goods Merchants.—The Yacht Sunbeam.—Main Street of the City.—A Grand Opera House.—A St. Giles in Malta.—Strada Santa Lucia.—Street of Stairs.— Thoroughfares.—The Military Hospital.—Characteristic Street Scenes.—Emigration.

As the Grand Harbor of Malta is entered and the white battlements of forts St. Elmo and Ricasoli are passed, one realizes the vast importance of the situation. Those heavy guns rising tier upon tier are silent now, but they are capable of doing fearful execution upon an approaching enemy. Probably the access to no other seaport in the world is more powerfully defended, unless it be that of Cronstadt, guarding the mouth of the Neva and the passage leading up to the city of St. Petersburg. Let us hope that such armaments may prove to be preventives and not incentives to warfare. "How oft the sight of means to do ill deeds make deeds ill done!" This is very true, and yet being prepared, fully prepared, for it has doubtless often prevented war. It is calculated that twenty-five thousand men would be required to properly man these defensive works which hem about the town.

Few persons visiting this capital for the first time are prepared, on landing at the broad stone steps near the Custom House, to find in this isolated place a large and beautiful city whose historic associations and architectural charms so admirably harmonize. Valletta is a genuine surprise. Whatever preconceived idea the stranger may have formed concerning it, he can hardly have approximated to the truth. Unique and mystical, it constantly appeals in some new form to the imagination. It strikes one at first as somewhat too pretentious in its endless fortifications, palaces, hospitals, churches, public institutions, theatres, and population, for a place so circumscribed geographically, and of such seeming commercial unimportance. It will appear, presently, as we progress in our Story of Malta, why and how such a full-fledged city should have sprung, Minerva-like, into complete existence, without experiencing the throes of incipient childhood, and the slow-ripening capacities of maturity.

The capital is well-built in solid masses of dwellings, presenting an unmistakable air of prosperity. One is reminded here and there of Oriental Tangier, with a suggestion of scenes borrowed from Spanish Granada. There are fascinating combinations everywhere, a succession of attractive novelties and surprises constantly greeting the eye. The town seems to be full of sunshine, of bright faces, and of flowers; at least it is so here on the Strada Reale. Everybody is gay and animated. The fountains laugh with rippling melody in the warm atmosphere, and the blossoms on the fruit trees are more lovely and fragrant than the bouquets which the pretty Maltese girls offer at such minimum prices. There is a rich and constant glow of shifting color, the yellow buildings reflecting light like burnished gold.

Surely it is good to be here, good to behold this charming phase of foreign life, and to contrast it with other scenes more famous but far less attractive. Paris is said to be the city of art and poetry, but Valletta embodies both within itself, adding a third allurement as being the city of romance and vivid history, which leaves upon the visitor's brain a memorable vision of light, life, and color.

Lord Beaconsfield wrote of Valletta as being equal in its architecture to any capital in Europe, but this is an exaggeration, and is incorrect. It may, however, be fairly said to vie with any town on the shores of the Mediterranean for the elegance of its construction and its general effect. "If that fair city," says the authority which we have just quoted, "with its streets of palaces, its picturesque forts and magnificent church (that of St. John), only crowned some green and azure island of the Ionian Sea, Corfu, for instance, I really think that the ideal of landscape would be realized."

The prevailing style of the edifices is Italian and Moorish combined, quite appropriate to the climate and habits of the people. The Knights are said to have brought with them from Rhodes the style of building which has been uniformly adopted here. The palaces now seen in the capital of Malta are reproductions of those left in the former home of the order, that "Garden of the Levant." There is an unmistakable flavor of the Orient in nearly everything which the fraternity brought hither from Rhodes, even extending, in no small degree, to their domestic affairs, manners, and customs. Valletta, including the immediate suburb of Floriana, is about two miles long and nearly a mile in width. After Venice we know of no other city more strongly individualized or more thoroughly mediaeval. There is no other capital with which it can reasonably be compared; it stands quite alone, a populous city and citadel combined. Like Gibraltar in purpose, it is as unlike that far-famed rocky fortress and town as can well be conceived. It was founded in 1566, by Jean de La Vallette, forty-fourth Grand Master of the Knights of St. John, whose statue, together with that of the brave and gallant L'Isle Adam, who preceded him in the important office, is to be seen over the Porta Reale. The latter was the able defender of Rhodes, the former was the hero of the great siege of Malta, in 1565.

Concerning the lives and achievements of both these remarkable historic characters, we shall have occasion to speak more in detail as we progress with our narrative.

The title proposed for the new capital by its founder was quite characteristic of the man and the priest. It was *Umilissima*, that is, "the humblest," but those who succeeded the Grand Master, and who faithfully carried out nearly all of his many purposes, saw the eminent propriety of calling it after his own name, and thus it became a fitting and lasting monument to his memory. La Vallette died in 1568, after a most remarkable and eventful career. In briefly reviewing his character, we find many contradictory traits. He was brave, but cruel; a warm and loyal friend, and yet a most determined and rigid disciplinarian with one and all. Only the renowned pirate chief, Admiral Dragut, who was his contemporary, exceeded him in terrible deeds of warfare, and yet he was always profoundly devout in his religious instincts, and specially observant of all the Romish church ceremonials and requirements. He is believed to have lived more in accordance with his religious vows than did nine tenths of the brotherhood over whom he presided. The Knights often curbed their vicious and licentious inclinations, checked by the force of his judicious example. He fearlessly led his people in every great contest, whether at sea, when he was commander-in-chief of the galleys, or on land, when contending with the Turks in a fierce hand-to-hand conflict. Being a powerful man physically and an expert swordsman, his flashing weapon dealt terrible execution wherever he appeared. He bore upon his body many scars which had been received in the van of battle, while gallantly fighting the infidel hosts for more than forty years: first in Rhodes under L'Isle Adam, afterwards upon the sea in the galleons of the order, finally and victoriously at Malta, where his management of the great siege placed him in the foremost rank of successful generals. This was the crowning heroic deed of his life. La Vallette was unquestionably the grandest of the Grand Masters of the order.

The original plan of the city of Valletta was not consummated until 1571, under the Grand Master Pietro del Monte, successor to Vallette, who imported masons and artisans of all sorts in great numbers from Sicily and Italy for this purpose. The original design was to cut down the ridge of rocks which form Mount Sceberris, upon which the city now stands, thus forming a plain only a few feet above the level of the Mediterranean. But this idea was abandoned as involving too much time and expense, and also on account of news received by the Grand Master from his spies at Constantinople, to the effect that another expedition was fitting out there to attack the island. So the new capital was finally built upon the sloping ridge which makes the natural conformation of the peninsula, rendering it necessary to build the lateral streets into stairways in place of roadways. Nevertheless, it is to-day the most attractive and interesting small city we have ever visited.

Mount Sceberris is an Arabic name, signifying "the jutting out of the cape." Like Asiatic names generally, it is very appropriate. Primitive races have a happy inspiration in this direction. Minnehaha, "laughing water," is an instance of apt and descriptive nomenclature born in the brain of uncultured Dakota Indians. The highest point of the city foundations is about two hundred feet above the level of the sea, into which it projects considerably over three hundred yards, with a width of twelve hundred, though it narrows at its seaward extremity and is lowest where it joins the line of the mainland. The fort of St. Elmo—the patron saint of mariners—crowns the narrowed point of the peninsula seaward.

The streets, running at right angles, divide the buildings into large, quadrangular groups. The houses, which are all flat-roofed, are guarded by low parapets, and are universally built of stone picturesquely carved, and ornamented by balconies of all sizes and patterns. The native stone masons are natural artists in the carving of stone. There is something in the very air of Italy, so close at hand, which engenders artistic taste even among the common people.

Within the dwellings, the rooms are quite large and lofty, insuring good ventilation. The floors, even to the upper stories, are composed of the same material as the main structure. This cream-colored stone is the outcrop of the latest geological period. The facility for obtaining this material where the whole island might be worked as a stone quarry has led to its general adaptation. It will be remembered that all wood, for whatever use designed, must be imported. Charcoal is used for cooking purposes, and so is anthracite coal. Wood is even more expensive than in Paris. The dwellings front upon thoroughfares of fairly good width, which are well paved and kept scrupulously neat and clean. When the building stone of which the houses are constructed is quarried, it is so soft that it can be easily moulded, or rather carved, into almost any desired shape, but exposure to the atmosphere hardens it gradually to the consistency of our American freestone. When newly quarried it is a light yellow, and under the midday sunlight it is somewhat trying to the eyes. Age tones down this effect to a sombre buff hue. It is found that exposure to the atmosphere, which at first hardens this stone, in the lapse of time causes the surface to peel off, or in other words a slow process of disintegration takes place, which gives, by the mouldering away of the surface of the stone, an appearance of great age. Any one who has noticed the action of frost upon brown freestone in our New England climate has a familiar example of what we describe.

The streets which run up the steep hillsides upon which the city is terraced have broad stone steps by which they may be ascended, but are quite inaccessible to wheeled vehicles, forming a sort of "Jacob's ladder," more picturesque than comfortable for one having to surmount them. The simile does not hold good as to angelic spirits ascending and descending, as those who are thus occupied here are very decidedly of mundane origin. These curious streets of stairs, over which Byron grew profane, with their quaint overhanging balconies, and life-size saints presiding at each corner, are indeed unique. Strada Santa Lucia, Strada San Giovanni, and Strada San Domenicho are among these, with their gay little shops opening upon the steps, while about the doors linger small groups of gossiping customers. These lateral streets are of easy grade, and if one does not hurry too much in coming up from the water front, they will safely land him at last on a level with the Strada Reale. It is easy to imagine one's self, for a moment, amid these curious surroundings, spirited away to another sphere, to some distant bourne whence travelers do not return to write books. At Bahia, in Brazil, the public ascend from the lower to the upper town, some two hundred perpendicular feet, by means of an elevator. Why might not Valletta be thus supplied?

The principal thoroughfare is the Strada Reale, lined on either side with attractive shops, which display choice fancy goods, jewelry, silks, photographs, gold and silver filigree work, and rich old lace. The goldsmiths of Malta are justly praised for the excellence of their work, original in design and exquisite in its finish. The ornamental articles of web-like silver are nowhere else produced in greater perfection. They recall the silver work found at Trichinopoli, India, the product of the natives there, and the more familiar manufacture of Genoa. The Maltese women are particularly skillful in the embroidery of muslin, and the scarfs and shawls which they produce are not inferior to the best which come from Turkey. They are often sold to foreigners as the work of Constantinople artists. We say artists, for these goods are as much a work of art as any piece of statuary, or a well-finished oil painting. One other specialty must not be forgotten, for which Valletta is noted just as that Rhine city of cathedral fame is for cologne. A preparation of orange-flower water is distilled here, which constitutes a most delightful perfume, very popular with strangers. It is a choice delicacy, suitable for many purposes. A wine-glass of this distillation added to a bathing-tub of warm water makes a bath fit for the gods, having an excellent effect upon the skin, opening the pores, and removing all foreign matter.

The shops on the Strada Reale are liberally patronized by visitors to the island, nearly all of whom are desirous of carrying away with them some attractive souvenir of Malta. It is computed that the passengers by each P. & O. steamship which stops at the port on its way east or west leave on an average five or six hundred dollars distributed among the fancy goods merchants, and we should say this is a very moderate estimate. A considerable amount of money is also expended by the owners of private steam and sailing yachts, which are constantly arriving at or departing from Valletta. The purchases of this latter class of customers are often of the most lavish character. A storekeeper on this thoroughfare told the author that the late Lady Brassey purchased goods costing her a thousand pounds sterling, during the few days in which the Sunbeam lay in the harbor. It is hardly necessary to remark that these accommodating and enterprising merchants do not part with their goods without realizing a handsome profit. There is a familiar saying among the English residents in the island to the effect that "a Gibraltar Jew starves alongside of a Maltese tradesman;" and still another, quite as significant, to this effect: "It takes seven Jews to cheat one Maltese."

It is well to remember one characteristic of the mode of doing business here. As in most of the Eastern bazaars, and also in the shops of Spain and Italy, the local merchant does not expect the purchaser of his goods to pay the first price which he names for them. It is often the case that he is quite prepared to sell at fifty per cent. less. A certain amount of dickering seems to be considered necessary, and it is in fact the life of trade in Valletta and Alexandria. The dealer, after he has specified the price of any given article, regards the customer with an air of serene indifference, as though it did not matter to him in the least whether he sells his goods or not. All the while, however, he is secretly exercised by an intense anxiety lest you should not purchase. If one really desires an article, it is pretty safe to offer half the sum which is at first demanded, and nine times in ten it will consummate the bargain. It is an illegitimate mode of doing business, but one which is common in many parts of the world.

Speaking of the yacht Sunbeam recalls some pleasant memories. It has been the author's privilege to meet that graceful craft in various foreign ports, and to have known its cultured mistress. The last time he saw this white-hulled rover was in the harbor of Sidney, Australia. It was on the passage thence that Lady Brassey died of malarial fever, and was buried in the bosom of the ocean which she loved so well.

Lord Brassey, who is an excellent seaman and practical navigator, fully shared with his accomplished companion this fondness for ocean adventure. The cabin of the Sunbeam was fitted with all the accessories of a lady's boudoir, and with charming good taste. It was a veritable museum of choice bricabrac, not an article of which was without its pleasant association, a token to stimulate agreeable memories. One who wrote so delightfully of her foreign experiences could not fail to draw inspiration from such surroundings. All parts of the known world had contributed to the adornment of her cabin, including domestic articles from the South Sea Islands, Fiji weapons, African symbols, Samoan curiosities, Chinese idols and oddities, Japanese screens, and Satsuma ware of rarest beauty.

Let us not wander too far afield. We were speaking of the main thoroughfare of Valletta.

This central street, which runs very nearly north and south, contains a number of fairly good hotels, three or four banks, besides several good restaurants and boarding-houses. It is a favorite promenade, day and evening, being well lighted by gas. A large and imposing opera house of the Grecian order is situated at the highest point of the Strada Reale, near to the Porta Reale,—"Royal Gate." The elaborate edifice is finely ornamented with Corinthian columns. If its traditions are correct, Adelina Patti made her début at this house. Patti was then quite unknown, and is said to have received one pound sterling for her part of the performance on the occasion; to-day she realizes one thousand pounds sterling for a similar service in America. Though her voice evinces the corroding power of time, she is unquestionably queen of the operatic stage. That there is excellent music dispensed at this fine Maltese opera house one can easily believe, remembering the proximity of the land of song. The edifice was originally built in 1864, but was partially destroyed by fire in 1873, a fate which seems sooner or later to befall all such places of amusement. It was promptly rebuilt, with many and costly improvements, so that it is now as complete an operatic establishment as those of Naples and Milan. It cost the Maltese exchequer over fifty thousand pounds sterling. So elaborate and pretentious a structure to be devoted to this purpose was hardly demanded in a community of the proportions of Valletta, and consequently, when the full amount of its cost was made public, there was considerable fault found with those officials who were responsible for such lavish outlay of the public funds. The opera season is from the middle of October to the middle of May, the performances being given three times each week. There is another theatre close to the square of St. George, known as the Teatro Manoel. This is a much older though quite as popular a place of amusement, and antedates the grand opera house a full century.

The edifices on the Strada Reale are generally three stories high, many of them large and luxuriously planned. They are mostly occupied as dwelling-houses above the first floor, the latter being usually devoted to some sort of shop. When they are not improved for this purpose, the lower windows are guarded with large, protruding iron bars, such as are commonly seen in the cities of Italy,—more suggestive than ornamental. It is probably custom rather than necessity which prompts to this fashion. There is a certain incongruity in passing through a populous thoroughfare where the lower windows are thus barricaded, while bright children and happy family groups are visible behind the frowning bars. There is no absolute danger of mistaking these residences for prisons or insane asylums.

The taste displayed in the architecture upon the Strada Reale makes it both quaint and beautiful; though it is very irregular in expression and after no fixed order, still it is not without a certain fascination and harmony of general effect. The façades exhibit here and there curious armorial bearings, emblems of their former knightly occupants, but atmospheric influences are gradually obliterating these interesting mementoes. Many were purposely effaced by the French during their brief mastership, who waged a bitter warfare against all titles or insignia representative of other than military rank. Judging by this immediate neighborhood alone, one would surmise that the town was especially cleanly and quite devoid of low or miserable quarters; but that there are vile, unwholesome dens here, where decency is entirely lost sight of, in certain lanes, narrow streets, and out-of-the-way places, no one can deny. So it is in all large capitals. Are New York, Boston, and Chicago entirely exempt from such conditions? We do not agree, however, with those who have given Malta a specially bad name in this respect. There is a section of the town leading from the Strada Forni, known as the *Manderaggio*, which signifies "a place for cattle," where the poor and needy of the lowest class herd together like animals. Why some deadly disease does not break forth and sweep away the people is a mystery. Yet even this questionable neighborhood is no worse in its debasement than the Five Points of New York used to be within the writer's memory. There can be no reasonable doubt that the average condition of the place, as regards morality, is of a far more desirable character than it was during the sovereignty of the famous—we had almost written infamous—Knights, whose priestly harems were simply notorious, and whose dissolute lives were unrestrained by law or self-respect. One thing we can confidently assert: there is nothing here so vile and so grossly immoral as Chinatown in San Francisco, and nothing worse than may be seen any day in St. Giles's, London, or the Latin Quarter of Paris.

How closely the lines of civilization and of barbarism intersect each other in all populous centres!

Valletta is well policed; rowdiness does not obtrude itself upon the stranger. Even the annoying importunities of the beggars in some parts of the town are not carried beyond the bounds of respectful, though earnest solicitation.

Along the course of the Strada Reale,—the Broadway of the capital,—which the French called, after the style of that period, Rue des Droits de l'Homme, at the corners where the cross-streets intersect it, graceful little kiosks are erected, painted in fanciful colors, whose occupants, like those seen upon the Parisian boulevards and the busy thoroughfares of Rio Janeiro, sell flowers, bonbons, coffee, fruit, and newspapers. The pretty Maltese girls, with dark, brilliant, beseeching eyes, who preside in these kiosks, are natural coquettes. Like the occupants of the tall booths in the flower market of Marseilles, coquetry is a most available part of their stock in trade. A winning smile will sell a bouquet more readily than the most eloquent oral appeal. These flower girls are kept quite busy making up and disposing of buttonhole bouquets at certain hours of the day, to adorn strangers and native dudes, from whose presence no locality is quite exempt.

This main avenue is the highest street in the city, and runs along the crest of the hill upon which Valletta is situated. The site gives the place natural facility for drainage, and the sanitary conditions seem to be excellent. Every one agrees that the capital is a healthy one, all things considered.

Let us enter, for a moment, one of the dwellings on the main thoroughfare, and leave behind the hot sunshine, which seems striving to set everything on fire in the Strada Reale.

Passing in through a lofty vestibule leading to an open court or patio, as the Spaniards call it, we come upon a maze of flowering shrubs, small orange-trees in boxes, and other floral charms. A miniature fountain in the centre of the area is very busy in sustaining at the apex of its tiny stream a hollow glass ball of vivid hue, an innocent act of aquatic legerdemain. The air is perfumed with fragrant flowers, and there is a cooling sensation in the gurgle of the fountain. There rises from this area a winding stone stairway, conducting to a gallery, from which doorways lead into the several apartments. These rooms can be thrown together so as to give the effect of a large hall, by opening the wide connecting doors. The apartments are spacious and lofty, being at least twelve or fifteen feet in height. There is not much in the way of furniture to describe in this reception-room which we have entered, which typifies the rest. It is lined with comfortable divans, and the glazed tiles of the floor are covered here and there with small Persian rugs. A few quaint old portraits of the Knights of St. John hang upon the walls, grim and ghostly in their expression, together with a large oval mirror of Venetian make. A lesser one hangs opposite, which plays queer tricks with the faces and figures presented to its glistening surface. A spacious table of dark wood occupies the centre of this spacious room, having four or five antique chairs with tall backs ranged beside it. There are no books, no small articles of bricabrac to be seen, and there is a sense of emptiness and bareness which oppresses one. It must have been the residence of some bachelor Knight, say a hundred years ago; to-day it is a boarding-house. Out of this large room a bay window or balcony opens, containing a mass of fragrant flowers gracefully disposed, showing a woman's taste and a woman's hand. Such is a Maltese drawing-room on the Strada Reale. One can take an apartment here and dine at a neighboring restaurant, and live very cheaply, if economy be a special object.

Each of the steep, narrow passageways which run down to the water's edge from the Strada Reale bears the name of some patron saint. Strada Santa Lucia is a typical street of this character, with its many tiresome stone steps, not one of which is level from end to end. The Imperial Hotel, so called, is upon this street. English and American visitors who are passing a few days here generally choose the Hotel Angleterre, on the Strada Stretta. There are half a dozen avenues which run parallel with the main thoroughfare of the city. Strada Mercanti is the most important of them. On this avenue there are several large public institutions, including the post-office, the Monte di Pietà, and the principal market. The latter is situated in the centre of the town, at the back of the governor's palace. Flies and beggars congregate here in almost equal numbers, forcing upon one's attention the puzzling problem of hunger and plenty existing in juxtaposition. Here and there are seen the spacious and elegant palaces formerly occupied by the rich, comfort-loving, luxurious Knights, which are now devoted to English government offices, as barracks, a public library, and law courts, or are improved for club purposes. It is a wealthy nation which holds sovereignty in Malta to-day, and her officials, civil or military, are lodged like princes. The original Auberge de Provence, with its cool, attractive corridors and lofty apartments, is occupied by the Union Club, and the Auberge de l'Auvergne, equally palatial, is now used as the Court of Justice.

The Order of St. John began its career humbly enough among the pilgrims of Jerusalem, by taking upon itself vows of chastity, self-abnegation, and poverty; but it ended in palaces, gross immorality, and undisguised debauchery. Its lowly birth in that sacred Syrian city was grand and noble in purpose, but ultimate success, together with the acquirement of power, fame, and riches, acted as adulterants to the original conception. Being only mortals, the Knights gave way freely to the weaknesses of humanity. This perversion of the fundamental design of the order was the natural presage of its gradual decline and final downfall.

The principal streets of Valletta which run parallel with the Strada Reale are Strada Forni, Strada Mercanti, Strada St. Paolo, Strada Zecca, and Strada St. Ursula. The second named, as we have already intimated, is the most important next to Strada Reale. Upon it is situated the large military hospital which was erected in 1628, and which contains four hundred beds. One apartment in this institution is nearly five hundred feet long, exceeding in size any room or hall in Europe. In this establishment the Knights were accustomed to serve by turns as day and night nurses,—as "Hospitallers," in fact, and thus to keep good their claim to the original title of the order.

Bonaparte, when he was in possession of Valletta, pronounced this civil and military hospital to be the most perfect institution of the sort in the world. It was lavishly conducted during the sovereignty of the Knights, no regard being had for expense, and there was no advantage known to the medical profession of the period which was not to be obtained within its walls.

Street scenes are always significant of the character of a people. Here, after the style which prevails in southern Europe, all sorts of trades are carried on in the open air upon the streets. As on the Neapolitan Chiaja, people live out of doors, invited by the mildness of the climate. Barbers, tailors, shoemakers, tinkers, and basket-makers ply their several callings in public, quite unsheltered by any sort of device, except that of seeking the shady side of the thoroughfare. The effect is at least to present an industrious appearance. It nevertheless seems rather odd to see a man, his face frosty with lather, in process of shaving under such circumstances, or to watch an individual posing upon the sidewalk while being modeled in wax by a native itinerant artist. This, by the way, is a specialty here, and its followers acquire great facility, with a true artistic touch.

Several of the minor streets are devoted to special occupations, such as the Strada Irlandese, "Irish Street," which, is well-filled with blacksmith's shops; in the Strada Levante dwell stone-cutters and ship-chandlers; another section is occupied by basket and chair makers, while in a fourth coffin-makers congregate. So, in the City of Mexico, one street near the great market is entirely devoted to the shops of coffin-makers, who have florid signs displayed which indicate their calling, and mural caskets hanging upon the shop fronts.

The crowded condition of the population suggests emigration, which is a necessary recourse in these islands. Many of the Maltese are to be found distributed among the several Mediterranean ports, especially at Gibraltar, Tangier, Tripoli, and Constantinople. They are quite unmistakable wherever they are met, retaining under all circumstances a strong individuality, and using only their native tongue. The men are sought for by sea-captains who navigate these waters, being as a rule excellent seamen, prompt and obedient. Like the Sicilians, they are quick-tempered and passionate, though not particularly quarrelsome. If they are allowed to carry a knife, they are liable to make use of it in a quarrel. As it is the men and not the women who emigrate, there is a preponderance of the latter sex in Malta.

These Maltese women are often very charming, especially in their figures and general bearing. No youthful person can be ugly while possessing such eyes as Heaven has been pleased to give them. They have almost universally a gentleness of manner which is in itself a great attraction in women. That their charms are evanescent must be frankly admitted; they marry early in their teens, and grow old quickly, like the women of the fellah class in Egypt, who when young are really beautiful, exquisite in form and graceful in every movement, but who fade rapidly under the cares of maternity and the labor of the fields. The occupations of the Maltese women, however, are of a far less wearing nature.

One never wearies of wandering about Valletta. There is somehow, amid the scenes encountered in these quaint streets, a suggestion of the Arabian Nights which haunts one all the while, only a degree less forcibly than at Cairo. It would seem to be quite the thing were Haroun-al-Raschid Grand Master here, accompanied by his favorite minister Jaafar, and there is ample material from which Ali Baba might recruit his Forty Thieves. May not this fellow who is crying in Arabic some mysterious merchandise upon the Strada Reale have new lamps to exchange for old ones? We only require a score of over-laden donkeys and a few mournful looking camels to complete the Oriental picture.

## CHAPTER IX.

Ophthalmia.—Profusion of Flowers.—Inland Villages.—Educational Matters.— Public Amusements.—Maltese Carnival.—Italian Carnival.—Under English Rule.— No Direct Taxation.—Code of Laws.—A Summer Palace.—Governor-General Smyth.—San Antonio Gardens.—Wages.—Oranges.—Life's Contrasts.—Swarming Beggars.—Social Problem.—Churches crowded with Riches.—Starving Population.— A Mexican Experience.

Nearly every locality which is visited by travelers is found to have some special annoyance which is active in its warfare upon humanity. Thus diseases of the eye prevail among the common people of Malta as they do in Egypt, a trouble in both countries which is caused by the fervor of the sun's rays and the general lack of shade, not forgetting also an evident want of cleanliness. The author has seen native camel-drivers come into Egyptian cities from across the desert quite blind for the time being from continuous exposure to the sun's rays and the powerful reflection of the heated sand. The same effect arises from the yellow stone dwellings of Valletta, and the bare rocks inland aggravate the prevailing trouble. So Arctic explorers, living amid the constant glare of the snow-fields, are subject to ophthalmia, an affliction which they guard against by wearing snow-goggles. In the Maltese capital, as in Cairo, there is a fine dust permeating the atmosphere when the wind blows, charged with silex and animal impurities, which finds lodgment in the eyes. The ordinary people have no predilection for the use of water wherewith to cleanse their hands and faces, consequently such matter accumulates in these delicate organs, first irritating, then poisoning them. Ulceration follows, and insects—especially flies, which are a great pest in Malta—carry the virus from one person to another, creating, in warm weather, an epidemic of sore eyes. Children are most frequently the sufferers; and this disease, commencing with them when they are of tender age, is liable to become chronic.

Nine tenths of the inhabitants of the group are professed Roman Catholics. One meets a priest or cowled monk at every turn in the public streets, as well as upon the roads inland. They usually wear a characteristic black robe, together with an impossible hat, very broad of brim and turned up at the sides. There are said to be about two thousand priests in these islands, whose physical appearance certainly indicates free and generous diet, not to say luxurious living. The reader may imagine what a strong contrast they furnish to the hungry, begging masses of the town whom they pass by with the most utter indifference. One is fain to ask, Does it ever strike the people, who are taxed so heavily to support these "walking delegates" of the church in idleness, that there must be something radically wrong in a system which fattens a priest by starving a laborer? The conduct of church affairs should be just as amenable to consistency and sound common sense as any of the affairs of life. The Maltese, unfortunately, have a paucity of reason and a plethora of priests.

Flowers are abundant in Valletta, and, as already intimated, are marvelously cheap and beautiful, thus arguing a certain degree of public taste and refinement in the community, which makes it profitable to raise them. "That man cannot be mean and deceitful," said a shrewd, cultured woman, and a good judge of human nature, "he is so fond and careful of flowers." Seeing a bouquet prettily backed with maidenhair fern, we asked if it was cultivated here, and were told that the plant grew wild in some of the caves of Comino, near at hand. In the environs of the capital there is a hamlet named Casal Attard, that is, "the village of roses;" there is also a Casal Luca, "the village of poplars;" and still another, Casal Zebbug, signifying, "the village of olives;" a simple but very appropriate system of nomenclature. Casal Luca is mostly inhabited by stone masons and quarrymen; indeed, the whole district about the hamlet is one large quarry. The church in this thrifty village contains three admirable and well-remembered paintings by that illustrious artist, Mattia Preti.

There are twenty-six small casals in Malta proper, the larger number of which are on the eastern end of the island, and all of them are very much alike. They are divided by narrow streets, designed to exclude the powerful rays of the summer sun, while the low stone houses are full to repletion of children and Arabic-speaking people with Oriental proclivities. Though there are beggars by the score along the roads and in the villages, there are no other obvious tokens of poverty. Indeed, there is a general appearance of thrift. It is in populous centres, in large cities, that real want and hunger are mostly suffered, where from force of circumstances the multitude of people cease to be producers, but are still consumers. Each of these casals has its school, wherein, it is said, the government tries to introduce the English language, but it would seem with indifferent success. Those who are sovereign here appear to be too indifferent in this matter. There is a well-organized college at Valletta, where degrees are conferred in divinity, law, and physic. To our inquiry of an intelligent citizen touching this subject, he promptly replied: "Education in Malta is cheap, bad, and neglected." This is only too true, though all the civilized world admits it to be the great and most effective weapon of Christianity and progress. The most effective missionary who can be dispatched to foreign lands is the competent school-teacher. Tenets of faith will adjust themselves in accordance with reason, among those who are rendered sufficiently intelligent to think for themselves. The ignorance of a large portion of the Maltese villagers is absolutely deplorable. They have no recognized language in literature; and if they had, they could neither read nor write it. They are quite uninformed even upon the most common current events. An English gentleman (Mr. Seddall), who lived some years at Malta, declared that they were not a whit better educated than the Bedouin Arabs. As a conclusive evidence of this, he tells us in print: "A laboring man once informed me that the Sultan was the supreme ruler of the island." The same author says: "The priests oppose all enlightenment of the masses." This is not anything new, as it is their known and admitted policy everywhere; but in the multitude of witnesses we arrive at the truth.

The school system of Valletta was reorganized a few years ago, but it is still far behind the general progressive ideas of our times. Education is not compulsory here.

The popular entertainments of a people form a good criterion for judgment as to their general character. The amusement which seems to be most generally resorted to in Malta is that of parading through the streets in a special garb, while displaying various banners in celebration of certain church festivals. As in the ritual of the Roman Catholic Church there are some two hundred such days in the year marked for similar displays, the festivities of this sort appear to be chronic, and absolutely pall upon one. The natives are inclined also to make these occasions an excuse for undue indulgences, and carelessness of conduct generally. The Carnival is also made much of by the common people, and indeed it would seem that all classes participate. It begins on the Sunday preceding Lent and lasts three days, during which period the populace engage, to the exclusion of nearly all other occupations, in a sort of good-natured riot, not always harmless. The most ludicrous and extravagant conduct prevails, the actors being generally masked and otherwise disguised. Hardly anything that occurs and which is designed only for diversion, and not instigated by malice, is too absurd for forgiveness. Ladies are ready to engage in a battle royal from their balconies, using confetti, dried peas, beans, and flowers, which they merrily shower upon the passers-by with all possible force. Sometimes, but this is not often, unpleasant missiles are employed and serious quarrels ensue. The day after the close of the Carnival, those who have taken any extravagant part in the revels, or who have been over self-indulgent, repair to the small church of Casal Zabbar, called Della Grazia, where they humble themselves by way of penance for their follies and excesses. It must be admitted that under shelter of the large liberty which the occasion of the Carnival renders possible, many otherwise quite inadmissible acts are perpetrated, and that as a whole this peculiar celebration is terribly demoralizing to all classes of the community.

A story of a tragic character is told, having a sad local interest, and which was a natural outcome of the carnival season. It happened not long ago. On the last day of the revels, when extravagance of costume and conduct had reached its climax, when the actors strove to so carefully disguise themselves as to render discovery impossible, a certain popular beauty of the humble class was being pursued, complimented, and plied with bonbons by a masked individual, to the great, disgust and annoyance of a youth who was her acknowledged lover. It seems that the conspicuous attention thus bestowed by a new aspirant for her favor was not entirely displeasing to the youthful beauty. The fact that her accepted lover evinced great jealousy at this condition of affairs seemed to spur on both the girl and her newly devoted companion. At last, jealousy so wrought upon the passion of the neglected lover that, seizing a favorable moment for his purpose, he plunged his knife to the hilt in the breast of the unknown rival. The wounded man fell to the ground, bathed in his own blood, and his mask was promptly removed to give him breathing space. He who had given the fatal blow escaped. To the amazement of all, the dying youth was recognized as the girl's own brother, who was merely enacting a Carnival deception. The man who dealt the murderous blow has never since been heard from, but the broken-hearted girl, who was by no means blameless, soon entered a convent and donned the irrevocable veil.

Once since the English held possession here, a Scotchman was sent to Malta as governor, a devout Presbyterian, who conscientiously endeavored to abolish the noisy celebration of the Carnival on the Sabbath. This so angered the people that it very nearly led to an open and general rebellion against English rule. The occasion was not without bloodshed, though the governor did not push matters to extremes. Their parishioners were secretly spurred on by the priesthood, who were only too happy to find an opportunity to make trouble for the Protestants.

Some of those who read these pages will doubtless remember the Carnival as it occurred annually in the principal cities of Italy a few years ago, in Venice, Naples, Milan, and Rome, but more particularly in the last named capital. The Italian populace would no more be content without the annual Carnival than the Spaniards would without their cruel bullfights. The difference between these nationalities is clearly evinced in these two exhibitions. The Italians are passionate and quick to quarrel, but as a rule they are not cruel, a trait which is, however, wrought into the very web and woof of Spanish character.

The Roman Corso is vividly recalled by the mere mention of the Carnival, a specially Italian celebration. Through that narrow thoroughfare the spirited and riderless horses, clad in barbed trappings which spurred them at every leap, rushed at wild speed until brought to a sudden halt by the heavy ropes stretched across the entrance of the Piazza del Popolo. In a similar manner, on high festive occasions the Strada Reale of Valletta was turned into a racecourse, though it is by no means level, like the Roman Corso. Intoxicated with mirth, frolic, and mischief, the motley Roman crowd, the better class of whom, men and women, wear masks, filled the atmosphere of the Piazza di Spagna with ribald songs and laughter. The streets which lead into and out of this central square were crowded with hilarious people dressed in caricature, all busily engaged in practical jokes and mimic warfare. Harlequins, gods and goddesses, clowns, spirits of good and evil, all were represented. Priests and peasants were depicted with their several belongings, together with members of the learned professions. Those who assumed these characters strove to be ludicrously consistent therewith. Foreign lookers-on sometimes mingled with the crowd, from which they were only too glad to escape after being decorated with mud, and having their tall hats driven down over their eyes and their coats turned inside out! To the crowd it was fun, but it was anything but amusing to the victims. Three days and nights of this pandemonium ended the mad frolic. To-day, in Rome as in Malta, the Carnival is losing its popular interest. Horses no longer rush furiously through the Corso, and there are but few maskers on the streets. The occasion is not forgotten in Milan, Florence, or Turin. It still lingers with some of its pristine extravagance in Venice, but its "glory" has departed.

The reader will perhaps sympathize with the exuberant memory of the writer, when it breaks forth for a moment recalling these vivid scenes of past experience.

Let us return once more to Valletta.

The British government seems willing not to interfere to any considerable extent in the domestic or religious affairs of the islands. An unequaled military and naval station is secured to England in the Mediterranean, that is the main point. The loyalty of the people to the British Queen is quite a secondary consideration. Were the Maltese to break out in a rebellious mood, they would be instantly and ruthlessly crushed. Their position would be in no way improved. The privileges which they enjoy would be greatly curtailed, and their political condition would assimilate to that of the subjected and down-trodden tribes of India. As we have said, there is no direct taxation imposed upon the Maltese. The rents of the government lands, together with customs, licenses, etc., bring in an annual revenue of about two hundred and sixty thousand pounds sterling, which is calculated to be quite sufficient. Malta is considered to be self-supporting, in the political acceptation of the term, so far as England is concerned. In fact, a small balance appears on the right side of the account toward the support of the large military organization held here in reserve at all times, and from which, in case of an emergency, she could draw for service elsewhere. Gibraltar, Malta, and Aden, the latter at the mouth of the Red Sea, form important links in the chain of British outposts guarding the route to her possessions in India. During the ninety-two years of English occupancy, the group has steadily increased in population, wealth, and productiveness. Were England to give up Malta, it would under some specious pretext fall into the hands of Germany, France, Italy, or Russia. It is far too insignificant in itself to maintain its independence, and too important in its strategic position not to be controlled by some one of the great nations.

As regards the code of laws recognized by the local courts, in conversation with a native advocate it was found that that of Malta was of a very confused character. These laws are based upon old Roman legislation, amended by ecclesiastical enactments brought hither by the Knights, and fortified by provisionary regulations issued by the several Grand Masters, and designed to meet special cases. The system is, indeed, a standing puzzle to the judges themselves. However, as the Maltese are not a contentious people, but on the contrary are most docile and easily governed, the authorities find no great stumbling-block in the legal code. When in doubt, they have always English common law to fall back upon, and being masters of the position, there is no appeal from the decisions rendered by the English judges. Here as elsewhere, litigation is an expensive luxury, in which only those with full purses can indulge. The petty courts are quite sufficient to keep the masses of the people in proper discipline. The large garrison constitutes the most restless element, but as its members are amenable to martial law, which is always prompt and decisive, good order is easily preserved. Trial by jury has been applied to all crimes since 1855. It was first introduced in certain criminal cases as early as 1829, but its scope was extended in 1844, and as we have said, it now applies to crimes of whatever nature.

The governor's summer palace is situated at Casal Lia,—known as San Antonio,—about five miles from the city, where the chief official makes his home during a portion of the year. The incumbent of the office at this writing is General Sir Henry Augustus Smyth, who receives a salary of twenty-five thousand dollars per annum. Sir Henry is also commander-in-chief of the troops stationed at Malta. San Antonio is on the road from Valletta to Città Vecchia, just before one reaches Casal Attard,—"the village of roses," with its fine old stone church. The "palace," as it is called at San Antonio, is spacious and handsome. Though it is quite plain architecturally, the surroundings are very beautiful, consisting of extensive gardens, artificial ponds, musical fountains, and myriads of thrifty fruit trees, the latter laden with blossoms or golden fruit, such as oranges, lemons, pomegranates, citrons, figs, and limes. The terraced grounds are connected by easy stone steps, inviting the visitor to ramble in all directions. A superficial view of the group gives no promise of such a lovely spot of ground, borrowed, it would almost seem, from fairy-land, or, as the Moors were wont to say of Andalusia, "a favored region dropped from Paradise." Gorgeous butterflies, fragrant geraniums, scarlet and purple verbenas, graceful lindens, glutinous honeysuckles, and ever-fragrant roses, all combined to attract the eye and delight the senses. One is reminded of the low lands of Florida and Louisiana, where the air at certain seasons is heavily laden with the perfume of the lotus-like magnolia, empress of the everglades. Very enchanting were the hours passed at San Antonio, beneath its cool green shades. One can never forget how brilliant was the floral display, how soft the atmosphere, and how glorious the sunshine.

Maltese gardeners understand their business, in the various combinations of which a tangible poem may be written by one loving his calling and with a genius for floriculture. Great care is taken as regards the fitness of one color or form placed in juxtaposition with another; a group of ornamental trees harmonizes with its surroundings, and even the fruits are classified with an eye to their fitness for companionship. An inartistic arrangement in a garden will jar upon the eye of a critical observer, even as the ear is shocked by a discord in music. It has been finely said: "To cultivate a garden is to walk with God, to go hand in hand with Nature in some of her most beautiful processes, and to learn something of her choicest secrets."

"How much is paid for the services of a capable gardener here?" we asked of the guide.

"About two shillings per day. How much is paid in America?" he inquired.

"Not less than ten shillings," was our answer.

The incredulity of the guide was written upon his countenance, but he made no reply.

The grounds of San Antonio, like all garden plats in Malta, are protected by high stone walls. Here, they reach upward eighteen or twenty feet, above which, here and there, a few towering dark green cypress-trees are seen, standing like watchful sentinels guarding the palace grounds. The large number of productive orange-trees makes the place like a garden of Hesperides. The Knights of old—this having been the summer residence of the former Grand Masters—are said to have realized a large income from the sale of the fruit ripened in these grounds. The orange grove contains over three thousand trees, which would excite the envy of a successful Florida cultivator by their thriftiness. In a favorite corner were some specimens of the evergreen loquat; its long, overshadowing leaves and peculiar yellow fruit reminded one of the attractive gardens of Hong Kong. At this season fine, luscious oranges sell in the market of Valletta at twelve or fifteen cents per dozen, while large quantities are packed and exported, realizing profitable returns. The royal family of England has a regular supply of this fruit forwarded from these islands, especially the fragrant and luscious tangerine, or mandarin species, which lies so loosely within its crumpled skin as to require only a touch to remove it. The natural covering of this orange is full of a highly concentrated and richly flavored oil, whence a superior perfume is produced, and also a flavoring extract. The fruits of Malta, being grown on an arid soil, are more juicy and savory than is usual in tropical regions, where they develop to an abnormal size, and where, if the soil is too rich, the pulp becomes spongy.

San Antonio is one of the loveliest and greenest spots on the island. The view of the sea, city, and harbor from some of the elevated points of the gardens is charming. Here the Duke and Duchess of Edinburgh resided for a considerable time, and here one of their children, Princess Victoria Melita, was born, in 1877. She is said to be the only British princess ever born in a foreign dependency of England.

The fee of the property of San Antonio is in the British government, having passed into its possession by right of conquest, like all other property formerly belonging to the Order of St. John in these islands. Pleasure unalloyed is not to be found on the earth. That we are in terrestrial regions, and not in Paradise, is made clearly manifest not only in this fruitful garden, but also in some decided form wherever we seek enjoyment. The prominent objection to this beautiful location is the maddening discomfort of flies and mosquitoes, for the place swarms with them during four months of the year. It is a happy provision of nature that we remember best the pleasures of our experiences in foreign travel, and soon lose the recollection of the annoyances which we encounter. One can dismiss the mosquito pest; but as we write these lines there comes back to us, like a half-forgotten strain of music, the recollection of sweet-smelling syringas, lilacs, and lemon verbena, mingled with the all-pervading Maltese orange blossoms. Taken as a whole, San Antonio is a perfect Gan-Eden, a garden of delights in which to linger and to dream, forming a sort of fairy world, peopled with blossoms, where wood-nymphs might hold their moonlight revels.

This is very pleasant to relate and to remember; it is enchanting for the time being, and puts one at peace with all human nature; but as we have just illustrated, in the instance of San Antonio, there is always a reverse side to the picture.

Let us glance for a moment at the every-day street life of the Maltese capital.

The observant stranger is struck with sadness upon first landing in Valletta at sight of the swarming hordes of the unemployed who throng the shore and some of the public squares of the city. He sees before him an ignorant, hopeless, poor, hungry mass of humanity, and wonders where these people can obtain sufficient bread to keep them from starving. The manifest poverty of the prolific lower classes of Malta is appalling to the political economist. Who would dare to sound the depth of this sea of human want and misery, the daily lot of these hordes of half-fed men? While looking upon such a scene, a resident with whom we were in company was asked: "Where can this army of poor, portionless creatures bestow themselves at night?" The reply was brief and significant: "They have always the sky over them!" Doubtless a large percentage of these people sleep on the bare ground, or rather on the flat stones leading up the lateral streets, with a step for a pillow, like homeless dogs, wherever drowsiness overtakes them. Fortunately, in this climate the poor do not suffer from cold under any ordinary circumstances. We were told by our companion that many of these lazzaroni were heedless rogues and professional thieves, without the least moral sense of right and wrong. Who can be surprised at the dishonesty of such poor, ignorant creatures? *Is* it dishonesty, this feverish, irregular, desperate struggle for existence? Must not food be had at any cost? Ah, the great social problem of dire poverty and purse-proud wealth, this startling inequality of possession and position, this paucity of sustenance on the one hand and plethora of means on the other, which presents itself in every populous community all over the globe!

It is to sever the Gordian knot of this confusing problem that the half-crazy, drinking socialist, the wholly reckless, unreasoning nihilist, resorts to the sword and the fulminating bomb. Far be it from us to sympathize with such disciples of anarchy; we only present facts to the mind of the thoughtful reader. Every one admits the incongruity of the situation. Many worthy persons give way to a false spirit of philanthropy in connection with it. One thing is certain,—the means adopted by these irresponsible agitators, socialist or nihilist, will never remedy, but only augment the difficulty.

There are many rich people in Malta, while the churches—supposed emblems of charity, peace, and good-will towards men—are uselessly decorated with gold and silver candlesticks, precious stones, costly marbles, valuable tapestry, and priceless works of art, articles as foreign to any true principle of devotion as snow is to the vegetation of the tropics. No one can travel in Spain, Italy, Mexico, or South America—all Roman Catholic countries—without being brought face to face with a similar state of affairs: costly cathedrals and churches crowded with gorgeous display, upon which gold has been recklessly lavished in all possible ways, often surrounded by a ragged and starving populace steeped in ignorance. Is there any amount of sophistry which can reconcile such incongruities?

On coming out of the magnificently adorned Cathedral of Guadalupe, situated a league from the City of Mexico, not long since, the author was literally dazed by the strong contrast which presented itself. Passing by a dozen steps from within this rich and gorgeous temple, upon which millions of dollars had been lavished, into an atmosphere of the most abject poverty and dismal want was like changing from brightest sunshine into the valley and shadow of death. A half-naked, starving army of beggars—men, women, and children—stared one in the face, their cadaverous features and attenuated forms, all too clearly defined, appealing for them with more eloquence than words could do. What sort of religion is that which can hoard jewels of fabulous value, together with plate of gold and silver, in its churches, while the poor, crippled, naked multitude starve outside of its towering and gilded walls?

The sense of outraged humanity was too strong for words. Even the sleek, well-fed priest, who had acted the part of guide through the church, looked abashed as we pointed to this tableau of misery, and then reproachfully at the gorgeously appointed temple whose portal we had just left behind.

How forcibly that Mexican scene is recalled while we write these lines. At each of the two corners of the plaza nearest to the cathedral stood a native woman beside a large receptacle of corn meal, from which, by adding a little water and salt, she was making what is here called polenta, or dough cakes, which she fried in small slices over a charcoal fire. Of this plain, simple food,—probably the cheapest which can be produced,—such of the poor creatures standing near as were possessed of the means ate a small portion, for which they paid one penny, devouring the cake with voracious appetite, while the rest looked on with hungry and longing expression. The reader may be assured that the half-starved crowd were supplied to the extent of their appetite for once with the nutritious though simple food, while thin-cheeked mothers were seen hurrying away with pieces of the polenta in their hands to feed their hungry children at home. The profuse blessings which were showered upon the "Americano" were cheaply purchased.

Within that pretentious church were idle treasures, the interest upon which, if the principal were properly disposed of, would feed the hungry people of Guadalupe for years. "Ah!" says the poet Shelley, "what a divine religion might be found out, if charity were really the principle of it, instead of faith!"

Does Christianity, as strikingly represented by gorgeous temples, filled with hoarded, useless treasures, while surrounded by a hopeless, naked, starving populace, render any real service to humanity? To the author's mind, religion of this sort, so far from preventing one crime, affords pretext for hundreds.

Let us now conduct the reader to more cheerful and attractive scenes, and describe the picture as presented by the main thoroughfare of the charming capital of the Knights.

CHAPTER X.

Broadway of Valletta.—Panoramic Street View.—A Bogus Nobility.—Former Grand Palace of the Knights.—Telegraphic Station.—About Soldier-Priests.—Interior of the Palace.—Ancient Tapestry.—Old Paintings.—Antique Armory.—An American with a Fad.—Ancient Battle-Flags.—Armor worn by the Knights.—Days of the Crusaders.—Bonaparate as a Petty Thief.—There are no Saints on Earth!—Dueling Ground.—Desecrating Good Friday.

The Strada Reale of Valletta is thoroughly kaleidoscopic in its gay and fascinating presentment of humanity, forming a strange medley of colors, while its variety of nationalities recalls Suez and Port Said, where representatives of the East and West are so confusingly mingled. Here one sees English ladies and gentlemen clad in fashionable London attire; soldiers in smart red uniforms; barefooted natives, whose lower garments are held in place by a gaudy sash tied about the waist; brown-skinned peddlers, with fancy wares, jostled by a dignified Hindoo, a turbaned Turk, or a swarthy Spaniard of questionable purpose. There passes also an occasional Greek in picturesque national costume; a white burnoused Arab; a native woman in sombre dress, with her face nearly hidden by a dark hood (a faldetta), which takes the place of a Castilian mantilla. Here, also, are noisy, half-tipsy blue-jackets, with broad collars, and straw hats, enjoying shore-leave after their ideas of pleasure. There are many plethoric, unctuous priests and cowled monks, all mingling indiscriminately; while persistent, whining, half-clad beggars are present everywhere. Verily, it is a motley group one encounters upon this principal street of the Maltese capital.

Having once promenaded the Strada Reale from the fortress of St. Elmo to the Floriana Gate, lined from the beginning to the end with quaint yellow buildings, green projecting balconies, prominent statues of saints, and filled with a variety of colors generally which a painter's palette could hardly excel, an American is not likely soon to forget the brilliant picture of foreign life which it presents. In our own country, nothing like it is seen off the theatrical stage.

As regards the faldetta, or dark hood, which screens the faces of the Maltese women, though a popular legend ascribes its origin to the time of the French invasion, our own idea is quite different. Its adoption is most probably connected with the Oriental veil or yashmak of the Eastern women. It came into use, doubtless, upon these islands during the dominion of the Arabs, and has been handed down from mother to daughter ever since. It is purely for street wear. Within the house, at the theatre, or other public entertainments, variety in dress is not wanting, nor the dazzling brilliancy of diamonds and other precious stones, to set off in attractive style the rich brown complexion, dreamy eyes, and fine features of the Maltese ladies. The effect of this peculiar hood as worn in public is both nun-like and coquettish,—a seeming anomaly; but it is quite correct. The average woman of this mid-sea group speaks a universal language with her dark, expressive eyes, though only Maltese with her lips.

Society, as the term is commonly used, is rather peculiar in Valletta, and is divided into many cliques. There is plenty of gayety, such as is always to be met with in a great naval and military dépôt. Many of the conventionalities of English home life are dropped here, as they are inevitably in Her Majesty's Indian possessions, or at Hong Kong. All colonial life is apt to be a little lax, so to speak, just a trifle fast. Ennuied by their semi-isolation and circumscribed resources, even cultured people are liable to grow careless as regards the nice refinements of society. There are several clubs whose object is of a literary character. A well-organized society for the prevention of cruelty to animals exists here, also one to promote agriculture, and another known as the Society of Arts. Each of these engages the attention of a certain set of people of culture, to their own advantage and indirectly to that of the community.

It is natural that there should be a certain exclusiveness observed between the Maltese families and those of the official English residents. Caste, so to express it, though not under the arbitrary conditions in which it exists in India, is not unknown here. Where is it not to be found under various forms throughout Christendom? It exists to a certain degree among the English themselves. The separation caused by the dissimilarity of language, religion, and education is also wide. There are, as already stated, a certain number of "nobles" who transmit their distinction to their sons. These are a bigoted, useless, and extremely ignorant class, generally possessing just enough inheritance to keep them from beggary, yet who are too proud of their empty titles to adopt any occupation. These individuals, together with the numerous native priests, as illiterate as their humblest parishioners, form the black sheep of Malta, equally useless and unornamental, illustrating the proverb that "Satan finds some mischief still for idle hands to do."

The quays bordering the harbor of the capital present a busy and picturesque scene well worthy of study. Next to the Strada Reale, they afford the strongest local color. They are dotted with fruit stands, refreshment booths, out-of-door cafés, piles of ship-chandlery, jack tars in white canvas clothes and beribboned hats, and native boatmen in scarlet caps and sashes of the same texture. One feels inclined to laugh at the queer little go-carts intended to carry three or four persons, and drawn by a dwarfed donkey. These vehicles are not unlike an Irish-jaunting-car, the passengers sitting sideways in the same fashion.

The former Grand Palace of the Knights of St. John is quite a plain structure externally, much less pretentious than the edifices devoted to the several divisions of the order. The Auberge de Castile, for instance, is a far more striking and ornamental palace, built at the headquarters of the Spanish language. The Grand Palace has an unbroken frontage of three hundred feet on St. George's Square,—Piazza St. Giorgio,—forming an immense quadrangle bounded on each side by large thoroughfares. Two centuries ago this was called the Piazza dei Cavalieri, or the

"Square of the Knights," and was held as almost sacred ground. No Maltese could resort to it without a permit in the early days of the new city. The French called it the Square of Liberty. On the opposite side of this esplanade is the main guard house of the garrison, also an establishment known as the Casino, a popular resort of the merchants and the public generally. Over the entrance of the building devoted to the guard is the following inscription in Latin: "The love of the Maltese and the voice of Europe confirm these islands to great and invincible Britain." In the Strada Vescovo, on the left of the square, is the house occupied by Byron while he resided here, a fact which your guide will be sure to mention, as though it were of some real importance. The old palace has two principal entrances in the front, each of which leads into an inner area or open court. There are two other entrances, one from the Strada Vescovo, and one at the back facing the public market. Centuries ago these spaces within the palace were improved, one for the storage of the sedan chairs belonging to the leaders of the several divisions of the Knights, and the other as a stable for the horses of the Grand Master. During the Carnival these dignitaries made a gallant show, drawn in the state carriage, to which six gayly decorated mules were attached, and preceded by a trumpeter. To-day these deliciously cool areas which lie within the palace are planted with orange-trees, tall scarlet verbenas, pink oleanders, hibiscus, rosebushes, and honeysuckles. A large and thrifty creeping vine, whose name we cannot recall, covered one whole side of a wing of the building, from foundation to roof, with a wilderness of green, together with a wealth of scarlet bloom, imparting an agreeable sense of beauty and fragrance. The liquid notes of a musical fountain also delighted the ear. In the right-hand court is a large Norfolk Island pine, planted by the Duke of Edinburgh, and this is called Prince Alfred's Court. The left-hand area is named for the Prince of Wales, and contains a statue of Neptune by Giovanni of Bologna.

This famous old palace is now occupied as the town residence of the English governor and commander-in-chief of the forces.

The upper portion is surmounted by a tall square tower, originally designed as an observatory, the obvious incongruity of which seems to indicate that it was probably an afterthought on the part of the architect. It is now used as a marine telegraph station, whence all arrivals are signaled as soon as the ships' flags and numbers can be made out. The view from this *torretta*, as it is called, drew forth the admiration of Lamartine, who visited it. "From the tower of the old palace," he writes, "Valletta is seen in all its original beauty, appearing as if cut out of a single piece of living rock."

The area in front of the palace—no longer exclusive ground—is now a favorite public resort, and contains two fountains brimming with sweet refreshment. Here one of the regimental bands gives out-of-door concerts twice a week. This is also made the headquarters of the annual carnival displays and frequent military reviews. The Spaniards would call it the plaza of the city.

It is true that the exterior of this historic pile is somewhat disappointing and commonplace in its architectural effect, but the interior more than compensates for this first impression. One enters the lofty corridors stimulated by a throng of active memories touching the romantic story of the chivalric order of the Knights. The impress of that seemingly incongruous combination, the soldier and the priest, is everywhere to be seen. We promptly recall their humble beginning centuries ago at Jerusalem, where, actuated by pious zeal, they fulfilled the duty of good Samaritans; how they grew in numbers and in importance until they finally became a warlike body of soldier-monks, knight-errants of the cross. We remember that for hundreds of years they fought incessantly against the active power of the Porte, and, almost single-handed, kept the Ottomans and the piratical Algerines at bay, an enemy who, uniting, strove to extend the creed of Mohammed westward by power of the sword, and to banish Christianity from the face of the earth; how, successively driven from Jerusalem, Cyprus, Acre, and Rhodes, they finally established a home for the order in this Maltese group, in defense of which they fought heroically, spilling their blood like water upon the ramparts of St. Elmo, and finally erecting this noble city, where they have left such lasting monuments of their bravery, enterprise, success, and decline.

Such thoughts are almost automatically suggested by the brain as one enters the portals of the interesting old palace, once the court of the now virtually extinct fraternity. Though occupied by the English officials and kept scrupulously in order, it has an unmistakable and most melancholy air of desertion in its stately hangings, its echoing halls, and quaint vestibules. It must all have been very grand when the renowned brotherhood were at the zenith of their fame and power, when the head of the order presided here and ruled the proud organization in regal state.

The interior of the palace is divided into broad passageways inlaid with colored marble, picture galleries, banqueting hall, hall of justice, hall of council, grand armory, and many other spacious apartments. Among the most meritorious paintings are a series of striking views representing the various sanguinary battles in which the Knights had from time to time been engaged. This series is the work of Matteo da Lecce. Other examples of superior workmanship are by Caravaggio, Cavalier Favray, Giuseppe d' Arpino, and so on. There are no modern paintings in the palace, all are mellowed by age. Indeed, there is nothing new here in art or furniture; such would be quite out of place; everything seems to have about it the tone of lapsed centuries, while exhibiting a lavishness of original expenditure which the most limitless means alone could warrant.

In one of the broad corridors near the armory hall, the gilded state carriage formerly used by the Grand Masters may be seen. Its gaudy construction shows the style kept up by the Knights in those days. The tawdry, lumbering, gold-decked state carriage one sees at the State Department of the City of Mexico, left by the ill-advised Maximilian, is no more extravagant in character. The idea of supporting an official carriage at all upon this circumscribed island is an obvious folly and straining after effect. The most extensive journey such a vehicle could make would be the length of the Strada Reale, or possibly from the palace square through the Porta Reale into the suburb of Floriana, about two miles. This useless carriage somehow recalled the ponderous gilded car of Juggernaut, seen at Tanjore, India, the structure in which the idol takes its yearly airing drawn by thousands of poor, deluded, and fanatical Hindoos.

This edifice in the Square of St. George, it will be remembered, was the official palace of the order, the headquarters of the Grand Master. Each "language" or division of the Knights had also its separate palace. Valletta, like Calcutta or Venice, was a city of palaces. In these latter days the members of the fraternity lived in great splendor; their tables were heavy with the richest viands to be obtained, while they were served in regal style by numerous slaves, male and female.

The council chamber of the Grand Palace is hung with ancient Brussels fabrics of great original cost and beauty. These pieces of tapestry, twenty-two in all, are each fifteen feet square. The figures are of life-size, representing typical scenes in India, Africa, Europe, and America, and depicting with considerable accuracy the fauna and flora of each section of the globe. In the representations of America, there are a few manifest incongruities and inaccuracies, but one should not be hypercritical under such circumstances. Little, comparatively speaking, was known three hundred years ago of this great western continent. These tapestries are in a state of remarkable preservation, both as regards color and texture. They are said to have hung in their present position for over two centuries and a half, exposed to a strong light, and more or less to atmospheric influences. These are rare specimens of the admirable work as well as of the durable colors produced by those early artists in textile fabrics. Connoisseurs whose interest is in this special line visit Malta solely to see them as they hang in the old palace.

The author chanced to meet a wealthy American gentleman in the city of Florence, lately, with whom this mania for ancient tapestry had become chronic, and was pursued to some purpose. The individual referred to was Mr. Charles M. Ffoulke, now of Washington, D. C. He had invested over fifty thousand dollars in the purchase of very old and neglected fabrics of this sort, found in various parts of Italy, notably at Rome. These were mostly from the looms of Gobelin and Brussels. Mr. Ffoulke had secured the services of a score of patient nuns in the convents of Florence, who were engaged in the careful restoration of the frayed and torn, but valuable fabrics. When every piece should be brought as nearly as possible to its original condition, the whole was to be shipped to America. One portion of this collection, valued at twenty thousand dollars, is already in this country, and was presented by its generous owner for the adornment of the sacristy of a prominent church in New York city.

The spacious dining-hall of the government palace of Malta contains among many other portraits one of Grand Master Vijncourt, by the famous artist Caravaggio. A master ruler of the order, as we have shown, always lived in regal style. When he went to church he was attended by a hundred Knights in full uniform, and half a dozen pages to hold up the bottom of his robes of state. When he dined in public, the Knights who formed the rank and file of the order ranged themselves about the hall standing, and no one moved until he gave the signal for doing so. He was addressed only in the most deferential manner, and the Knight doing so must uncover his head and bow submissively. No royal court observed more strictly the etiquette of profound respect, as evinced towards the reigning sovereign of the realm.

There is also in the old palace a gorgeous throne-room and ball-room combined, sometimes used for the latter purpose to-day. The several private apartments are all richly frescoed by the best exponents of the art who could be obtained in Italy, when frescoing was held to be one of the highest branches of pictorial illustration. Many of the scenes are very elaborate and quite unfaded, representing events in the early history of the Order of St. John, including tableaux of the famous defense of Rhodes, together with many sea-fights between the galleys of the order and the piratical crafts of the Barbary coast. The Knights prided themselves upon being as good sailors as soldiers. It was in their galleons that they captured their richest spoils from wealthy Ottomans, who often carried with them to sea not only much personal property and convertible wealth, but also a portion of their slaves and the favorites of their harems. It was thus that each capture of the Knights represented a considerable amount of real wealth.

In visiting the Grand Palace of Malta, the apartment which is sure most to interest and occupy the stranger is that of the elaborate armory of the ancient order, a spacious hall, two hundred and fifty feet long by forty wide, wherein are exhibited the steel harness, mailed gloves, crossbows, javelins, halberds, pikes, arquebuses, and battle-axes which were used by these soldier-monks in actual service. Like Falstaff's sword, the edges of these weapons present tokens of having given and received many shattering blows, but one feels no doubt that the evidence here displayed is genuine. History in this connection is quite vivid enough without seeking to heighten its color by any subterfuge. In the days when these weapons were used, conflicts were mostly at close quarters, hand-to-hand. Cavalry and long range cannon were of little account; indeed, the latter did not exist, and in siege operations the former were almost entirely useless.

In this interesting and curious armory are many torn flags, Turkish robes of military rank, and other trophies of war captured from the infidels in various conflicts.

A critical eye will observe that most of the armor must have been designed for men of smaller physical development than the average soldier of our period. There is one mail suit in the hall, to wear which, a man must have been at least seven feet in height, and of corresponding physical development, the helmet alone weighing thirty-five pounds, which would soon exhaust the strength of an ordinary man. There are said to be over three hundred suits of armor preserved and mounted in the collection, though we should not have thought there were nearly so many. The average weight of these must be considerably over forty pounds each. Many are constructed of the finest quality of steel, elaborately engraved, and inlaid with gold and silver. The author's attention was called to one suit, which was so heavily ornamented with the precious metal that the original cost must have been at least a thousand pounds sterling, including the artistic and mechanical labor involved in its production. This armor, it should be understood, was only designed to protect the front and side of the wearer's person. Here and there are seen a breast-plate with indentures evidently made by an enemy's bullet or spear-thrust, which would doubtless have proved fatal to the wearer but for this metallic protection. The armory is also hung with an interesting series of grim old portraits of the Grand Masters of the Order of St. John, dating back to the earliest days of the organization. As here represented, they must have been men of decided character, the traits of decision and firmness being those most prominently delineated by the artists. One or two were evidently persons of fine and commanding personality, notably L'Isle Adam and La Vallette. There is, somehow, a sternness and spirit of aggression pervading all these counterfeit presentments.

Some of the firearms in the Knights' armory are very curious weapons, closely resembling the principle of our modern revolvers and breech-loading guns, although it must be remembered that these specimens are three or four hundred years old. When one pauses to consider the matter, this seems to make the late Colonel Colt more of a discoverer than an inventor. A most curious cannon preserved among the rest of the arms, small in calibre and of Turkish workmanship, is particularly interesting. It has a barrel which would take a ball of about an inch and a half in diameter, and is made from closely-woven tarred rope, with a thin metallic lining, the whole so strong and compact that it would sustain a discharge of gunpowder sufficient to propel a shot with fatal effect a hundred yards at least. This singular weapon seems to have been used for belligerent purposes, and it purports to have been taken from the Mussulmans during the famous siege of Malta, in 1565, when an enemy forty thousand strong, with a hundred and fifty galleys, invested the island and besieged it for three months, being finally defeated with a loss of three quarters of their army. Thirty thousand men are said to have lost their lives on the part of the Turks, by the sword and camp fevers, not to enumerate those disabled by wounds.

As regards this strong and compact rope cannon just spoken of, so far as we know it is unique, and would seem to belong to an earlier period than is claimed for it. Probably it was brought by the Knights from Rhodes. Few people are aware how strongly tarred rope can be bound together by seamen and others accustomed to manipulate it. When thoroughly worked into shape, it becomes almost as solid as iron.

The rusty old lances, broken spears, and dimmed sword-blades hanging beside tattered battle-flags bearing bloody marks of the fierce contests in which they took part, are silent but suggestive tokens of the Crusades, recalling the names of Saladin and Coeur de Lion, when Christians and Mohammedans were arrayed in bitter sectarian warfare against each other upon the plains of Palestine,—romantic and historic days rendered thrice familiar to us by the captivating pen of Scott. Here we pause for a moment before the trumpet which sounded the retreat from Rhodes. These instruments close beside it are the batons of office which were used on state occasions by Aliofio Wignacourt and La Vallette. Those curious in such matters find the place full of interest while carefully examining these warlike appurtenances, which as a whole form a collection unequaled in its line by any armory in Europe. There are many interesting relics of the famous Order of the Knights in this apartment, besides those of the battlefield. The hall is a veritable museum, containing many illuminated books, manuscripts, sacred emblems, ancient Phoenician, Arabic, and Maltese coins, with curious church paraphernalia which were in constant use centuries ago, each article forming a page, as it were, in the history of those Knights of the church. Among the treasures preserved in the armory was the costly and artistic sword given to the Grand Master, La Vallette, by Philip II. of Spain. The golden hilt was set with large diamonds of purest water, and the workmanship was of exquisite finish. This sword Bonaparte stole and appropriated to his private use, wearing it ostentatiously when he departed from Malta on his way to Egypt,—a mean and petty sort of thieving which this man constantly practiced.

Among other valued curiosities, one sees in a glass case the deed of perpetual sovereignty granted to the Order of St. John by Charles V., dated March, 1530. Nothing upon earth endures for long. The formal deed of gift is here, but the title is extinct, and so is the order of the Chevaliers of St. John.

The English government have stored in the palace a large collection of firearms, including some twenty thousand muskets, which were manufactured in the Tower of London. Such have been the improvements made in this weapon, however, that these guns would hardly be considered suitable arms with which to furnish a body of infantry in time of war. The old smooth-bore, muzzle-loading firearm is now entirely obsolete. Even the African tribes, who have so lately fought the French in Dahomey, were supplied with, and used effectively, breech-loading rifles.

It appears, as we have felt it our duty to make plain, that these church-robed warriors were very human in their instincts, and by no means exempt from the average sins that flesh is heir to. Some outspoken historical writers have recorded acts of debauchery perpetrated by them which we should certainly hesitate to reprint. All this, too, notwithstanding their pretended sanctity and discipleship, together with the stringency of their priestly vows. We may be sure that there are no saints on this mundane sphere, and that those who pretend to the greatest degree of sanctity are mostly those who possess the least. Experience never fails to furnish proof of this. Our most cherished idols have feet of clay. Nothing known to civilization is more debasing to morality, truthfulness, honor, and chivalrous manhood than the holding of slaves. The Knights of St. John were open and undisguised slave traders,—slave traders in the fullest sense of the term, reaping therefrom not alone constant additions to their material wealth, but also all the miserable consequences contingent upon so vile a connection. This was perhaps the greatest promoter of the sensuality, gluttony, and gambling propensities which prevailed to such a demoralizing and shameful extent among the members of the brotherhood.

These famous champions of the church had also their schisms, their petty jealousies and quarrels, like all the rest of the world. There were in the code of laws, to which they solemnly subscribed, stringent rules against premeditated dueling, but these were easily and frequently evaded. Fatal infractions often occurred, the outcome of quarrels started over the gaming-table or the wine-cup. Punishment was somehow escaped. The law was plain enough, but the misdeed seems always to have been condoned. Men who live by the sword are very liable to die by it. Deaths arising from personal conflicts were by no means rare among this priestly fraternity. If a Knight was challenged by one of his brotherhood for what was deemed to be good and sufficient cause, and did not promptly respond, no matter why, he was denounced among the fraternity as a coward, and was punished by social ostracism. The inconsistency of such a state of affairs, existing in a pretended religious community, will at once suggest itself to the reader. The profession of Christianity did very little to separate the armed priest from the brute. This fact was not only illustrated in this dueling propensity, but in the recklessness of their daily habits. Human life was held at the lowest possible estimate, and its sacrifice for trivial causes was taken little if any notice of by those in authority. Men who make a profession of arms are very liable to resort to weapons of warfare, rather than to reason, in the settlement of any question which may arise among them.

There is a narrow street which runs the whole length of the city, parallel with the Strada Reale, which was celebrated as the dueling ground of the Knights. The reason for this selection was because a combat in this circumscribed passageway might be looked upon in the light of a casual encounter, or an accidental collision. This was a very weak deduction, but it appears to have sufficed for the purpose. The fact was, that a challenge which had passed between two Knights, no matter what the circumstances were, could not be ignored by them, or a personal encounter avoided, any more than such an occurrence could be disregarded among the swashbucklers of Dumas's musketeers. The instinct of the sword, so to speak, was stronger with these professed religionists than was any other recognized principle. The combatants were bound, however, by some recognized palliating rules: for instance, to put up their swords upon the interference of a brother Knight, an officiating priest, or a woman, which may be interpreted as an attempt to draw a line of prevention about this barbaric custom of settling private disputes with the sword.

When a fatal conflict occurred on the Strada Stretta, a cross painted or cut upon the house front nearest to the spot ever after indicated the event. There used to be a long line of these significant signs upon this thoroughfare, but nearly all are obliterated, some by design and others by the wear of time. The records of the sixteenth and seventeenth centuries teem with entries of stabbing, wounding, and killing among the Knights, the result of encounters upon the Strada Stretta. When there was a common enemy to encounter, and upon whom to expend their surplus energy, the Knights were as one man, living together in comparative harmony, but in days of peace they were only too ready to turn their weapons against each other in heated quarrels.

Washington Irving relates a veritable ghost story concerning a fatal encounter which took place in this notorious Strada Stretta, as related to him by an old Knight who once lived upon the island of Malta, and whom he met somewhere in Italy. The basis of the story was the fact that two Knights of the Order of St. John, one of Spain and one of France, met and fought a duel here on a certain Good Friday, the latter losing his life in the conflict. There was always more or less active rivalry existing between the French and Spanish divisions of the brotherhood. In the instance referred to there was a woman in the case, for the Knights were as famous for their gallantry towards the ladies as for prowess in battle. In times of peace they occupied their leisure, not with any intellectual resort,—alas! that the truth must be told, few of them, comparatively speaking, could read and write,—but nearly all seem to have been experts at domestic intrigue and gambling, at wine-bibbing and dueling. Their only study was the effective handling of warlike weapons. The fencing-master, not the schoolmaster, was constantly "abroad."

The story, which Irving tells at considerable length, represents the victor in the duel referred to as having suffered infinite remorse for his murderous act, and that he was pursued night and day by a terrible phantom visible only to himself. In vain was the severest self-imposed penance, in vain the confessional, in vain his prayerful regrets. He seemed doomed as a just punishment to endure a purgatory upon earth. The great onus of the whole affair, however, as made to appear in the narrative, was not the sacrifice of a human life under such circumstances, but that the act should have been committed on Good Friday!

## CHAPTER XI.

The Famous Church of St. John.—By What Means it was Decorated.—Grand Mosaic Floor.—Roman Catholic Ceremonials.—Remarkable Relics.—Chapels of the Languages.—A Devout Artist.—Church Treasures.—Thieving French Soldiers.—Poetical Justice.—The Hateful Inquisition.—Churches of Valletta.—A Forlorn Hope.—Heroic Conduct.—A Maltese Pantheon.—A Rival Dome to St. Paul's, London.—Some Fine Paintings.

After the Grand Palace of the Knights, described in the last chapter, the next place of interest to a stranger in Malta is the church of St. John, which stands upon an open square, shaded by graceful trees, opposite the head of the Strada Santa Lucia. It is a little over three centuries old, having been built by the order about the year 1576, at great cost. The members of the fraternity vied with each other in its elaborate adornment, and lavished untold sums of gold for this purpose. Robbery upon the high seas, predatory invasions of unprotected coast towns, and the sale into slavery of the captives—men, women, and children—whom they thus got possession of, served to keep the purses of the Knights full, and enabled them to indulge their wildest fancy to its full extent. Perhaps the expenditure of their ill-gotten wealth in this direction was the least harmful of all the ways in which it was squandered. The piratical manner in which they procured the means for the costly adornment of the church of St. John did not militate against the acceptability of the same, on the part of the priesthood immediately attached to the cathedral. What a satire upon the "holy" character of this Romish temple, this church of St. John! "The church," says Goethe, "has a good stomach; has never known a surfeit; the church alone can digest such ill-gotten wealth." In Mexico, Sicily, and Spain the banditti go to the priests when contemplating murderous crimes, and pay to be shrived of their sins before committing them, promising also to hand over to the church treasury a liberal portion of the proceeds of their robberies!

But let us return to our description of this marvelously decorated church of Valletta.

Below the cross which forms the apex of the front is a statue of the Saviour, a masterpiece of art from the hand of Algardi, a famous Bolognese sculptor. There are two heavy square towers, containing numerous bells, whose metallic tongues are perfectly deafening on all festal occasions, giving utterance at early morning hours, intended by nature for sleep, and continuing all day long, the dread of unaccustomed ears. They are not rung in the manner commonly adopted elsewhere, and after what would seem to be the most legitimate fashion, but are beaten with a hammer, in the stout hands of a native islander. In Japan they ring their ponderous, low-hung bells, placed in front of the temples, with a battering-ram of timber, driven by many hands, which, though it sounds like veritable thunder, is no more malicious than the Maltese sledge-hammer method.

The clock of this church has three faces, showing the current hour, the day of the week, and the day of the month. It is a curious, though not remarkable, piece of work, interesting, however, as being the product of a native Maltese mechanic. This edifice was intended to be the Westminster Abbey of the order, where the mortal remains of its members should find a lasting and monumental sepulchre. The architect, Girolamo Cassan, was a famous artist of his day, who laid out and designed the city of Valletta as a whole, with its many palaces, under the immediate direction of the Grand Master whose name it bears.

As we draw aside the heavy matting which always hangs before the entrance to the church, it is impossible not to be impressed by the magnificence which is everywhere displayed.

An oppressive odor of floating incense at first salutes the senses, as is the case in all Roman Catholic churches; but a few moments serve to accustom one to the musty, unventilated place. It does not seem to occur to the custodians of these edifices that such a place of public assemblage requires change of atmosphere just as much as a domestic residence. Architecturally, the church of St. John has no pretension whatever, either inside or out, though its proportions are very grand. The mosaic pavement is doubtless the most perfect specimen of the kind in existence,—a mosaic of tombs, and an example of sepulchral magnificence. The whole effect is rich beyond description, from pavement to roof. Yet there is, strange as it may seem, a cold emptiness, not to say gloom, which overcomes the stranger amid all this plethora of furnishing and fresco. The detail is too infinite to be taken in as a whole. Only a general impression of the place is retained by the average visitor. To the thoughtful and unprejudiced it must surely prove to be more pagan than Christian.

Where we stand upon its tessellated floor, each square yard is sacred to the memory of some departed Knight; the marbles bearing their names are also emblazoned with their arms. One can readily imagine the many festive occasions, elaborate and pompous ceremonials, military, civic, and religious, which have taken place within these walls while the Knights were at the acme of their power. The chairs of state were then filled with gaudily dressed officials. Priests, in glittering robes, bearing gold and silver mitres, filed hither and thither in long processions, accompanied by banners, and preceded by youths in spotless white, who swung burning and pungent incense in silver vases, while the ponderous organ breathed forth its solemn, reverberatory notes. The tapestried alcoves were brilliant with numberless candles, and the high altar was ablaze with burning wax, while the figures in the sacred paintings must have looked down from their canvases with weird and cynical expression. No doubt these church ceremonials were solemn and impressive, where one and all assumed a virtue, if they had it not. Is it surprising that this cunningly devised and gaudy display, these elaborate performances, should be awe-inspiring to an ignorant and superstitious people? One can even conceive that the actors themselves, in such a theatrical show, having been brought up in the Roman Catholic faith, may believe that they, poor, finite creatures, individually glorify the great and good God by this hollow mummery.

To-day, only a score of nun-like Maltese women, clad in black, kneel here and there before some favorite saint. If the stranger catches a glance of their dark eyes from behind the screening faldetta, he finds them more redolent of earth than of heaven,—dreamy, persuading eyes, glancing from beneath downcast lids, and shaded by long lashes. Only two male visitors are present,—the author and his guide, while a single priest, robed in a velvet surplice, goes through a pantomime of kneeling and crossing himself in front of the high altar, with his back toward the scanty audience. This man's voice is so low, if he speaks at all, that the solemn silence of the place is quite unbroken. If he could be heard, no worshiper of the class who come hither would understand the Latin tongue in which he is supposed to read the service.

We can remember but two other churches of its class which equal this of St. John in tawdry, yet costly and useless decorations, namely, those of Burgos and Toledo, in Spain. It was the former church that was considered so exquisite, and delicately artistic in every appointment, that Charles V. said it ought to be placed under glass. The Toledo cathedral rivals any Romish church we have visited, in its riches of gold, silver, precious stones, and art treasures. It contains also more stained glass windows than any other ever built, with the possible exception of St. Peter's. Statues and pictures abound in the church of St. John; gold and silver accessories, added to the original expense of the carved lapis lazuli, render the high altar, as a whole, of great aggregate cost. The railing in front is composed of solid silver. The keys of Jerusalem, Acre, and Rhodes, esteemed of priceless value as memorials, are deposited beneath the high altar,—relics of the early possessions and the old chivalrous days of these warriors of the cross. Just behind the altar hangs a famous painting of the Beheading of St. John, by Caravaggio, painted in 1609. There is also an elaborate group, in marble, representing the Baptism of Christ. It is the work of Maltese artists of the seventeenth century, forming a remarkable monument of native talent.

Before the altar of this Valletta church, on the right and left, richly upholstered chairs are placed, raised above the level of the floor, and draped with canopies of rich crimson velvet. These chairs are designed for the bishop and the representative of the sovereign power in Malta. They are occupied only on state occasions. Over the last mentioned is placed the British coat of arms. In the spacious sacristy are a score or more of fine old paintings variously ascribed to great masters. One or two of these are very old, and were brought by the Knights from Rhodes when they evacuated the island.

The most celebrated relic of this Maltese cathedral was the reputed right hand of St. John the Baptist, brought originally from Antioch to Constantinople by the Emperor Justinian, who, in the intensity of his veneration, built a church expressly for its preservation. After the capture of Constantinople by the Turks, the Sultan Bajazet gave it to the Grand Master D'Aubusson at Rhodes, whence it was brought to Malta by L'Isle Adam. The hand was incased in a glove of wrought gold covered with precious stones, among which was a large diamond of unusual value. This gem, Bonaparte, as usual, stole and placed upon his own hand. "You may keep the carrion," said the French general flippantly, as he handed the relic to the Grand Master, minus the ring. It was a curious act of destiny that the Corsican scourge should have carved his name upon this rocky island of Malta,—this granite page of history.

When Hompesch treacherously and in the most cowardly manner surrendered the Maltese group to the French, he carried the hand of St. John away with him, and afterward presented it to Paul I., Emperor of Russia, when he was chosen Grand Master of the order, under peculiar circumstances. This singular relic is still preserved in the Winter Palace at St. Petersburg.

The tapestries in the church of St. John are known to have cost originally thirty thousand dollars, and were from the famous manufactory of De Vas Frères of Brussels, for whose looms Rubens did not disdain to work. On the way to Malta they were captured by a Moorish corsair, and ransomed by the payment of their full value in gold. Thus they cost the church just sixty thousand dollars.

Among other relics which are shown to the visitor is a thorn from the crown worn by Christ, a fragment of the infant Jesus' cradle, one of the stones which slew St. Stephen, the foot of Lazarus, some bones of St. Thomas of Canterbury, and so on.

On either side of the nave of the church of St. John are dome-crowned chapels, each having its special altar elaborately ornamented with paintings of more or less merit, together with bronze and marble statues. These chapels were devoted to the several divisions of the Knights,—the different languages, comprising those of France, Provence, Auvergne, Aragon, Castile, Italy, Germany, and Anglo-Bavaria, eight in all. In the French chapel is a sarcophagus in memory of the Duke de Beaujolais, brother of Louis Philippe, who died of consumption at Malta. This tomb is ornamented with a full-length recumbent statue of the youthful prince, and is a fine work of art. From this chapel there are marble steps leading to the crypt in which are the tombs of twelve of the Grand Masters, including those of L'Isle Adam, first Grand Master in Malta, and his successor, La Vallette. The sarcophagi in this place are elaborate works of more than ordinary merit, and are said to have come from Florence, Milan, and Rome. The sepulchre of La Vallette interested us most, as does the life of this remarkable soldier, commander, and prelate. The pedestal is of bronze, upon which the Grand Master is represented as reclining in the full armor of a Knight of the order which he had served so long and so faithfully. At the foot of this tomb lies the body of Oliver Starkey, La Vallette's trusted secretary, who, had he possessed the ambition, might have aspired to almost any post of honor within the gift of the brotherhood. In the silence of this sepulchral chamber, one naturally falls to musing upon the vanities of life and the stern reality of the end. The tomb is the great leveler; the emperor and his humblest subject must alike crumble to dust.

As we ascend once more to the nave of the church, the brain becomes very busy with thoughts suggested by the surroundings, where there is such an incongruous blending of religious with warlike associations. Everything speaks of the brave but heedless Knights, and their common pride in and devotion to this ostentatious temple.

Besides the chapels which were assigned to the several languages of the order in this church of St. John, here called the cathedral, each division had also some church in the city devoted entirely to its service. Thus to the Knights of Provence belonged the church of Santa Barbara, in the Strada Reale; that of Italy possessed the church of Santa Catarina, in the Strada Mercanti; the church of Our Lady of Pilar, in the Strada Ponente, belonged to the language of Castile and Portugal, the other divisions being similarly supplied with separate churches.

We have several times referred to the divisions of the Knights; this should perhaps be made clearer by a few words. In consequence of the admission to their ranks of kings, princes, and nobles from all parts of Christendom and speaking various tongues, they divided themselves into what was called "the eight languages," each, as we have shown, having its special chapel and palace. In the Grand Master, however, who was nearly always an accomplished linguist, rested supreme power over each and all. No vow which the members of the fraternity took upon themselves was deemed more binding than that of implicit obedience to the presiding head of the order. The importance of discipline was thoroughly recognized, and there was no possibility of appeal from a decision of the Grand Master. By no other means could so heterogeneous an assembly of men from different nations be controlled, especially when consisting of individuals whose sense of moral rectitude was of the feeblest character, and whose principal occupation was that of arms.

We were speaking more particularly of the cathedral of St. John, in describing which many pages might be easily if not profitably filled.

The roof of the edifice, which is divided into zones, is superbly painted in elaborate designs, representing hundreds of figures of such proportions as to appear from the floor to be of life-size. The subjects are mainly Scriptural themes, especially relating to the life of St. John, painted in oil laid on the stone, which the artist prepared by a peculiar process devised for this purpose. At the corners of each of the arches are a score of figures representing martyrs and heroes, illustrative of the history of the knightly order. The real genius displayed in the designs could only be born of one inspired by a true love of art, together with a devoutly religious spirit. The excellence of the designs and the naturalness of the army of figures challenge both surprise and admiration. They are so artistically done that it is difficult not to believe them to be in bas-relief. The whole was the patient work of one prolific artist, Mattia Preti, an accomplished and enthusiastic Calabrian, who spent forty years of his life in the special adornment of the church of St. John, refusing, it is said, all pecuniary remuneration for the same. He was quite content to live frugally, exercising strict self-denial, that he might thus exemplify his art and his religious devotion. Preti studied the rudiments of his chosen calling with his brother, who was director of the Academy of St. Luke, at Rome, and brought with him to Malta not only ability and experience, but a devout love of art for art's sake. His body lies buried before the entrance to the vestry, the artist having died in 1739, well advanced in years, and leaving behind him, in Malta, a vast number of examples of his ability, which form an appropriate monument to his memory. As evidence of his indefatigable industry, it should be mentioned that in the cathedral of Città Vecchia in the centre of the island, other specimens of Mattia Preti's work in the same line of church adornment may be seen, together with some fine individual pieces of composition.

The treasures still remaining in the church of St. John are of great intrinsic value, notwithstanding the fact that Bonaparte's soldiers, after the usual fashion of the French in these days, robbed it of nearly all portable articles which were of a salable nature, during their brief stay upon the island. Their stealings included the twelve life-size statues of the Apostles, which were of silver. These statues are said to have been ransomed by some rich prelate, and are now in the old cathedral of Città Vecchia, if common report may be credited. The author, however, did not see them there. A golden lamp of great size and value was also purloined by the same freebooters when they robbed St. John's church of other effects. Many articles which it was not desirable to carry off, these vandals wantonly destroyed. One of the Venetian chandeliers, thus sacrificed, when lighted burned several hundred candles at a time. The guide points out the balustrade before the altar already spoken of as consisting of solid silver, which escaped the observation of the soldiery. This was brought about by the ingenious act of a thoughtful priest, who, to hide the true character of the material, painted the precious metal black. It has in our day assumed its true argentiferous appearance. It was this shameful thieving propensity of the French, that of pillaging all the churches, art galleries, and charitable institutions of those upon whom they made war, which finally led to their expulsion, causing the Maltese at last to rise in a body and declare a revolution. This inexcusable pilfering was begun before Bonaparte left the group; indeed, he set the example himself, though he was only six days on the island. Leaving a trusted general in charge, he hastened onward with his ships and soldiers to Egypt, which was the objective point of the expedition. The invasion and capture of the island of Malta was, as it were, only incidental. The treasures stolen from Malta were placed on board L'Orient, a vessel which was lost in the sea,—it was blown up, in fact, and now lies on the bottom of the bay where the battle of Aboukir was fought. It was destroyed by the British fleet under Nelson in that memorable action, and forms an example of poetic justice with which one cannot but heartily sympathize. When Bonaparte left Malta he impressed the native regiment which formed the guard of the Grand Master into the service of France, promising to pay a certain sum regularly to the families whom they left upon the island; a promise which was never fulfilled by Bonaparte, and was never intended to be. The French were liberal in promises and agreements duly drawn up and signed—then totally ignored.

Sometimes Providence chooses to employ peculiar agents whereby to accomplish its purposes. Thus the French, who were birds of ill-omen wherever they appeared in those days, were the means of bringing about one great and much-needed reform during their sovereignty here in 1798, for which they deserve much credit. They promptly banished from the island that hateful and bloody agent of the Romish church, the Inquisition, which had taken deep root in Malta, and which was reveling in its bigotry, cruelty, and despotism, defying the authority of all recognized and regularly constituted laws. The spacious stone edifice formerly devoted to the use of these inquisitors, situated in the Strada Porta Maggiore, is now occupied as barracks for an English regiment. So it is with those priestly harems of Mexico, the late convents and nunneries, which, having been forbidden by the national government to be used for such purposes, are now improved for district schools, hospitals, libraries, and sundry other useful and respectable purposes, much to the improvement of the morals of the community.

An impressive personal experience in the church of St. John occurs to us as we write.

The soft light from the wax candles did not banish the sombre hues inside the ancient place, though it was midday on one occasion as we stood examining the rich old tapestry near the high altar. It was very still, and we were quite alone. No services were going on. Suddenly a strong ray of sunlight penetrated some opening from above and rested upon the illumined hangings. It brought out the dim colors and figures as though they had been touched by the wand of an enchanter. The eye involuntarily followed this shaft of light to its source, the rays being made up, apparently, of buoyant and infinitesimal sands of gold. The translucent column slowly changed its angle, until it rested for a moment, like a halo, upon the severed head of St. John, in Caravaggio's canvas, then suddenly disappeared. It seemed like an artificially produced theatrical effect, cleverly managed, but the memory of the singularly impressive experience is indelibly fixed upon the brain.

There are between thirty and forty churches in and about Valletta, none of which merit special attention for their appointments. It would seem as though there were more than the number named, since in wandering about the town one is constantly coming upon a fresh one, whose crumbling walls, however, are anything but "fresh." Two or three of these churches were founded by Roger, when King of Sicily and Malta, and were liberally endowed by him about the beginning of the eleventh century. There is also a Jewish synagogue of modern construction, to accommodate the followers of that faith, who, although not numerous, are still represented by considerable numbers in the city. The architecture of the churches is mostly of the Renaissance, presenting each a great dome flanked by two heavy towers. Besides these churches, there are several minor chapels within the fortifications. Particular interest attaches to one of the latter, which for many years was hidden by the debris of the fallen walls of St. Elmo. The episode which makes this small chapel so specially worthy of mention forms one of the bright, chivalric pages in the too often darkened career of the Knights of St. John.

When the capture of this fort by the Turks, in the famous siege of 1565, became at last inevitable, after months of stout defense and gallant fighting, the few surviving Knights who so bravely held the position against immensely superior numbers retired to this small chapel within the fort, where they received the viaticum, solemnly embraced each other, and then, although many of them were already grievously wounded, went forth upon the ramparts to die. In the general defense of the island it was all-important,—nay, imperative—that St. Elmo should hold out as long as was possible. Every hour that it delayed the enemy was of the greatest importance.

Reinforcements from Italy were anxiously expected, and the fleet which should bear them might heave in sight at any moment. The walls of St. Elmo were already honeycombed by the shot of the enemy, but the idea of surrendering to the Turks did not even enter the minds of its brave though weary defenders. The Grand Master demanded of them, if it became necessary, to die sword in hand, fighting the infidels to the last gasp. This order was literally obeyed. Communication with the other forts was entirely cut off, so that it was impossible to reinforce those who were left within the crumbling walls, but the gallant defenders managed to send word to headquarters by employing an expert native, who made his way across the harbor in the night, swimming mostly under water, so that the Grand Master was informed of their exact situation. By the same means of communication, the order was sent to them, "Hold the fort, or die fighting," in obedience to which, every Knight faithfully laid down his life!

We know of no parallel case in warfare. Indeed, there are few more heroic pages in history than those which record the gallant defense of the Maltese fort of St. Elmo, before which, not only hundreds, but many thousands of frenzied Turks, the flower of the Ottoman army, were slaughtered in vain but savage assaults upon its walls. The few chivalrous Knights who constituted the forlorn hope left to the last in the fort sold their lives to the enemy at such fearful cost, killing so many of them outright,— quarter being neither asked nor given,—as to spread consternation among the whole army of besiegers, the remnant of whom not long after withdrew from the island in despair. The frenzied recklessness of the Turks was no match for the cool, determined purpose of men who had consecrated themselves, as it were, to death.

The leader of the infidel forces, Mustafa Pasha, when surveying the scene of the last terrible conflict, and realizing that more than half of his invading army had been sacrificed before the walls of St. Elmo, is reported as having said, while looking toward the other and greater forts still held by the Knights, "If the child has required the spilling of such rivers of blood and such myriads of lives to conquer it, what sacrifice will not the parent demand before yielding?" Nothing but Mohammedan frenzy, a wild, unthinking, religious zeal, infatuation pure and simple, could have sustained this long, destructive, and fruitless siege on the part of the Turks.

St. Elmo to-day is considered to be the most perfect and the most absolutely impregnable of all the fortified points of the Maltese capital. It requires two regiments of artillery and one of infantry to man the extensive walls of this fort in war time. It was, comparatively speaking, an infant in arms, in those early days. Now it is like a full-grown giant,—a man-of-war in size and strength. Its original form was almost exactly like a star, but ample additions have somewhat changed its outlines.

Speaking of the several churches of Valletta and its environs, the remarkable dome of Musta is recalled. It covers a Pantheon-like edifice, situated in a village a league or so from the capital. The church is visible from a lofty point in the city, and was built by the labor of the poor peasantry of the neighborhood, patiently and resolutely continued through a period of thirty years. Yet, speaking of these peasants, Mr. Henry

Ruggles, a late American consul to Malta, says: "They are so poor that the most opulent has not sufficient income to purchase a goat." The Musta church was originally designed by a devout and conscientious priest, who inspired his helpers by his self-devotion to the purpose which he had conceived. But he did not live to see it finished. It is curious that the dome of this village church, on a Mediterranean island, should be a widespread, lofty structure, larger than that of St. Paul's, London. The span of the latter is ten feet less than that of the former. It is a round edifice, composed of the yellow Maltese stone, and of such majestic proportions as to be very pleasing to the critical eye. The church is dedicated to the Madonna. The extreme height from the ground to its apex is about two hundred feet, the walls being very thick. The diameter of the whole is about that of its height, which are the same proportions as the Pantheon at Rome, from which many of the features are evidently copied. It has a couple of large bell towers placed at either end of a Corinthian portico which forms the main entrance, but they are rather diminutive compared with the central dome.

This, as well as all the village churches in the group, is plentifully ornamented with images and paintings, the latter mostly of a very ordinary character. Occasionally a fine one arrests the visitor's attention, and such examples are generally attributed to some famous artist; whether correctly or not, it is impossible for any one but an expert to decide. The date of these works, the proximity of Italy, and the liberality of the people in artistic decoration of the churches render quite possible the originality claimed for many of the best paintings found in Malta.

Several legends are current as to the origin of this Musta temple, but they would hardly interest the average reader, though possessing a certain emphasis and fascination when related to one standing beneath the shadow of its lofty walls. When it was decided to erect the church, for some special reason it was particularly desirable to have the new edifice occupy the same site as the ancient structure already upon the ground. The question arose as to how this should be brought about. Knowing that the new temple must be years in course of construction, it was thought best not to destroy the smaller existing church until a new place of worship was completed. To meet this exigency, the one now bearing the grand dome was built outside and over the old one, the latter remaining undisturbed during the process. The dome, it is said, was thus constructed without raising any staging around it. When the walls and all of the new temple were finished, the old church was demolished and the debris promptly removed. This was certainly a remarkable architectural achievement.

There are a dozen domes within the city walls, of less size, in view from the same point which takes in the Musta Pantheon, as it is often called. Many of the edifices to which they belong are costly structures, but they are not elegant or attractive. There are a few fine paintings in these city churches. One by Guido Reni in the church of Santa Maria, representing Santa Ursula, is highly prized, and is often visited by connoisseurs in art. It is doubtless an original. Unless one has a considerable amount of leisure time to dispose of, after a thorough inspection of the grand church of St. John, there remains little in the same line worthy of attention in Valletta. A careful study of this structure and the cathedral of Città Vecchia will doubtless satisfy the average traveler.

There are said to be two hundred churches and chapels in the group, but this is, we should think, an exaggeration. Nevertheless, it is certainly true that a few less churches and a great many more schools would redound to the well-being of the inhabitants.

## CHAPTER XII.

The public library and museum of Valletta are in the same edifice, adjoining the Grand Palace, the entrance being under the arcades facing the Café de la Reine. This was the last building erected by the fraternity of St. John in Malta. It contains a collection of over fifty thousand volumes besides many choice manuscripts. The library is mostly composed of the individual collections once owned by the Knights, each of whom agreed to bequeath, at the close of life, his private possessions in this line. Of course there were some studious and scholarly men as well as many charlatans in the brotherhood. It now forms a library of much more than ordinary importance, to which valuable books are still added from time to time. The printed works can be taken out for home use by any resident of Malta, under reasonable restrictions, and even strangers are permitted this privilege, if they are properly introduced by any responsible citizen. The shelves, as might be supposed, are particularly rich in the literature of the Middle Ages, containing some extremely interesting volumes, the work of zealous old monks, some few of which are illumined with rare artistic ability. The department of engravings is quite extensive, embracing some examples of very ancient origin, especially curious and valuable. It is true that nothing could possibly be cruder than some of these specimens, wherein the rules of perspective, after the Chinese fashion, are entirely ignored. Indeed, some of the objects attempted would seem to require labeling to fix their character and purpose.

This library was founded by Bailli de Tencin, who started the institution with ten thousand volumes, his entire personal collection of books, freely contributed for this purpose. It is true that comparatively few persons avail themselves of the advantages here offered, but an occasional priest, an elderly citizen, or a foreign student is seen turning over the leaves of the ancient tomes. Specialists sometimes visit Malta, coming from long distances solely to consult this collection of books and manuscripts. An individual was pointed out to the author who seemed to be very much interested in the library, and who was said to be here in behalf of the British Museum, London, to effect the transfer or exchange of certain duplicate volumes in the collection to the grand, monumental library of the great English metropolis. Our companion was a cultured Englishman, who spoke with just pride relative to the London library. "Do you realize," he asked, "how many books that noble institution contains?" We confessed a lack of exact knowledge in the matter. "Well," said he, "there are to-day upon its shelves, properly classified and catalogued, over one million and a half of printed books, not to enumerate its many thousands of rare manuscripts which are held of priceless value."

The books in the Valletta collection are principally in Latin, Italian, and French, but there is also a large assortment in other European and in Asiatic tongues.

The English residents maintain a well-supplied and constantly growing subscription library, known here as the Garrison Library, situated in St. George's Square. This resort forms a sort of ladies' club, where the gentler sex congregate daily; they come to read, write, and to learn the news. Here they have access to all the latest magazines and newspapers, and here they gossip to their heart's content. Like Viesseux's Circulating Library in Florence, or that in the square of the Spanish Stairs, at Rome, such an institution is of as much benefit to travelers as to the local inhabitants. There are a dozen newspapers published in Valletta, about half of which are in English and the rest in Italian. The number of volumes in the Garrison Library is about thirty-one thousand. It is an indispensable acquisition in such an isolated spot, helping to reconcile one to the fate of being forced to make Malta his home. Army officers look upon an assignment to either this group or to Gibraltar as anything but desirable, while entertaining a strong preference for Malta. With the facilities and gayeties furnished by the Union Club, these gentlemen of the sword and epaulet manage after a fashion to exist. Public dinners are given, as well as balls and assemblies, both by the governor at the palace and by the managers of the club, each week during the season. This Union Club of Malta is favorably known all over the continent of Europe for its hospitality and general excellence. The hall of entrance to the club is very artistically ornamented, and so is its elegant and spacious ball-room.

The museum of Valletta did not escape the outrageous cupidity of the French soldiery, who perpetrated more mischief in their senseless destruction of antiquities than will ever be known in detail. Plunder and spoliation were second nature to them, but they also spitefully defaced escutcheons and armorial insignia which were the only available keys wherewith to unlock the mysteries of the past. The Valletta museum, notwithstanding its misfortunes, contains many curious and unique specimens of antiquity, being almost entirely composed of such as have been found upon the islands of this group. These consist of statuary, vases, illumined marbles and very ancient coins, amphora of Egyptian shape and mural urns. A considerable number of these and also some beautiful Etruscan vases were found on the island of Gozo, and were unearthed quite recently. One of the marble groups represents the familiar subject of a wolf suckling the infants Romulus and Remus. Another marble figure is a bust representing Zenobia, Queen of Palmyra. This is in alto-relievo. Some of the metallic objects are too much corroded by time and rust to enable one to divine their original purpose, like the specimens seen in the museum at Naples exhumed from buried Pompeii. There are three or four interesting medals exhibited which are in excellent preservation, bearing Phoenician characters, and some other articles which are inscribed in the same language. There is one monument which evidently belongs to the period of the Goths, besides a fine marble statue of Ceres, the product of the same period. This was exhumed on the island of Gozo. A few medals bear Greek inscriptions. There are some lachrymals and sepulchral lamps which came from Roman tombs near Città Vecchia, the ancient capital, also a couple of terra-cotta sarcophagi from the same neighborhood. A square stone slab of great interest bears a legend in Punic characters, designating it as cut to mark the burial place of the famous Carthaginian general, Hannibal. This was found in a natural Maltese cave near Ben-Ghisa.

It is claimed that Hannibal was born on this island, and there is a respectable, intelligent family now living near the city of Valletta who bear the name of Barchina, and who assert themselves to be his posterity. Menander, the celebrated orator, was born at Malta. Aulus Licinius, whom Cicero styled the Aristotle of Malta, and Diodotus, the philosopher and intimate friend of Cicero, were also born here. The latter died half a century or more before Christ was born, which reminds us that the "Sons of Malta" were representative men in Rome about two thousand years ago.

We were shown a small but highly valued and curious gold coin, which must have been issued by the Arabs about the year 1090, though its date could not be distinctly made out. It was in the possession of private parties. On one side was an Arabic legend: "There is only one God, and Mohammed is the prophet of God." On the reverse side was: "King Roger." It will be remembered that Count Roger the Norman, son of Tancrede de Hauteville, was declared King of Sicily and Malta about the close of the tenth century. We were told that a hundred pounds sterling had been offered for this coin not long since, by an agent of the British Museum, London.

The curiosities in this collection are not very numerous, but they are extremely interesting. It is especially remarkable that so many highly choice examples of antiquity should have been obtained in so limited a space as the Maltese group, nor is the field exhausted. One cannot but be impressed by these silent witnesses of the mutations to which these islands have been subjected.

A pawnbroker's establishment on an extensive scale occupies a long building in the Strada Mercanti, opposite the city post-office, and is under special government charge. It is an institution very similar in its purpose and management to one existing in the City of Mexico, and was established in 1507, its object being to afford prompt pecuniary aid when needed by the native people, who are often in temporary distress. The government regulates the rate of interest, which is placed at the lowest figure compatible with the purpose of making the institution self-supporting. It was in the first place a private enterprise, and high rates of interest were charged for the use of money, but as it grew in means and usefulness, it was taken in hand by the government, or sovereign power for the time being. The Maltese women who have inherited from parents or grandparents cherished articles of personal adornment, such as jewelry and the like, prize the same far beyond the intrinsic value, and if they are forced to pawn them for a period, they are very sure to redeem them when they possess the means to do so. Since 1833, solely with a philanthropic purpose, a savings bank has been added to the pawn establishment. After half a century of experience, this branch of the institution has proved to be of decided public benefit, promoting frugality, industry, and self-respect among the common people of Malta. It has been the means of changing the daily habits of many careless, heedless individuals, who through its agency have gradually laid by a foundation for acquiring a competency. In 1891 the deposits had reached an aggregate of over two million five hundred thousand dollars. This is a very large sum for such a community as constitute the humbler class of Valletta. The number of depositors is set down at six thousand in the last annual report. Any native may place here a sum as small as one dollar, to which he can add from his savings similar sums at his pleasure. When these deposits amount to one pound sterling, the money begins to draw interest. Being under the control of government, it is safely and honestly administered for the public good. An unsuccessful effort was made by the author to obtain other details, as it seems to be a subject of general interest, and a progressive move worthy of imitation.

The French, who respected neither religious nor charitable institutions, even robbing the hospitals, and stealing right and left wherever they appeared under Bonaparte,—the Alaric of his age,—plundered the Monte di Pietà of Valletta, purloining therefrom about one hundred and fifty thousand dollars, in small securities, left on deposit as collaterals by the poor men and women of the capital! This ruined the institution temporarily; and it was compelled, for the first time in about three centuries, to close its doors. Such an unfortunate experience served to confirm many of the ignorant Maltese in the Arab passion for burying their money in the earth for safekeeping. This is a practice which they have not wholly outlived, even at the present time, showing the tenacity with which a people will adhere to the customs of their ancestors. After the much-hated French were driven out of the island, a few liberal men, who possessed the means, capitalized the Monte di Pietà at once, and by energetic and honest effort it steadily regained its former position, proving itself to be indeed a public charity. It benefits all classes, makes no distinctions, and loans as high as three thousand dollars to one individual.

There are two Baraccas or parterres in connection with the line of fortifications surrounding Valletta, which form favorite promenades of the citizens. They are known as the Old and the New Baraccas, from either of which fine and comprehensive views may be enjoyed. The latter is preferable on account of the great extent of land and sea which it commands, as well as for its beautiful garden. A study of the topography of Malta from this point will enable the visitor to bring away with him, impressed upon the tablets of his memory, a truthful map of the group. Experience soon teaches the traveler to adopt this expedient when he finds himself in any new locality which admits of so doing, until he finally possesses many photographic pictures stored within his brain, forming delightful reminiscences of which no misfortune can rob him.

One of the most charming pictures which lives in the author's mind is that of a bird's-eye view enjoyed from a lofty standpoint in the Maltese capital, on a beautifully clear afternoon in early spring. The larger portion of the yellow-hued city lay far below, with its myriads of cream-colored, flat-roofed houses, and its thrifty, business-like boulevard; while its many blooming fruit trees afforded warm bits of color here and there. The Strada Reale recalled the Via Victor Emanuel as seen from the top of the Milan cathedral. Both harbors of Valletta, with their numerous shipping and stately warehouses, were in view. Half a dozen iron-clads with their grim, threatening batteries formed a prominent feature. The broad Mediterranean stretched far away to the horizon, dotted at intervals by the picturesque maritime rig of these waters, its placid surface now serene and quiet, radiating the afternoon light like liquid sapphire. A fleet of gaudily emblazoned native boats shot hither and thither over the near surface of the bay. Large, broad-winged sea-gulls sailed lazily through the air, dipping now and then into the water, and rising again upon outspread pinions of stainless purity, dazzling as new-fallen snow. One or two long, irregular lines of dark smoke, floating among the distant clouds, pointed out the course of the big continental steamers bound east or west. Far away to the northward, the conical outline of grand old Mount Ætna, king of volcanoes, was faintly limned upon the sky which hung over the Sicilian coast.

How soft and summer-like was the still atmosphere, how suggestive the comprehensive view! Can one who was brought up on these islands ever be content to live in the cities of the mainland? How they must hunger for a horizon!

As we viewed the scene, the hum of the busy town rose upon the air like the drone of insects in a tropical forest, mingled at the moment with the soft chimes from the church of St. John. It was a fête day in Malta, and other bells joined in the chorus which floated upward with mellow cadence, creating a tender glow of peacefulness. While we gazed half-entranced upon this varied scene, the sun declined serenely toward its ocean bed, and slowly disappeared. At the same moment a sharp, ringing report was heard from the flag-ship of the squadron, preceded by a small puff of white smoke, which rose in circling wreaths from the evening gun. Then the national colors came gracefully down by the halliards from each peak and topmast head, and the brief twilight following was steeped in the red and yellow afterglow of the departed day, always so beautiful where sea and sky make the horizon, fading into each other's embrace.

How full of vitality and animated contrasts seemed the small world that lay within the scope of vision as we gazed! But now it was the close of day; both man and beast were ready to seek repose. Nature had set the example. Even the sea-birds turned toward their night-haunts, where they might fold their busy wings, as the war-ships had just furled their pennants.

What a delightful picture it was to hang in the gallery of one's memory, often to be recalled by a single word or sound.

Let us look inland from an advantageous point in the city of Valletta; an undulating country presents itself to the eye, sparsely settled, with here and there a small village, always dominated by its quaint stone church, and divided round about, as already described, by high stone walls designed to shelter the vegetation. A central rocky ridge is observed running north and south, which divides the island of Malta proper near its middle, the eastern side being the most extensive and populous. This view does not reveal any of the small groves; these are hidden in the few valleys where they exist, and the landscape is almost entirely devoid of arboreal ornament.

The people are few and the churches many, the latter quite out of proportion to the number of the population or their pecuniary means. In no other country, unless it be Mexico, is there such a manifest disproportion in this respect.

Two leagues away to the westward, upon a prominent elevation, the highest point of the ridge referred to, Città Vecchia is seen breaking the line of the horizon. It is called the "old city" to distinguish it from Valletta, the modern capital. At this distance it appears dim and dusty, almost like a mass of ruins, and, indeed, in some respects it is but little better. The stones of its best edifices are corrugated by the finger of Time, for the old capital of Malta was founded many centuries before the advent of Christ upon earth. One writer states that its origin dates back to 1804 B. C., but upon what authority we know not. It is a hill city, founded upon a rock, originally proud and pretentious in its design. We can easily imagine its grandeur when ten times its present population dwelt within the walls, and it was at the zenith of its prosperity. To-day, hoary and decrepit with age, it is rich only in the traditions of its past. Situated near the centre of the island, it was under various sovereignties and during many ages the honored capital of the group; but to-day, its dirty, gloomy, silent streets are comparatively abandoned, and a general somnolence reigns in its thoroughfares, though it is connected with Valletta by a narrow-gauge railway, built some few years since,—the only one on the islands. This is a mere toy railway, so to speak, after leaving which a broad, well-kept road leads up a gentle ascent to the brown and dingy walls of the crumbling old city.

As we enter the ancient metropolis by its principal gate, a time-worn, battered statue of Juno is passed, a figure which dates back to the Roman period of possession here; and just within the walls the guide points out the remains of a temple dedicated to Apollo. Everything is gray and picturesque; dilapidation and neglect are everywhere apparent. There are probably four or five thousand people still residing within the city limits, not a tithe of the number which were once to be found here. It is said that the walls which encompass the town formerly embraced three or four times the present area, but they were contracted to the present dimensions during the sovereignty of the Arabs, to make them more easy of defense when besieged by an invading enemy. Città Vecchia flourished in times when might alone made right, and warfare was the normal condition of the world. Malta was specially exposed to invasion from various quarters by those who sought its capture, or for purposes of plunder. Greek, Turkish, and Algerine pirates swarmed from the Dardanelles to the Straits of Gibraltar, and when satisfactory prizes were not to be found upon the open sea, inroads were organized upon the land. It was therefore necessary for the people of Città Vecchia to be always prepared to repel an active and daring enemy, and even to withstand successfully a protracted siege.

Only the skeleton of a once great and thriving metropolis now remains. The place has no commerce and no special industry, but is slowly fading away into the dimness of the past.

In wandering about the doleful streets of the ancient capital to-day, one meets a swarm of plethoric priests, sandaled monks, and hooded friars, while escorted from point to point by sad-looking, ragged, importuning beggars. Where the first of these elements abound, the other is sure to do so. This is a universal experience. Nowhere are the people more absolutely subservient to the control of the priesthood, or more completely subject to the exacting ordinances of the Roman Catholic Church. The priests receive rental for at least one third of the land which is occupied or cultivated on the islands. Unfortunately, this money is not expended in a way to benefit, even indirectly, the inhabitants of Malta. Nearly all the income from this source flows into that great pecuniary receptacle and avaricious maw, the pontifical treasury at Rome. There is no other palace in the world which is so rich in hoarded treasures as the Vatican, the thrice voluptuous Roman home of the Pope, where he lives surrounded by a populace which leads a life of penury and semi-starvation. Little heeds he of such trifling matters, while he "quaffs his Rhenish down." Appreciative travelers speak of the "cold wilderness of the Vatican." This sensation is easily accounted for. It is because this grand palace is so much more of a museum than a home, or human habitation. It has been called, not inappropriately, a congress of palaces, and, with two exceptions, is the largest in the world. The Royal Palace at St. Petersburg and that of Versailles exceed it somewhat in proportions, but by no means in the richness and intrinsic value of its hoarded wealth. The accumulation of original paintings and statuary, by the great masters of art, which are stored in the Pope's palace would alone bring over thirty million dollars, if sold to be added to the grand national collections open to the public in various European cities. The value of other treasures of the Vatican one would hardly dare to estimate, but the aggregate figure would far exceed that named in connection with the paintings and statuary. The gold in the Pope's plethoric treasury is to be added to this estimate. With this enormous amount of riches lying perdue, and being constantly added to, myriads who look upon the Pope as their spiritual father actually starve on the banks of the Tiber, at his very gates.

But let us return to Città Vecchia, whose site upon one of the spurs of the Bingemma Hills was so well chosen.

Much interest is felt by visitors in the ancient cathedral of the old city, its mouldering monasteries, its convents, its theological school, its hospitals, and its bishop's palace. The cathedral is said to be built upon the site of the house formerly occupied by Publius, the Roman governor of the island at the time of St. Paul's shipwreck, and who, if tradition may be believed, was his ardent friend and follower. It has two tall bell towers, a hundred and thirty feet in height, from which a grand view of the Maltese group is enjoyed, the elevation being over seven hundred feet above sea-level. The length of the edifice is nearly two hundred feet, and it is about half as wide as it is long. The form is that of a Latin cross. In effecting an entrance, one passes through an army of mendicants, poor, miserable creatures, who with blind credulity come hither in the hope of obtaining relief from their sufferings, the most prevalent of which is gnawing hunger!

The interior of the cathedral is very rich in gorgeous decoration. Like the church of St. John, its roof is superbly painted. This work was done by Vincenzo Manno, an eminent Sicilian artist, and represents scenes in the life of St. Paul. The high altar is composed of the finest marble, artistically wrought, and must have been very costly. The mosaic tombstones which form the flooring, after the style of the Valletta cathedral, are a marvel of patient workmanship, and produce a fine effect. A picture of the Madonna is pointed out by the guide, which is said to have been painted by St. Luke, and there are several presumed relics of the Apostle Paul. In one of the chapels is a painting representing the Apostle miraculously routing twenty thousand Moors, who came to besiege the city. The site upon which the cathedral stands is so elevated as to afford a most extensive view even from the terrace.

Beneath the ancient Court of Justice near at hand, there are some damp and dreary dungeons where human beings used to be confined ages ago, dungeons which rival in horror those of the Doge's Palace at Venice, or the direful cells beneath the Castle of Chillon, excavated under the Lake of Geneva.

CHAPTER XIII.

Ancient Catacombs.—A Subterranean City.—Phoenician Tombs.—Grotto of St. Paul.—A Crumbling Old Capital.—Dreary and Deserted.—Bingemma Hills.— Ancient Coins and Antique Utensils.—Ruins of a Pagan Temple.—A Former Fane to Hercules.—A Garden of Delights.—Druidical Circles.—Beautiful Grotto.—Crude Native Dances.—Unique Musical Instrument.—Nasciar.—Suburb of Floriana.—A Capuchin Convent.—Grim Skeletons.

The stranger who comes to Città Vecchia seems to inhale an atmosphere of the Middle Ages which pervades everything in this quaint dwelling-place, almost as old as the sacred city of Benares, the Hindoo Mecca, which was famous before Rome was known, and when Athens was in its youth. Medina was the old Arabic name by which it was known, but probably it had other names in the far past. Phoenicians, Greeks, and Romans reared their dwellings upon its site, and have left evidences of their departed glory. Historic memories and suggestions hang about its crumbling monuments, its ruined ramparts, and its narrow footways. One of the most remarkable attractions in the vicinity is the extensive system of catacombs, which are very similar in many particulars to those of Rome, and which, if we may believe local tradition, were once connected with Valletta by a spacious tunnel. This would require a remarkable piece of engineering. To perfect such a passageway through solid rock, though it was comparatively easy to work, would involve a cost of time, labor, and money which would be hardly at the command of a primitive race. If such a tunnel did exist, it would nearly equal the Hoosac Tunnel of Massachusetts, and would be at least five miles long. The entire length of the catacombs as they now exist is computed to be fifteen miles, though there are no authentic statistics about them. Their size and regularity of construction have caused them to be called the Subterranean City. They are hewn out of the rock at a depth of from twelve to fifteen feet below the surface, small openings upward at suitable intervals admitting the necessary fresh air. Torches or lanterns are quite indispensable in visiting them, and a competent guide should always be taken. A stranger might easily become confused and lost among the intricacies of these dim, subterranean passages. Tradition tells of a schoolmaster who attempted to explore these catacombs without a guide, in company with a troop of his pupils, and, according to the story, the whole party lost their way and perished miserably.

There are several spacious halls among these underground galleries, the roof of one being supported by a line of many fluted columns wrought out of the solid rock, just as they stand. Here it is supposed that religious or pagan ceremonies of some sort took place. A solid stone, which might have served as a rude altar or place of sacrifice, was found in the centre of the hall referred to. Portions of these catacombs have been walled up in modern times, since a second party of visitors became lost in them. Along the sides of the passages there are occasionally excavations which seem to have been used for sleeping purposes, or possibly for burial nooks, wherein the bodies were hermetically sealed after death. There are places also which appear as if designed for baking ovens; indeed, there are many special arrangements of so peculiar a character that it is difficult to imagine their several uses. The origin of the catacombs and their real design are lost in antiquity, but they are known to have existed in the days of Roman sovereignty here, that is, over two thousand years ago. They may have served both as tombs and as hiding-places. The primitive Christians are believed to have fled to them for refuge, and are thought to have used them also as tombs, and yet if they ever contained any mural appointments they must have been long since removed. There is nothing in these subterranean passages now but the mouldering stones and an atmosphere of an earth-impregnated character, suggestive of humanity turned to dust. Upon the whole, one cannot but rejoice at leaving these damp, gloomy, mysterious passages far behind.

It suggests itself to the visitor that the large amount of rock which must have been removed in the formation of this Subterranean City was used for building purposes upon the surface of the island. Probably Città Vecchia itself, so near at hand, is largely composed of the natural stone thus procured. A double purpose may thus have been served,—the obtaining of means for building substantial habitations above ground, and the forming of sepulchral avenues for tombs, hiding-places, or for secret rites, either pagan or Christian. There were times when Christians were compelled to worship here in secret.

Near the entrance to the catacombs is the Grotto of St. Paul, over which an unpretentious chapel is built, dedicated to the memory of the Apostle to the Gentiles. He is supposed to have lived here during his three months' sojourn upon the group, in which time he not only converted Publius to Christianity, but also sowed the seed which bore fruit to the same effect among nine tenths of the population. According to all accounts, Christianity, as we construe the word, thus made its advent in Malta with the shipwreck which took place in St. Paul's Bay, so many centuries ago. In the middle of the grotto just spoken of is a crudely executed statue of the Apostle. The visitor is assured that the stone of this cavernous apartment is remarkable for its efficacy in the cure of fevers and of poisonous bites. Credulous people secure pieces thereof, and keep them on hand for use in an emergency. A story is told of the miraculous nature of the grotto stone, to wit: it seems that, although it is constantly cut away to supply the demand for it as a remedial agent, yet it never becomes less, but is always replaced by unknown means. The many legends relating to St. Paul and his stay upon the group are most religiously cherished and believed in at Malta, and it would be considered little less than an insult, by a native, to question their verity. If there is any truth in profane or sacred history, we are quite ready to believe that St. Paul was wrecked on the island of Malta, and that the outline of the story as handed down to us is veracious; and yet, who is it that says, "History is only a fable agreed upon"?

Some few descendants of the old Maltese nobility, as empty in purse as are their titles in any real value, keep up a degree of appearances in their moss-grown and decaying "palaces," so called by courtesy, while other edifices, once grand and pretentious, are either quite untenanted, or are occupied for commercial purposes. The town forcibly reminds one of Toledo, on the banks of the Tagus in Spain, which is equally dead and deserted, and probably of as ancient origin. Its grand edifices are now diverted to storage purposes, and its palaces closed. Here, in the day of Spanish glory, royal pageants alternated with ecclesiastic parades, and grand military displays often varied the scene. Coveted by various conquerors, she too had been besieged more than twenty times. Like Città Vecchia, her glory was at its acme in mediaeval days.

In an endeavor to keep up the importance of the old Maltese capital under the rule of the Order of St. John, it was required that each new Grand Master of the Knights should come hither to be inaugurated, and here, the precedent having been established, each new bishop of the island is still consecrated. There are several other official acts which are not considered binding unless they are first promulgated at Città Vecchia. So in Russia there are certain state ceremonials, such as the crowning of a new Czar, or the marriage of a royal pair, which must be performed at Moscow, the ancient metropolis of the empire, notwithstanding the fact that St. Petersburg is so much more populous, and is the capital as well as the royal residence. But in this instance the old Muscovite capital is in perfect condition, so to speak, picturesque and beautiful, and never more populous and prosperous than it is to-day. Città Vecchia, one can easily see, must once have been a proud and stately city, surrounded by high walls and stout bastions, but its glory has long since departed. Ptolemy eulogized it in his day under the title it then bore,—Melita. The once formidable walls are now in a crumbling, neglected condition. Indeed, the charm of the old place consists in its memories alone. It was growing less populous yearly when Valletta was begun, more than three hundred years ago; the completion of the new city acted as a finishing stroke to its social and commercial interests. So rapidly was the ancient capital deserted by its inhabitants, who sought homes in the new metropolis, that, as we have intimated, ingenious laws were devised to make it more attractive to its residents.

During the dominion of the Knights, Città Vecchia was governed by a ruler chosen from the native Maltese citizens by the Grand Master, a custom which was cunningly designed to satisfy the native population by holding forth the idea that it was an independent, self-governing district. When the Knights first came to Malta, they were specially considerate of the native people, conciliating the populace in every possible way, but after they had thoroughly established themselves upon the island and become firmly seated, they ruled the natives with a rod of iron. In later years they had become so arbitrary and exacting that the Maltese were quite ready, when the time came, to bid them farewell, and to welcome their new masters, the English.

The Grand Master, Matino Garzes, made Città Vecchia a place of refuge, as it were. It was decreed that all persons who lived permanently within its walls should be free from arrest for debt during a certain period. If any of its citizens committed an offense outside of its walls, giving cause for civil complaint, the case must be tried only in the local tribunals of Città Vecchia. These and many other special enactments, though designed to particularly favor the residents of the old capital, failed to have the desired effect. The people gradually removed to the more attractive seaport, fascinated by its scenes of busy life, its freshness and cleanliness, together with its charming site, all were in such broad contrast to the drowsy, cheerless inland resort which crowns the Bingemma Hills.

There is plenty of evidence hereabout to show that this was of old the great centre of life upon the island of Malta, and that more than one race was here in large and thriving numbers, each of whom ruled for a period of longer or shorter duration, and then passed away. Conjecture alone can fill up the gap between the known and the unknown, traceable by crumbling monuments and suggestive ruins.

Not far from Città Vecchia, clearly attesting to the great antiquity of this mid-island neighborhood as a populous centre, the hills—Bingemma Mountains, the Maltese call them—are thickly occupied by Phoenician tombs excavated in the solid rock, "pathetic monuments of banished men." Out of these tombs curious articles have often been taken, and such are still occasionally found in them. It is plain that the primitive people who formed these rock-tombs possessed good tools and an aptitude for using them; also that they had a cultured taste in architecture, adhering to a certain purity of order in their designs wherever exhibited, whether in tomb or temple. The resemblance of these caves at Bingemma to the sepulchral grottoes which still exist in the environs of Tyre and Sidon is remarkable. The latter, it will be remembered, was the early seat of the Phoenician kingdom, in which fact we have evidence of a common parentage between the two people who built them.

Strangers are offered apocryphal coins by itinerant peddlers, which purport to have been current in Malta when ancient tribes were masters of the group; but common sense teaches us that original and genuine articles in this line must have been exhausted centuries ago. There are also urns and domestic pottery on sale at Città Vecchia, supposed to have been in use among the Phoenicians. The survival of such articles for the period of two or three thousand years is too great a tax upon one's credulity to be patiently entertained. While in Egypt, the author saw an insignificant article purchased of a peddler by an English lady, which was said to have been exhumed at ancient Thebes, and for which she paid five pounds sterling. An expert in such matters afterward showed the lady certain unmistakable marks upon the object she had purchased, which proved to her that it had been manufactured at Birmingham, England, for this purpose. There are other articles offered for sale at Città Vecchia, which are after the Greek style, and still more which are Roman in design. Some of the latter appear to be genuine, but who can tell? The imitation serves every purpose, one must freely admit, provided only the imitation be correct.

Many ruins of temples, tombs, and prehistoric monuments exist between the site of the old city and the coast, especially toward the south, most of which are attributed to the Romans; but there are also others which the Romans must have found here when they came. Antiquarians believe they can identify the period to which most of these "black-letter records of the ages" individually belong. Without doubt sufficiently complete portions of some of them are still extant to serve for this purpose, though the rust of twice ten centuries has crumbled and disintegrated some of the largest stones.

So late as 1839, a very spacious edifice was exhumed south of the ancient capital, which, so far as regards its almost complete preservation in all essentials, together with many antiquities which it contained, proved to be even more interesting than the greater Giant's Tower, on the island of Gozo. It closely resembled that structure, and is believed beyond doubt to be the work of the same race, though it is not of such mammoth proportions. Implements of husbandry, domestic utensils, and large jars formed of baked clay, supposed to be designed for oil and wine, were found in this singular structure. To us it seemed to be clearly of Phoenician origin. It is thought by many that this people had their capital in the group near this spot, possibly antedating Città Vecchia, but this is all conjecture. In the neighborhood of these ruins, considerably nearer to the sea, are more remains of a similar character, which have not yet been so fully uncovered, and there are many other indications showing that this vicinity must once have been a populous district. The shore for some seven miles in either direction is so precipitous as to form an inaccessible barrier on this side of the island. Vestiges of a fane to Hercules are also found near the coast. Quintius speaks of this temple, and describes it as embracing a circle of no less than three miles! Cicero speaks of a temple of Juno, at Malta, as being remarkable for its splendor in his day, but one naturally hesitates at entertaining the theory of a temple existing here whose base covered a circle of three miles.

Less than a league from Città Vecchia, in nearly the same direction, the visitor will find a delightful valley, forming a garden-like expanse, called El Boschetto, or "little forest," where inviting shade trees, fruits, flowers, and fountains abound. This is sure to prove an agreeable surprise to the stranger. A superficial view of Malta gives no promise of any such gem as this oasis in the rocky expanse of the island. Had Homer chosen El Boschetto for the abode of his Siren, it would not have been necessary to draw upon his poetical fancy to make its attractiveness apparent. Like San Antonio, it is a small rural paradise, watered by artificial canals, and having an abundant spring and fountain combined. Picnic parties are made up in Valletta to visit this charming spot, and others sometimes come from the old city on the hill, just as the populace used to do, no doubt, hundreds of years ago. On the festal days of St. Peter and St. Paul, this valley is thronged. The place is overlooked by a large square tower, which was formerly one of the summer resorts of the governors of Malta, but which is now in a crumbling condition. It crowns Monte Verdala, named for the Grand Master who built the tower, and was once a palatial residence occupied by Hugo de Verdalle, who gathered about him various skilled artisans from Italy to ornament, fresco, and beautify the place. Some of the evidences of his regal manner of living here are still extant within the spacious walls. The site was shrewdly chosen, and from its windows the view is both rural and lovely. Verdalle is represented to have been a man of the most selfish and sensual nature, who thought of little else except his own personal enjoyment. He died in 1595, tormented if not absolutely killed by gout, induced by riotous living and constant self-indulgence. He was truly a typical Knight of St. John, but as Grand Master, how unlike La Vallette!

A little south of El Boschetto is the palace, so-called, which was once occupied as the summer resort of the iniquitous and jesuitical crew who represented the Inquisition for a considerable period in Malta, but who were finally expelled in disgrace from the island. It was here that a vile and characteristic conspiracy was hatched by several members of the institution in connection with some Spanish Knights, to murder the Grand Master, La Cassiera, in 1657, but this purpose of cold-blooded assassination was discovered and frustrated. It was no new thing for the officers of the Inquisition to resort to secret murder to further their vile purposes. Like the Council of Ten in old Venetian days, the assassin's dagger was made one of their ordinary instruments by which to rid themselves of enemies whom they feared to attack openly. This building, with its vile associations, is now the property of the British government. The immediate vicinity is a very fertile and fruitful region, and contains a famous spring called Ain-el-Kibra. Irrigation is systematically applied all over this district. Two miles or less from the inquisitor's palace is a place known as Fanara. It overlooks the sea, and is much resorted to by picnic parties. Here is the head of the new aqueduct, called new in distinction from the old one already described.

Some of the most remarkable ruins in Malta are to be seen within a mile of this spot, consisting of masses of Phoenician masonry, called by the natives Gebel Quim, that is, "stones of worship," reminding one of the ancient Druidical circles, forming a strange jumble of rude altars, colossal stones, and mysterious nooks and niches.

At El Mnaidre, which signifies "the sheepfold," are more ruins of a similar character, said to be the remains of a temple originally dedicated to Æsculapius. We are here near the brink of the cliff overlooking the sea, taking in a distant view of the rocky island of Filfla, which looks like a huge whale come up from the depths to blow, and pausing for a few moments upon the surface of the blue expanse. In the face of the perpendicular rock sea-gulls find a safe home, where they lay their eggs and rear their young. Instinct teaches them that this abrupt cliff-formation is inaccessible to man. Flocks of these white-winged birds are seen wheeling round about the locality, especially at night and morning, together with the so-called rock-pigeons, a sea-bird which also abounds upon the coast. It is a lonely shore hereabout, with only an occasional ancient stone tower commanding a view of the far-reaching Mediterranean. In troublous times watch was kept from these stone structures, for the coming of Barbary corsairs, or a possible Turkish inroad. There are a dozen or more of these lookout stations, placed at suitable distances from each other. They were built by Grand Master Martin de Redin more than two hundred years ago, at his own expense, and form conspicuous objects on approaching Malta from the northwest. They are now occupied by the coast-guard placed here to watch for smugglers.

In the southwest part of the island, besides many more rock-cut tombs, there are also some conspicuous ruins, showing the former existence here of a large town, concerning which no other information survives. This may also possibly have antedated the Phoenician period. One is led to marvel that even the destructive power of time could have swept a large and fixed population from the island, and have left no clearer record of their existence behind them. The vicinity in which these ruins are found affords a dreary prospect at present, whatever it may have been at some former period. There is a trying meagreness in the landscape. One is homesick for want of color. Everything except the sea is gray, while the broad-spread rocky surface of the island is cheerless and repelling. There are many caves on this southwest coast, some of which seem to have been utilized as dwelling-places by a primitive people. Here and there the calcareous rock has been worn into singular forms by atmospheric influences and the incessant wash of the sea for ages, as one sees the same material wrought upon at Biarritz, on the boisterous Bay of Biscay. In one inlet there is a cavern very like the Blue Grotto of Capri, in the Bay of Naples. Not far away is a natural arch, so broad and high that a full-rigged ship of six hundred tons might sail through it, with all her canvas spread and yards squared.

There are numerous heaps of ruins besides those we have mentioned, on this side of the group, each one a history in itself, though nearly effaced by time, written in a tongue which our scholars strive in vain to unlock. The neighborhood is a Sahara of solitude, the scene of gardens deserted long ago, abandoned vineyards, and palatial edifices now nearly or quite crumbled to dust.

About six or seven miles from Valletta, near the hamlet of Casal Crendi, there is a most singular oval depression of the land, about a hundred and forty feet in depth, at the bottom of which is an orchard of fruit trees. The ground about the grove is quite level, and measures over three hundred feet in length by two hundred in width. Rugged and uneven stone steps lead down the precipitous sides of this land basin. Nature must have been in a very erratic mood when she created this singular depression, at which the average visitor gazes with curious and puzzled eyes. There is a gradual sinking of the country round about, until it centres abruptly in the manner described. The place is known as Tal Macluba, that is, "the overturned." The natives have a tradition about the place to the effect that a casal once existed here, but the people being unbelievers, and defiant towards the Almighty, the earth suddenly opened, swallowing the village and the occupants thereof at a single gulp.

Geologists explain the creation of this cylindrical hollow in a much more reasonable and satisfactory manner.

These islands, as we have shown, are full of caves, formed by the processes of nature, especially on the shores, where they are multiplied by the ceaseless action and combinations of chemicals. Probably a cavern, which had been ages in forming below this spot, finally collapsed, and let the surface earth sink to fill the space it had so long occupied. There is no evidence of any village or hamlet having ever been situated near to this depression of the earth.

A similar hollow, of nearly the same dimensions, exists also in the island of Gozo, at Kaura.

In the neighborhood of this chasm, of which we have spoken at length, and of Casal Crendi, one is besieged by a swarm of beggars. The latter place is a small agricultural village of more than usual importance. Its ancient stone church contains some very interesting paintings, the principal one of which bears the name of Rocco Buhagiar, who has also some meritorious pictures in the churches of Valletta.

There is an ancient quarry near Crendi, in one of the cavities of which some curious Roman remains have been found. A small bronze statue of Hercules, perfect with the exception of one foot, was exhumed from this place. It is a highly valuable memento of the far past, and should certainly be in the museum at Valletta; but it is in private hands at present. A very singular medal was also discovered in the crevices of the rocks near the place where the Hercules was found. It has on the convex side figures of soldiers in armor, and on the concave a group which is supposed to represent Lot and his daughters. This medal is not in the museum; but the custodian of the institution will give any inquirer such information as will enable him to get sight of it.

In the little inland villages of stone cabins a pastoral air prevails; but one occasionally witnesses novel scenes and unique performances, such as small groups of peasantry dancing after a style erratic enough to suit a Comanche Indian. The accompanying music, on the occasion we refer to, was produced by a home-made instrument, which reminded one of a Scotch bagpipe, only it was, if possible, still more trying to the ears and nerves. It is known here as a *zagg*. It is made of an inflated dog-skin, and is held under the musician's arm, with the defunct animal's legs pointing upward. A sort of pipe is attached to this air-bag, which is played upon with both hands. It is hardly necessary to say that a more ungainly instrument could not well be conceived. A tambourine accompaniment, performed by another party, is usually added to the crude notes of the dog-skin affair. To the music of these simple instruments the bodies of the dancers sway hither and thither in a singular and apparently purposeless manner. There was, however, a certain uniformity in the movements of the participants which showed design of some sort. The dancers seemed to lose themselves in the process, and to enjoy the queer pantomime, after a fashion. For significance of purpose, or poetic design, this exhibition will not compare with the tarantella, which the peasantry dance in southern Italy, or with the dashing firefly dance of the common women of St. Thomas, in the West Indies.

A league to the westward of Valletta is situated Casal Nasciar, which is perched upon a steep hilltop, and forms a good type of an ordinary Maltese village. Its stone church is nearly two centuries old, and contains some interesting relics. The people native here claim for their ancestors that they were the first in the group to receive Christian baptism, a matter which they deem to be of immense importance. Just outside of the village there is a statue of St. Paul, who is said to have preached upon the spot where it stands. The site of this Casal Nasciar is peculiar, being upon the summit of a great geological "fault," of which there are two or three striking examples in the group. The view from this village is far-reaching and beautiful, embracing certain portions of the island which are under high cultivation.

One sees a different people in these interior towns or villages, the inhabitants being more thoroughly Maltese than those of cosmopolitan Valletta. After once looking upon the rich and fertile plains of Nasciar, one no longer feels inclined to call Malta "only a sterile rock."

Among the peasantry, stalwart, light-haired fellows are often met, with bright faces and clear blue eyes, quite in contrast to their companions. To account for the presence here of this type, we must go back and inquire of the gallant, priestly Knights of St. John, whose elaborate vows of celibacy were thinner than the parchment on which they were written. The roads between the casals are, as a rule, excellent, the rocky surface making them, as it were, naturally macadamized; but they are so dusty as to be very trying to the eyes and lungs, impregnated as the atmosphere is all through the dry season with the fine silex of the friable surface rock. The dwellings of the people are flat-roofed and all of stone, the abundant native material.

To reach Città Vecchia from the present capital of Malta, one leaves Valletta by the Porta Reale, the outlet of the city proper toward the country. The town is closed by three gates,—that which has just been named, the Porta Marsamuscetto, leading to Quarantine Harbor, and the Marina Gate, conducting to Grand Harbor. Having crossed the broad drawbridge which spans the deep, wide, artificial ditch, on looking back one realizes how thoroughly the city proper is cut off from inland access when this drawbridge is raised. There is no part of the elaborate system of engineering for defensive purposes which does not seem to be as nearly perfect as is possible for such works. The entire design is masterly, and the consummation admirable.

After crossing into Floriana, we are still surrounded by a cordon of elaborate fortifications, demi-lunes, curtains, and ditches. This suburb is so named for the engineer who planned this curious and intricate maze of ravelins and bastions. This was Pietro Paolo Floriani. The place might have been thus appropriately called on account of its gardens, verdure, and flowers. As soon as the bridge is crossed, there lies before us a level space designed for military parades, an esplanade large enough for manoeuvring two or three thousand troops. The ditch which separates the city from Floriana is intended as a final barrier to any invasion from the land side; it is nearly a thousand yards long, sixty feet deep, and thirty wide, cut out of the natural rock, and reaches from Quarantine to Grand Harbor.

It is customary for strangers coming hither to visit the church of San Publio, a curious old sanctuary full of altars, pictures, and cheap images, together with any amount of tawdry gilding. Here one sees innumerable emblems, such as arms, legs, ears, feet, and hands, represented in wax, silver, and wood, hanging upon the walls, thus placed as thank-offerings for cures experienced by various sufferers. So the temples of Japan represented centuries ago, and do so still, a similar custom, each emblem being specially dedicated to the deity or spirit which received credit for the donor's cure.

The streets of Floriana intersect each other at right angles. The central and principal one, Strada Santa Anna, is a broad thoroughfare, with attractive and sheltering arcades on either side. In the Piazza Maggiore is the Soldier's and Sailor's Home, an excellent charitable institution, furnished with a good serviceable library, a reading and writing room, smoking and other rooms. This admirably conceived and philanthropic organization is calculated to greatly benefit and improve the class for whom it is designed, affording them not only respectable accommodations, but occupation for their leisure hours. There is a similar institution in the city proper, which we should not fail to mention. It is situated in the Strada Cavaliere, "Street of the Knights," forming a resort for sailors, soldiers, and marines, and conducing to their moral and intellectual improvement. It is very judiciously managed by a committee of European citizens, and to strangers is certainly significant of the spirit of progress which seems to prevail among the officials at Malta.

There is a well-arranged theatre in Floriana, the Princess, where amateur performances mostly occupy the stage. The botanical gardens of this section afford a charming exhibition of a floral and arboreal character, where the genial climate seconds the tasteful efforts of the intelligent florist. This suburb of the capital contains many fine dwellings, shops, and manufacturing establishments. There are also extensive barracks, and one or two regiments of English infantry are always quartered here.

In Floriana are situated the numerous spacious vaults, cut out of the solid rock, for the storage of grain to support the garrison and populace in case Malta were compelled to sustain a long siege. Here, too, are the catacombs belonging to the old Capuchin convent, founded in 1588, where the dead bodies of the brotherhood are preserved, clad in their usual robes and arranged in sitting postures, filling nooks in the walls. Here and thus they remain for many, many years, until the slow process of decay crumbles both body and bones to dust. This is a Sicilian idea early imported into these islands, "a custom," we should say, "more honored in the breach than the observance." These dreary, cadaverous corpses are supported in the positions which they are made to assume by means of steel wires hidden beneath their scanty robes. If this strange mode of disposing of human bodies after death has any really worthy and reasonable purpose, or if it is of any possible advantage to the quick or the dead, we are too obtuse to believe it. Sightseers call a visit to the sepulchral chamber, "going to see the Baked Monks," it being generally believed that the bodies go through some toasting or drying process which preserves them.

About the walls of this mortuary chamber myriads of bleached human bones of beings who died centuries ago are fantastically arranged. From this collection ghostly skulls peer at the visitor with a sort of derisive, satanic grin. Perhaps it will be argued that all this is calculated to suggest the fleeting nature of earthly things, but the moral is too far-fetched. The uncanny smell of the place still haunts us, like the mummy flavor from certain receptacles in Cairo and Alexandria. We were told that this mode of disposing of the deceased monks had been discontinued, that they were now buried like other bodies after death, and that the Church of Rome tolerated such exposure of the mortal remains of the faithful simply as a check to human pride. "To this complexion must we come at last." We were not convinced by the explanation of the propriety or desirability of these mummy exhibitions.

A somewhat similar display of skeletons, but without drapery of any sort, may be seen under the Hospital for Incurables at Valletta, in what is termed La Chapelle des Morts, where bleached skulls and whitened bones are stored in fantastic shapes by the thousand. Both this and the Floriana chamber naturally recalled the charnel-house of the Capuchin church in Rome. This church, it will be remembered, contains Guido's renowned Archangel Michael.

CHAPTER XIV.

The Chivalric Order of St. John.—Humble Beginning of the Organization.—
Hospitallers.—Days of the Crusades.—Motto of the Brotherhood.—Peter Gerard.—
The Monk lost in the Soldier.—At Acre, Cyprus, and Rhodes.—Naval Operations.—
Siege of Rhodes.—Garden of the Levant.—Piratical Days.—Six Months of
Bloodshed.—Awful Destruction of Human Life.—A Famous Fighting Knight.—Final
Evacuation of Rhodes by the Order.

Our story of Malta would be incomplete unless we gave a succinct and
consecutive account of the famous Order of the Knights of St. John, to whom we have
so often alluded in the foregoing pages, and who have left upon this island more of
their personality than all the other sovereignties that preceded or have succeeded
them. While we freely reprehend their many and glaring faults, we are forced to
admire and praise their energy, their heroic bravery, and their undoubted spirit of
enterprise. Providence saw fit to raise up this fraternity for its own good purpose, and
perhaps it was the one element needed to cope with the exigencies of the troublous
times in which they flourished. They played their important and tragic part in the
great drama of the ages, and passed away. The ashes of their last representatives now
lie beneath the mortuary mosaics of the church of St. John.

The beginning of the organization was, as already intimated, of a very humble
character, but being in its purpose founded upon true Christian principles, it
challenged at the outset the just admiration of many sincere and devout people, who
gladly joined in furthering its estimable object, and thus it grew, though very slowly at
first, until finally it became a great power throughout the civilized nations, exercising
in its day a vast degree of both religious and political influence. The Grand Masters of
the order took position among the highest potentates of the age, and were given the
post of honor next to that of royalty itself, at all assemblies of state to which they were
called.

A few sincere, energetic, and practical individuals, said to have been Italian
merchants from Amalfi, then belonging to the kingdom of Naples, impressed by the
peculiar exigencies of the time and place, solemnly joined themselves together as a
sacred fraternity, at Jerusalem, by taking upon themselves vows of indissoluble
brotherhood, and of chastity and poverty. Little did the pious, self-abnegating Peter
Gerard, the accredited father of the Hospitallers, when collecting a few friends
together at his own humble dwelling in the latter part of the tenth century, realize that
he was then and there founding an order whose power should presently become the
main prop of Christianity, as sustained against the energetic inroads of the Ottoman
power. The avowed purpose of these men thus banded together was to devote their
lives to the care and protection of poor, oppressed, and sick pilgrims, who had come
from afar to the sacred city as the Mecca of their religious faith. After a considerable
period of usefulness in the direction indicated, and seeing the possibilities before them,

they obtained permission from the Caliph of Egypt to found a hospital for the use of the sick and the needy, but especially in behalf of those who came from foreign lands to visit the Holy Sepulchre. The rapid increase in the service they had assumed soon demanded the erection of a second hospital, or annex, one being devoted to women and the other to men. This enlarged capacity soon rendered it necessary to create a sisterhood of regular nurses, composed of self-devoted women actuated by the same Christian sentiments which had given rise to the formation of the brotherhood. The hospice prospered beyond the most sanguine hopes of its originators. Grateful pilgrims who had shared its hospitalities, on returning to their distant homes, spread the fame of its charities all over Europe, thus arousing the warmest enthusiasm, and liberal contributions of money were freely given in its behalf. To meet the necessities of the case, a chapel was in time duly added to the hospice, thus forming a very complete and well-organized whole, which may be said to have been the cradle of the afterward famous Order of the Knights of Malta.

There can be no reasonable doubt that the early members of the fraternity, when they were best known as Hospitallers, were entirely consistent in their object, as it was announced to the world, and that they were actuated solely by the highest sense of duty and of Christian endeavor. The sick were healed, the hungry fed, an economical and unostentatious hospitality was exercised toward one and all, and good, effective, charitable work was constantly performed. These self-appointed servants of the poor and unfortunate were sincere followers of the Master, and devoted to his service. Those who were at this time in power at Jerusalem, though professed Mohammedans, were apparently won by the liberality of the organization, in freely extending its charities to all of the native population who applied for aid. Christian and infidel fared alike in sharing the benefits of the hospice. No unfortunate one was turned away from its gates empty-handed, when actual want drove him to supplicate for the Christian's aid. If such were poor and needy, these were the only credentials required to command the free services of the brotherhood of Hospitallers, who derived this name from their special care of the sick, and by it they were solely known in the early days at Jerusalem. Their governing motto was: "Inasmuch as ye have done it unto one of the least of these, my brethren, ye have done it unto me."

As we have said, generous, sympathetic people all over Europe subscribed liberally toward the support of this sacred charity; the Hospitallers became the almoners of their spontaneous bounty. Prince and peasant alike contributed, each one in accordance with his means. All were enthusiastic and cheerful givers. This condition of affairs was, however, abruptly changed by the new conquerors of the country,— warlike Turks, who ignored the tolerance of their Mussulman predecessors. They at once instituted a system of persecution with regard to the Christians which became intolerable, and which almost entirely obstructed the design and the operations of the organization of the Hospitallers. It was thus in self-defense that the fraternity gradually developed into a band of soldier-monks and armed physicians, adding to their original vows a new and important clause, binding themselves to combat with warlike weapons on all suitable occasions in behalf of their religious faith, and to protect themselves with arms in their hands from their infidel oppressors.

It was not long after the Hospitallers were driven from the sacred city, and their leader, Peter Gerard, imprisoned, that the remarkable expeditions known in history as the Crusades were organized, their object being the rescue of Jerusalem from the possession of the Turks. This uprising of Europeans finally resulted in the capture by them of the ancient city, under the command of Godefroi de Bouillon, the illustrious leader of the first Crusade, in 1099. All Christendom rejoiced. Peter Gerard was released from his dungeon, and the banner of the cross superseded that of the crescent in the province of Judæa. One of the great epochs of history at the close of the tenth century was when Godefroi was proclaimed first Christian king of Jerusalem.

Nearly eight hundred years have passed away since this interesting era of the world's progress, and one pauses reflectively to realize and to moralize over the fact that the "Holy Land" is still Mohammedan. It is the crescent, not the cross, which floats to-day upon the breezes of Palestine. No Peter the Hermit preaches a new Crusade in this nineteenth century, to recover possession of the Holy Sepulchre.

We are writing of a period when personal prowess was considered the great essential of true manhood. Learning and the sciences were left to monks and the cloister. The profession of arms, therefore, attracted all noble and ambitious youths,— it was in fact the only path open to chivalric purposes, and which led to high preferment. The spirit of the age was one of superstition and veneration combined, so that it was easy to raise a host of brave followers for the purpose of fighting the Moslems, and of rescuing Jerusalem from their possession. A belief that the shedding of one's blood in such a cause not only purchased forgiveness for all sins, but also insured to the soldiers of the cross the future joys of heaven, prevailed in those days among high and low, throughout Europe. Recruits for the ranks of the Crusaders required no urging. They marched at first, like an impetuous mob, in myriads toward the East, and were defeated, as a matter of course; but learning wisdom by experience, they duly organized themselves, and victory followed.

Though the avowed purpose of the brotherhood of whom we write was one of charity, peace, and good-will toward men, of self-abnegation and devotion to good works, especially embracing the idea of nursing the sick, still, owing to the exigencies of the situation, as we have shown, the organization gradually developed into a complete military order, and presently came to be known the world over as the Knights of St. John; the significant and at first strictly appropriate title of Hospitallers was over-shadowed by the more soldierly one of Knights. Their first military duty was that of escorting pilgrims to and from the coast, guarding them from the frequently fatal violence of the natives. The field of their operation became rapidly enlarged, and they grew to be more and more warlike, until presently the soldier got the better of the monk, and from acting only in self-defense at the outset, the order eventually became boldly aggressive. Their ranks were recruited by soldierly additions from among the Crusaders, and their banner of the white cross floated victoriously over many a hard fought field of battle, when the Christians were fiercely struggling with the possessors of Palestine.

From Jerusalem the order removed to Acre, in Syria, about the year 1187, where Richard Coeur de Lion established a headquarters for the Knights, and here they remained as an organization for about one hundred years, devoting themselves only in part to their original design as a religious and charitable body, but redoubling their belligerency toward the Moslems. An opportunity for conflict was never avoided by these military monks, and unless they were beset by ten times their own numbers, the Knights were almost certain to be victorious. Finally, overpowered by the Turks, in a terrific and decisive battle, they were expelled from Acre, those who escaped the awful massacre taking refuge in Cyprus. This was in the year 1291. In this island, which Richard I. of England captured from the Saracens, the order maintained itself for the comparatively brief period of twenty years; but at last, forced to abandon the place, they seized upon the island of Rhodes, about the year 1310, which was then in the possession of Mohammedan pirates and Greek rebels. The Knights were not in open warfare against Greece, though they bore its people no special good-will. The Greeks had secretly opposed the Crusaders, and by treachery had aided the Turks on more than one important occasion.

We were speaking of the seizure of the island of Rhodes, which was a matter of no small importance, and to accomplish which involved herculean efforts at the very outset.

The enemy were so well organized and so thoroughly equipped with defensive material, that it required four years of incessant and vigorous warfare before the Knights finally gained undisputed sovereignty on the island. In this sanguinary and protracted struggle the order was nearly exterminated, losing hundreds of its best and bravest members, but their places were gradually filled by fresh acquisitions from Europe. There was a spirit of emulation in the ranks of the Knights, as to the exhibition of bravery and prowess exercised against the enemy, which often led them to great personal exposure, and to the performance of heroic deeds. The individual conflicts were frequently characterized more by rashness than by good judgment and bravery. In the period of which we write, the mode of warfare and of military organization left much freer scope for individual gallantry and originality of purpose, much freer play for personal prowess. Men fought less like machines and more like heroes than it is possible for them to do under our modern system of combinations and of implicit obedience to orders. The hope of successful and gallant adventure spurred on the most indifferent to do something which should lead to distinction. Emulation is an instinctive quality in those who make a profession of arms, and fighting is an appetite which grows by what it feeds upon. Emulation and imitation have been called twins.

It was after almost incredible suffering and persistency of effort that the Order of St. John was finally settled at Rhodes upon a firmer basis than it had ever before enjoyed, and here it remained sovereign for over two centuries, becoming so identified with the place as to be known throughout Christendom as the Knights of Rhodes. They had little opportunity for the exercise of those Christian virtues which they had heretofore claimed for their fraternity, but their character as a warlike brotherhood did not suffer by want of aggressiveness upon their part.

This most beautiful island of Rhodes, which was about one third larger than Malta, embowered with palms and citron groves, flourished wonderfully under the sovereignty of the Knights, while the order itself steadily increased in numbers, power, and wealth. The neighboring islands of Telos, Syme, Nisyros, Cos, Leros, and Calymna, known on the old charts as the Sporades, were conquered one after another and annexed to the island of Rhodes, thus coming under the governorship of the Grand Masters of the Knights. While establishing themselves in this island and strengthening its half-ruined defenses, the most profitable employment of the Knights was privateering, or, more correctly, active piracy. They cruised against all Mohammedan and Greek vessels. True, their vows only bound them to perpetual warfare against the Turks, but a very little stretching of their consciences enabled them to see no wrong in capturing the commercial property of the Greeks also. It must be admitted that the latter people, as a maritime nation, were themselves ever a predatory race. Might alone made right in the waters of the Levant, and especially so in the Grecian archipelago. No candid writer can defend the marine policy of the Greeks, and perhaps the Knights of St. John only meted to these rovers the same treatment which they (the Greeks) were used to accord to others. All history shows that the eastern basin of the Mediterranean was for centuries a swarming nest of corsairs of various nationalities, Greeks, Turks, and Algerines. Any attempt to transfer a legitimate cargo of merchandise from an Asiatic to a European port by way of the Straits of Gibraltar was to run the gauntlet of a fleet of piratical vessels which preyed indiscriminately upon the commerce of all nations. Those we have named were the most numerous among these sea robbers, the Turks and Algerines making war together upon the Knights of Rhodes, who retaliated upon them with interest, both on the land and on the sea. The Knights pursued these powers with most unchristianlike vengeance, pertinacity, and success.

The adventurous life followed by the order proved to be terribly demoralizing to the individual members, and especially incompatible with the observance of their religious vows and discipline. The frequent division of prize money, the constant capture of luxuries of all sorts, and of female prisoners, led to gambling, drinking, and debauchery on shore, until all semblance of respect for monastic ties utterly vanished. This was not because the Knights were so much worse than the average people of their time, for lawlessness was the characteristic of the age, but it was the natural outgrowth of the extraordinary circumstances in which they were involved,—circumstances which created an overstrained energy neither natural nor healthful. Insubordination and jealousies frequently broke out among the order, to quell which the severest measures were promptly adopted. The Grand Masters more than once resorted to the extremest punishment, even including the death penalty.

Following up their supremacy on the sea, the Knights continued to fight the Turks and Greeks, wherever found, until at last scarcely a vessel bearing the flag of either of them dared to venture out of port. Four times the Mussulmans made prodigious efforts to dislodge the Knights from Rhodes; but on each occasion they were signally defeated. The warlike Turks grew more and more formidable, while they were constantly goaded by the fresh aggressions of the Knights.

Besides being actuated by a desire for revenge upon an enemy who had not only so nearly ruined the commerce of Turkey, but who had raided so many of the unprotected coast towns, carrying off the inhabitants and selling them into slavery, Solyman, Sultan of Turkey, was burning with envy. He coveted the island, which, under the Knights of St. John, had been made to "blossom like the rose." So he "swore by his own head," says an ancient writer, that he would possess Rhodes, if it cost the lives of half his army to conquer it. Vast preparations were therefore made to carry on, if necessary, a protracted siege. At great labor and expense all the available forces of the Ottoman navy and army were brought together and organized for this purpose, in the year 1522. The writers of that period tell us that two hundred thousand men were transported to Rhodes from Constantinople, commanded by the emperor in person. To oppose this gigantic host the order could bring but six or seven hundred Knights and less than six thousand men-at-arms. But every Knight was a host in himself, while the common soldiers were well armed and thoroughly disciplined.

The army of the Sultan took position before the fortifications of Rhodes with all their implements of war, in a manner which showed that they had come to stay until victory should perch upon their banners. They stormed the stout defenses again and again, with great loss of life on their part. The Knights gallantly withstood all their furious and frenzied efforts for a period of six months, often sallying forth and slaughtering myriads of the Ottomans in hand-to-hand conflicts. The Turks did not lack for courage. They always fought with desperation; but in personal conflict, man to man, they were no match for the stout cavaliers of the white cross, who, besides having the advantage of weight and physical strength, were protected by impenetrable steel armor, while the Orientals wore only their flowing robes and turbans of linen. Vastly outnumbering the Knights, this very disproportion was to their disadvantage, often causing them to be swept out of existence by the score, from the solid phalanx which they presented to the keen weapons of the Christians. The light arms and the agility of the soldiers of the Sultan were of little comparative avail when met by the heavy blows and ponderous battle-axes wielded by stout Europeans. Among the vows of the Knights was a most significant one, namely, "never to reckon the number of an enemy." Vast superiority of numbers, however, told at last, for the besieged were utterly worn out. Quarter was neither asked nor given by either side; but when the combatants met, they fought to the last gasp. It was a war of extermination on the part of both Christians and Turks. The latter, being really the weaker party, went down by hundreds.

Including the killed and severely wounded, together with those who died of fever and various diseases incident to camp life, it is authoritatively stated that the Turks lost one hundred and sixty thousand men in the six months' siege of Rhodes, showing a dogged persistency which was probably never surpassed, if it has been equaled, in warfare. It should be remembered that the enormous host of the Ottomans was opposed by only about five or six thousand men, who, however, mostly fought from behind protecting stone walls.

In order to show the spirit which actuated the Knights, and their unscrupulous mode of warfare, we will relate a well-authenticated instance connected with this remarkable siege.

One of the famous fighters in the ranks of the Order of St. John was a Frenchman who bore the name of Fornonius, who is declared to have killed over six hundred of the enemy during the six months' contest! His prowess was not only marvelous in the open field and upon the ramparts when engaged in repelling an assault, but he would lie in wait, like a hunter of wild beasts, for hours together, to obtain the chance of killing a Mussulman. When a sortie was made against the besiegers, Fornonius was always found in the van, rushing among the enemy, and with one terrible sweeping reach of his keen-edged battle-axe, he would sever three or four heads from their bodies, keeping up a shower of these frightful blows, aimed right and left, until the astonished Ottomans, notwithstanding their usually reckless bravery, fled in utter dismay before what seemed to them a superhuman power. Even his comrades believed that he bore a charmed life; for, although he received many slight wounds, he was never touched in a vital part, and he boasted that he had not been out of "fighting trim" during the whole of that long siege, night or day. His example was in a degree contagious, and the Knights, thoroughly trained to the use of arms, vied with each other in their murderous efforts against the common enemy.

This gallant, though in one sense useless defense of the island was sustained so long and so successfully against such desperate odds, as to establish the fame of the Knights for persistent bravery, commanding even the respect and admiration of their enemies. The Turks had resolved upon the conquest of the place, let it cost what blood it might, and were constantly reinforced by fresh troops from Constantinople. Although the Knights were finally obliged to yield, they were enabled to retire from Rhodes upon advantageous terms, or to use the military phrase, upon "honorable" terms. It was on this historic occasion that Charles V. exclaimed in admiration: "There has been nothing so well lost in the world as Rhodes."

The Sultan of Turkey, to the great surprise of all the world, which had been looking on with deepest interest at this sanguinary struggle upon the most beautiful island of the Levant, proved himself to be, as an enemy, brave and persistent; as a conqueror, mild and merciful. The Knights, during the long period in which they had possessed Rhodes, had not failed to attack every galley bearing the Ottoman flag which they sighted, nor hesitated to destroy every coast town belonging to that power which they could reach, or to burn any Mohammedan mosque when they got near enough to apply the torch. Added to all this, they had constantly captured and carried into slavery Turkish men, women, and children by the hundreds. The Sultan, under such aggravating circumstances, would have been fully justified, according to the code of warfare practiced in those days, in putting every belligerent whom he found in Rhodes to the sword. To conquer the island had cost him a vast amount of treasure, together with a hundred and sixty thousand of his best soldiers,—a terrible price to pay for victory. Notwithstanding this long list of bitter aggressions, according to our idea, Sultan Solyman showed himself to be far more humane and generous than did the professed Christians of the Order of St. John.

The liberal and remarkable terms granted by the conquerors of Rhodes were in brief as follows:—

The Knights agreed to promptly and peaceably evacuate the island and its dependencies within twelve days, being permitted to take with them their arms and personal effects, even including such church ornaments and treasures as they chose to move. Those of the citizens of Rhodes who desired to do so could depart in the same manner, while the Christians who remained were to be unmolested, and permitted to worship in their usual manner. The Sultan was to provide ships, and to provision them, with which to transport to Crete all who desired to go thither. These liberal, not to say generous terms were faithfully adhered to, except in one instance,—all the Christian churches in Rhodes were promptly turned into Mohammedan mosques.

It is said that less than a hundred of the Knights of the order remained alive to avail themselves of the Sultan's clemency! What a comment upon the gallant and protracted fight which they had made! Of course there were numerous men-at-arms attached to the brotherhood, who also followed its fortunes into exile, saying nothing of the non-combatants who accompanied them.

The fall of Rhodes left Sultan Solyman for the time being sole master of the eastern basin of the Mediterranean. There were now none to dispute his power in the Aegean, Ionian, or Adriatic seas. The Greeks were of small account, while the Algerines were in fact his allies. The Turks, who were by no means originally a maritime people, had gradually, by force of circumstances, become so, and at this time they were as daring pirates as the dreaded Algerines of the African coast.

From this period the Order of St. John was homeless, and continued so for six or seven years, maintaining temporary headquarters at Candia, Messina, Cumæ, and Viterbo. Its officers, dispersed among the several courts of Europe, strove ceaselessly for recognition and reorganization. The long siege through which they had so lately passed had quite exhausted their immediate resources, and reduced their number to a mere nucleus. It had been, as we have shown, a fearful and most destructive warfare. The aged Grand Master, L'Isle Adam, repaired to Rome, where he did not cease his endeavors to influence the Pope in behalf of the order; that functionary either did not desire, or does not seem to have been able to do anything in its behalf. Finally, the island of Malta, having fallen into the possession of Charles V. of Germany, was presented by him in perpetuity to the homeless Knights of St. John. To an order which had no local habitation, and which was just then so universally ignored by the reigning monarchs, and even by the Pope, this was seemingly a great boon, a noble gift; but the real facts of the case rob the act of any spirit of true generosity. The royal owner cared very little for the possession of Malta, Gozo, and Tripoli, the latter situated on the adjacent coast of Barbary. He was in reality glad to get rid of dependencies which cost him a large sum of money annually to garrison and maintain, but from which he received no equivalent whatever. They were empty possessions to him, ministering neither to his pride nor his treasury. The emperor, nevertheless, made a virtue of their relinquishment, and bound the order, as a condition of the gift, never under any circumstances to take up arms against his lineage. These terms were acceded to, and were ever after scrupulously observed, though on more than one occasion the loyalty of the Knights was sorely tried.

As to Tripoli, the order did not desire to possess it at all, and would have been glad not to have taken charge of it. Tripoli was indeed a white elephant, to speak figuratively, but the emperor was persistent,—the three dependencies must go together. His pride would not permit him to abandon the place to the Turks, so he insisted on its going with Malta and Gozo into the custody of the Order of St. John. He knew very well that the Knights were in no condition to dictate terms, and he took advantage accordingly. So the fraternity in their then weakened condition were forced to take charge of a distant dependency, the maintenance of which must draw heavily upon their circumscribed resources.

The order is said to have been upon the point of making a permanent settlement at Genoa, where it had long before established one of its most successful commanderies, but the decision was finally made in favor of Malta. The Grand Master was influenced by the strategic situation, and also on account of the advantages it presented for being most effectually fortified. Against these considerations, however, he was obliged to weigh the sterile character of the rocky group, which at that time presented a most inhospitable aspect. The latter cause so affected a large portion of the Knights, who looked more to the present than the future, that a strong party was raised in open opposition to the choice of this group for their future home, but the decision of the Grand Master was final; there was no appeal from his mandate when it had been issued. L'Isle Adam's decision proved ultimately to be the grandest move ever made by the order, viewed from the results which were thus brought about.

As regarded Tripoli, its situation was more than precarious from the very first, having often to be defended against savage onslaughts made by the warlike Algerines. It was an outpost which only a rich and numerous people could afford to hold, and to the Knights of St. John it was worse than worthless. When the loss of the place occurred, therefore, some twenty years subsequent, in 1551, at which time it was surrendered after much hard fighting, to Dragut, the most daring and successful corsair of the century, it was a positive advantage to the Knights. Thereafter they were enabled to concentrate all their energies and means upon what was of infinitely more importance, namely, the fortification and strengthening of their principal holdings, the islands of Malta and Gozo.

CHAPTER XV.

Settlement of the Order at Malta.—A Barren Waste.—A New Era for the
Natives.—Foundling Hospitals.—Grand Master La Vallette.—Sailors and Soldiers.—
Capture of Prisoners at Mondon.—A Slave Story in Brief.—Christian Corsairs!—The
Ottomans attack the Knights in their New Home.—Defeat of the Turks.—Terrible
Slaughter of Human Beings.—Civil War.—Summary Punishment.—Some Details of
a Famous Siege.

When the Knights of St. John accepted the gift of Charles V., and removed to
their new island home in October, 1530, they came in small numbers. Their fleet
consisted only of three galleys, one galliot, and a brigantine. Malta was then
comparatively a barren waste; nothing could appear less inviting. With the picture of
verdant, sunny Rhodes still fresh in their minds, these bare rocks must have seemed
terribly inhospitable and dreary to the new-comers. The very title of Rhodes is of
Greek origin, having its appropriate appellation, and refers to the great number of
wild roses which grow spontaneously upon that lovely island. The Knights had lived
long and prosperously upon what was and is still known as the "Garden of the
Levant," hence the contrast was naturally disheartening. Here the rocky surface was
treeless and white with desolation. In Rhodes they had left whole forests of sycamores,
planes, and palms, together with groves of olive, almond, and orange trees, while in
Malta arboreal ornamentation was literally conspicuous by its absence.

The thirty-fourth parallel of north latitude intersects both of these famous islands,
which are, however, separated by six degrees of longitude, the climate being nearly
identical. Rhodes was larger than their new island home, its earlier history showing it
to have been, like Malta, at one time in the far past, a prosperous Phoenician colony.
There was no alternative for the Knights except to make the beat of the situation, and
so without wasting time in useless regrets, or repining, they set to work energetically
to introduce improvements, and to adapt the locality to their most urgent necessities.
The present site of Valletta was then sparsely occupied by a few poorly constructed
cabins, Città Vecchia, situated two leagues inland, being the capital of the island. The
Knights first selected their headquarters at Borgo, on the shore of the present Grand
Harbor. After the decisive victory over the Turks in 1565, Borgo was named Città
Vittoriosa, that is, the "victorious city," in honor of the gallant defense it made on that
memorable occasion, and thus it is known to-day.

As to the Maltese peasantry, who were thus summarily transferred from one
mastership to another without being permitted any voice whatever in the matter, they
naturally received the new-comers at first with considerable reservation, but were soon
on friendly terms with them, and erelong they cordially joined interests. At the first
coming of the Knights, it is true, the Maltese were not in a condition to dispute the
new authority placed over them, yet they had influence enough to exact from the
brotherhood certain satisfactory terms as the price of their yielding ready submission.

The Grand Master, in behalf of the order, solemnly swore to "preserve inviolate, for the inhabitants of the group, all of their present rights, customs, and privileges." Realizing the importance of retaining the good-will of the people, the fraternity as a body were careful to exercise towards them, in these early days of their settlement here, great consideration and generosity. They did not bear themselves as conquerors, but rather as friends, a community having a common interest, and they demanded no service from the Maltese for which they did not honestly pay. They encouraged them to till the ground by introducing new seeds, and by giving the natives valuable and practical information. They brought fruit and ornamental trees from the mainland, and in many ways stimulated the islanders to adopt progressive and profitable ideas for their own special benefit. The Maltese were a coarse, uncultured race, scarcely amenable to argument, and difficult to reason with. They followed in the footsteps of their forefathers, and ignored all experiments, however promising. But tangible results were convincing, and so steady improvement followed the efforts of the Knights to enlighten the dull native brain.

It was the beginning of a new era for this isolated people. The spirit of neglect which had so long reigned supreme upon the group was now superseded by another instinct with life and enterprise. Though the natives had not sufficient intelligence to originate ideas, yet when placed before their eyes they could appreciate and adopt them. The mass of the people seemed neither to know nor to care about the government under which they lived, provided they did not experience any personal harm or undue restrictions at the hands of those in power. They appeared to be content so long as they were permitted to join in the almost daily church processions and festivals, always remembering and demanding the utmost freedom at recurrence of the annual Carnival. They entertained no spirit of loyalty except towards themselves and their hereditary forms and ceremonies. This was nearly four hundred years ago, but almost precisely the same spirit prevails among the Maltese to-day.

At the time when the Knights first came hither, Malta was hardly fortified at all. True, Fort St. Angelo existed in name, and it mounted a few small guns, but a score of Algerine pirates could have landed and taken possession, so far as any protection was afforded by this apology for a fort.

The thin layer of soil which covered the rocks of the island here and there was hardly sufficient to till, and no extensive effort at agriculture or gardening seems to have been made by the natives before the Knights came to Malta, or at least not for centuries. In any other hands save those of this thrifty and determined semi-military organization, the island would have been but a sorry gift. It is described by a popular writer of that period as being "nothing better than a shelterless rock of soft sandstone called tufa." Subsistence for the dwellers upon the group, with the exception of fish, which were plenty enough, was brought almost entirely from Sicily, or the mainland. Frequent invasions of Saracens and Turks, continued for so many years, had devastated the islands, discouraging and impoverishing the natives, large numbers of whom had been carried away by the invaders and sold into slavery. This was the usual mode of disposing of prisoners of war in those days among people of the East.

According to the authority from which we have just quoted, Malta was in 1530 "intensely dry and hot, with not a forest tree, and hardly a green thing to rest the eye upon." This barren waste, however, was destined in the course of a few years to put on a very different aspect, and to become an attractive example of fertility and fruitfulness; in fact, a dépôt of vast importance, by the exercise of energy and engineering skill.

The material improvements thus introduced, together with the protection from foreign enemies which the Maltese gained, was to be considered with many qualifications. Magdalen asylums and foundling hospitals, to which priests and Knights could recommend their favorites for shelter, became most suspiciously numerous. The inference is only too plain. The native population, as usual, emulated not the virtues, but the vices of the new-comers. That the group must have flourished greatly under the Phoenicians, Greeks, Carthaginians, and Romans, there are plenty of monuments still extant to prove; but under the Arabs and Sicilians it had gradually declined, until the period when it came into possession of the Knights of St. John, who began promptly to restore its fallen fortunes, though, as has been intimated, at the expense of the morals of the people.

The galleys of the order did not lie idle after the fraternity had become fairly settled at Malta. They were promptly put in fighting condition, and constantly swept the neighboring seas, capturing prizes in all directions, even seeking the Turkish craft at the very mouth of the Dardanelles, and the Algerines on their own coast. The Knights filled the fighting ranks of the crews in their ships with Maltese, who were admirable sailors, and reliable for all sorts of sea-service. A score of Knights were quite sufficient to man each galleon, aided by a hundred or thereabouts of the trained seamen of the island. The slaves at the oars were not depended upon to act as belligerents, nor were the few hands who managed the sails and the running gear of the vessels. The Maltese had long before signalized themselves for valor and skillful seamanship under their own commanders, by capturing the entire Venetian fleet, together with Andrea Dandolo, the admiral who commanded it. At another time they destroyed the large flotilla of the Republic of Pisa, and thus raised the siege and blockade of Syracuse. Though the protection afforded the inhabitants of the group by the Order of St. John was ample, and freed the people from all fear of predatory invasions, still the influence of the Knights was less for peace than for war, and, as has been shown, was not calculated to permanently improve the material condition of the common people of Malta.

The renowned Dragut, daring and reckless pirate as he was, shunned a meeting with the red galleys of the Knights. "Fate is with them," said this dreaded corsair, referring to the armor-clad Knights, whom he had so often met in battle. "Our swords will not wound, nor our spears pierce them."

La Vallette, who was at this time "General" of the galleys, proved himself as successful at sea as he did afterwards upon the land, when, as Grand Master, he conducted the famous and successful defense of Malta. His career was a remarkable one. He became a Knight before he was of age, and was conscientiously devoted to the order, body and soul, to the very last of his life. A predatory warfare both on land and sea was carried on incessantly by the Knights against the Turks, in which they were almost always successful. The historians tell us that during the sixteenth and seventeenth centuries, Valletta became a vast slave mart, supplied with human merchandise by means of the invasions and sea-captures of the order. On one occasion a thoroughly organized and well-equipped force engaged in an expedition by which the Knights surprised and captured the city of Mondon, in Morea, whence they brought away a large amount of riches. We find enumerated in the list of their booty, eight hundred Turkish women and girls, whom they enslaved! The reader will please remember that we are writing of a fraternity,—a so-called religious brotherhood,— whose solemn vows bound them to charity, poverty, humility, and chastity. One feels not a little inclined to moralize, in this connection, upon the contrast between profession and practice, and on the weakness of human nature in general. These Knights of the cross reveled in cruel warfare; it was recreation to them. They displayed no want of valor, but they did exhibit "a plentiful lack" of Christian charity.

Among the beautiful women who fell into the hands of the Knights at the capture of Mondon was one possessed of marvelous loveliness both of form and features. Soon after her capture she became the property of Viscomte Cicala, who finally made her his wife. Being his slave, there could be no choice on her part, whether she would consent to the arrangement or not. The fruit of this marriage was a son, whom the father named Scipio, and had baptized into the Roman Catholic faith. This boy, when he grew up to man's estate, as the story runs, to fulfill a solemn vow made to his mother hastened to Constantinople, where he enlisted in the Ottoman army, and promptly embraced Mohammedanism. By his extraordinary valor and intelligence as an officer in the Sultan's service, he rose rapidly to the command of the Turkish army. In this position he proved himself one of the most able and active enemies the Christians had to contend with. He caused great destruction in their ranks, because of the knowledge he possessed of their modes of warfare. When he was engaged in battle with the Christians, his war-cry was, "Remember Mondon!"

In the lapse of years, aggravated by the numberless onslaughts of the Knights upon their commerce, also envying the great improvement and manifest prosperity evinced at Malta under the management of L'Isle Adam and his successor, La Vallette, Turkish jealousy was aroused to the highest point of endurance. The commerce of Egypt and Syria was in danger of annihilation. The Knights of St. John were virtual masters of the narrow seas,—they were the "Christian" corsairs of the Levant! In the forty-three years which had transpired since the Knights were driven from Rhodes, the Turks had many times seen cause to regret the clemency which had been exercised toward the Christians in allowing them to depart from the island in peace. The Sultan's royal liberality, it must be confessed, had been ill-rewarded. The Order of St. John had proved to be more of a thorn in the side of the Ottoman power than when its stronghold was on the nearer island. It is not surprising, therefore, that the Sultan resolved again to attack the Knights in their more recent home, and thereby not only to avenge the great losses which his people had sustained on sea and land, but also so effectually to demolish the power of the Knights as to disperse and break up the order altogether. Twice the Sultan brought large, well-organized forces to Malta for this purpose, first in 1546 and again in 1551, on both of which occasions the Ottomans were ignominiously defeated, and as usual with great slaughter. Their admitted losses aggregated from ten to twelve thousand men, killed outright, on each of these occasions. Their perseverance under such discouraging circumstances was marvelous, yet only characteristic of the race. The Turks always fought bravely, hand to hand, spurred on by a religious frenzy which led them to disregard all personal danger. They had no fear of death, which to the faithful Mussulman only signified instant transportation to the Mohammedan paradise, with them "a consummation devoutly to be wished."

The Ottomans stormed the fortifications of the Knights at great disadvantage. Inspired by their fanaticism, they advanced over the dead bodies of their comrades, which formed a bridge across the deep ditch, while the defenders were sustained by a lofty and heroic resolve to conquer or to die. The meeting of such opponents caused blood to flow like water, while the sacrifice of human life must have been enormous. It was the calm, unshrinking determination of the soldiers of the cross that rendered them so invincible, both on sea and on land, and that insured them victory, though they were always outnumbered in every conflict. A few score of men inspired by such a strong will as actuated the Knights of St. John, and so well versed in the use of deadly weapons, became a host in themselves. It was in the siege of 1551 that the order lost one of the most active and important of its members in the person of the Cavalier Repton, Grand Prior of England, whose prowess as a soldier of the cross was long remembered by his brethren in arms.

This frenzy, leading to the sacrifice of one's life in the hope of gaining Paradise, as exhibited by the Turks, seems ridiculous, no doubt, to the average reader, but it exists to-day in various forms among Eastern nations. The devout Hindoo solemnly believes that the shortest road to eternal life is to be submerged in the all-cleansing, sacred Ganges. His body is in the ordinary course burned upon its banks, while the ashes are carefully gathered and cast into the flowing tide. So infatuated were the pilgrims at one time, who came to Benares to bathe in the sacred river, that the English police were obliged to use force to prevent them from drowning themselves and their infants in these waters. It was so with the Turks, who believed themselves to be serving Allah and dying in his service, when they fought the Christian soldiers. "These infidels seem to welcome death," said Grand Master La Vallette, while at his advanced age he was wielding the deadly battle-axe upon the ramparts during the siege of Malta.

In the two attempts upon the island in 1546 and in 1551, the Mohammedans outnumbered the Maltese garrison ten to one. Having so often tested the prowess of the Christians in battle, the Turks would not attack the Knights except with a force much superior in numbers. In their most prosperous days in Malta, the Knights proper, that is, those holding full membership in the order, never numbered more than six or seven hundred, but there were various grades of men-at-arms, and of trained native Maltese, attached to the service of the Knights, thus swelling the fighting force to a fairly effective body. Many of the Knights were distributed over Europe, the order having "chapters," or "commanderies," as they were called, in France, Germany, England, Spain, and Italy, from which the headquarters at Malta drew pecuniary support to meet all ordinary demands upon it. But the treasury of the order was amply supplied in reality by preying upon the commerce of the Mediterranean between Sicily and the Levant. Occasionally, when seriously weakened by warfare, fresh members from these European dépôts joined the main body on the island for more active duty. A requisition to that effect being issued by the Grand Master, it was responded to with alacrity by the home members. It was a period when chivalry flourished in Europe, as we have already indicated, when warfare against the Mohammedans was deemed among the Christians an absolute service to God.

There was undoubtedly an *esprit de corps* among the Knights of St. John, which was strong enough to hold them in the ordinary bonds of brotherhood, and to keep up the forms of their religious vows and purposes. Yet those who knew their history at this period do not credit them with much consistency or pious devotion to the sacred obligations which they had voluntarily assumed. They were often anything but harmonious among themselves, requiring the intervention of stern rules exercised by an unquestionable authority.

While L'Isle Adam was alive, bending under the accumulated weight of many years, and still suffering much pain from the wounds he had received in various battles with the Turks, he was nearly disheartened and broken down with sorrow at the growth of domestic quarrels and jealousies among the fraternity over which he presided. In vain were all his earnest admonitions and pacific attempts at reconciliation. The time had come for exemplary action. He was severely just in administering the duties of his responsible office, and was both respected and feared by all backsliders. One cause, and perhaps the principal one, which induced quarrels among the Knights was that of the difference of language. There was a certain national rivalry which was ever coming to the surface, and which proved a chronic source of trouble. This spirit finally broke forth in open warfare, civil war, and was conducted with deadly hostility between the several factions. Duels and personal conflicts were of daily occurrence. It was a crisis in the history of the order, but L'Isle Adam, notwithstanding his physical infirmities, was fully equal to the trying occasion. He had faced the furious enemy in too many a hard fought battle to know anything like hesitancy at a critical moment. A brief court-martial was promptly held; the trial of the accused Knights was short and decisive. The reckless and guilty culprits found that they had been playing with fire. Twelve of the accused were ordered to be stripped of their official garments and insignia, and were ignominiously expelled from the order and the island, while an equal number were condemned to immediate death. These last were inclosed in canvas bags, after they had been securely bound with ropes, and, similar to the Turkish fashion of treating unfaithful women, they were thrown into the sea to drown! It was the iron hand of discipline, Oriental and heathenish in the character of the punishment, but it was effective in its results. Any halting in purpose on the part of L'Isle Adam at that critical moment would have proved to be the death of the order. We may be sure that there were no more attempts at civil war among the Knights. Order was firmly reëstablished. The vows of the members bound them to the most implicit obedience. They were rebellious; they disregarded the Grand Master's commands, and consequently they suffered condign punishment.

A terrible example having thus been made, the members realized thereafter both the certainty and the severity of the punishment which awaited those who indulged a like rebellious spirit. Four years after the settlement of the order in the island of Malta, L'Isle Adam died. This was in 1534.

It was in 1565 that the Porte made its greatest and final effort to capture Malta from the Knights of St. John. The Sultan determined to crush out the life of a fraternity which for centuries had been so persistently arrayed against his race. The immediate circumstance which at last awakened the fury of Solyman, and brought matters to a climax, was the capture by the Knights of a Turkish galleon, on the Ottoman coast, richly laden, and belonging to the chief black eunuch of his royal establishment. Enraged at this, the Sultan vowed to bring about the destruction of his old enemies, if it cost the lives of half his subjects. In pursuance of this resolve, after a full year occupied in elaborate preparations, one hundred and thirty vessels, carrying about forty thousand men, sailed from Constantinople, under command of Mustafa Pasha, who had grown old in the wars of his country, and having been joined by an Algerine flotilla manned by piratical crews, and led by the notorious corsair Dragut, appeared in due form, May 18, 1565, upon the Maltese coast. The force thus organized on the part of the Turks was one of the most complete, in its warlike character, which had ever floated in the eastern basin of the Mediterranean Sea. Its success seemed to be a foregone conclusion with all except the gallant Knights themselves.

In the mean time, while this grand expedition was being organized, La Vallette, then Grand Master of the Knights, was kept well informed of every movement at Constantinople, and he was by no means idle. Every exertion was made to place the island in a good condition of defense. A general summons was issued, recalling all Knights who were absent in Europe. A large body of infantry was raised in Sicily, two thousand men and more, who were gradually transferred to the island. Ample quantities of provisions, arms, and ammunition were accumulated. The native militia enthusiastically joined the service of the Knights, and were carefully trained to the handling of weapons preparatory to the arrival of the enemy. Thus, when the Turks made their appearance, the Grand Master had at his command a force of about nine thousand men, well prepared to meet them. Nearly six hundred of this number were Knights proper, full members of the Order of St. John. These latter had been trained from boyhood to the use of warlike weapons, and each man was equal to a score of ordinary soldiers, as organized in those days. Still, it must have been an anxious occasion among the Christians and their allies, the Maltese, especially so to those who remembered the siege of Rhodes. The Ottomans were much more formidable now than they were then. They conquered in 1522. Who could say what would be the result in 1565? The Mohammedans, as usual, vastly outnumbered their opponents;

indeed, it is reported that Solyman declared: "I will send soldiers enough to walk over the bodies of these proud Knights without unsheathing their swords to fight." The Sultan was so confident of victory that all his arrangements were made for the future occupancy and governorship of the Maltese group.

The Grand Master assembled the Knights to an extraordinary meeting. He bade them reconcile themselves with God and with each other, and then prepare to lay down their lives, if necessary, in defense of the faith which they had sworn to shield. All schisms were forgotten, as might naturally be expected. The order, in face of an enemy, was as one individual. After renewing their vows in the most solemn manner, they joined hands and hearts in the great purpose of defense, resolving to inflict dire destruction upon the common enemy. There was no more jealousy or rivalry between individuals of the order, except as to which should exhibit the greatest and most effective bravery upon the ramparts, or on the occasion of a sortie. This spirit of chivalrous emulation among the Knights cost the enemy daily many scores of lives.

Thus began one of the most sanguinary sieges ever recorded in history. It lasted for nearly four months, and was characterized by unrelenting desperation on both sides, reviving again the bloody scenes which were enacted at Jerusalem, Acre, and Rhodes. The thirty-five years which had transpired since the Knights took possession of Malta had been largely devoted to strengthening their means of defense, and in supplying their armory with the most effective death-dealing weapons. The present site of Valletta, it should be remembered, was then simply the bare promontory of Mount Sceberris.

The Grand Master knew every movement of the enemy, through the capable spies whom he maintained at Constantinople, and was promptly informed by them of the sailing of the expedition. The Christian forces, therefore, were in no wise taken by surprise, while the Turks were amazed at the ample preparation evinced in the manner their first onslaught was received, and the terrible slaughter of their forces, while the cheering battle-cry of the Knights of St. John rang ominously in their ears. They could not have hoped to take the Christians wholly unawares, but they had no idea that the Knights were so thoroughly prepared to receive them with stout arms, keen-edged weapons, and an abundance of death-dealing missiles. The invaders had brought siege artillery with them, and after the first assault, from which they had hoped to achieve so much, but in which they were tellingly repulsed, leaving hundreds of their best soldiers dead in the trenches and upon the open field, they resorted to their reserved means of offense. Some of their cannon were of such enormous calibre as to throw stones weighing three hundred pounds. Yet so clumsy was this primitive artillery, and so awkwardly was it served, that it often inflicted more destruction on the Turkish gunners themselves than on the Christians.

The struggle raged fiercely day by day, and the victims were reckoned by hundreds among the enemy every twenty-four hours. The carnage among the besiegers was awful. Their close ranks were mowed down by the Knights, as grass falls before the scythe of the husbandman.

When the Ottoman soldiers came in a body, bearing scaling-ladders wherewith to reach the top of the rampart of St. Elmo, and while they were in the most exposed situation, sharp-cornered stones, as heavy as two men could lift, were launched suddenly upon those ascending the ladders, forcing them to the ground, and killing them in large numbers. Boiling pitch was poured upon the upturned faces of the assailants, blinding and agonizing them. Iron hoops bound with cotton thoroughly saturated with gum and gunpowder were set on fire, and so thrown as to encircle the heads of three or four of the enemy, binding them together in a fiery circle which they could not extinguish, and which burned them fatally before they reached the ground below. Many other horribly destructive and fatal devices were adopted by the defenders, which spread death in all directions among the Turks. When one of the enemy succeeded in reaching the top of the ramparts, he was instantly met by a Knight, whose keen battle-axe severed his head from the body, both head and body tumbling back into the ditch among the assailants. Still, the indomitable Ottomans renewed their attacks from day to day, hoping to carry the fort at last by exhausting the physical endurance of the defenders, though it should cost ten Mussulmans' lives for one Christian. Each time they marched to the assault, the death-dealing rocks, the boiling pitch, and the fiery hoops did their terrible work, in connection with the ordinary weapons of war, in the use of which the Knights were so expert. It is said that in the hands of a powerful man familiar with it, no weapon is so destructive at close quarters as the broad-bladed, keen-edged battle-axe of those days. The Orientals depended almost solely upon their crude firearms,—the blunderbuss,—together with their light swords and spears.

Early in the siege of which we are speaking, the commander of the Mohammedan army resorted energetically to mining, in furtherance of their attack upon Fort St. Elmo, but the Knights were no novices at counter mining. On one occasion the Turkish engineers had sprung a device of this sort so near to the defensive bastions as to make a wide breach in the stout walls. This was not unexpected by the Knights, who had, in fact, been on the watch for just such an opportunity. Hardly had the shower of the debris ceased to fall, before the enemy rushed forward to enter the fort by the newly made breach. The turbaned throng, a thousand men and more, with waving banners and upraised swords, crowded together upon the spot, little heeding what was to follow. And yet there was a moment's pause, a moment of utter silence, as though those soldiers of the crescent instinctively waited for something to happen, they knew not what. It was like the awful stillness which precedes the hurricane at sea. The moment this pause occurred, the Knights sprung a well-prepared mine beneath the very feet of the densely crowded body of the enemy, blowing nearly two thirds of their immediate assailants to instant death! Seven hundred Turks are said to have lost their lives at that terribly fatal explosion, as though struck by lightning. The whole Ottoman force rapidly withdrew in utter confusion and amazement.

The moral effect of this frightful catastrophe to their army led to quiet in the Turkish camp for several days, though it did not fail to create among the invaders a spirit of revenge which amounted almost to madness.

Jean de La Vallette, Grand Master of the order, was well fitted for his position in this great emergency. He was seen everywhere, even in the thickest of the fight, praising the valor of the Knights and leading the most hardy. Though he was gray with age, being threescore years and ten, still his practiced arm was stout and able to wield the terrible battle-axe with dire effect. He had always been famous for his expertness with this weapon. He was the *beau idéal* of the soldier-monk, and the true embodiment of a spirit of chivalry which was fast passing away. At this special time his experience was of the greatest advantage, and his judgment was always sound. Having once been a captive among the Turks for a considerable period, he knew their mode of warfare, and spoke their language. Though stern and inflexible in character, and often charged with cruelty, he is represented to have been always just, and devoutly religious. To his skill, courage, and iron will, together with a spirit of tireless energy, more than aught else, the Ottomans owed their final defeat. His very name has become a synonym with the Maltese for genius, piety, and courage.

It is true that on the closing days of the siege, the Knights of St. John were joined by long-delayed reinforcements sent from Italy, but so far as we can discover, these fresh troops were not called upon to go into action with the enemy. The siege was virtually already at an end when they arrived upon the scene. The Turkish army had suffered beyond all precedent. Three quarters of their number had laid down their lives in this sanguinary and useless siege. The fort of St. Elmo had finally been captured by the enemy, but forts St. Angelo and St. Michael still remained intact. These forts were also stormed again and again, but the now weary and disheartened Ottomans were repulsed each time with awful slaughter. At last, when it became known that reinforcements sent to the Knights had actually landed upon another part of the island, Mustafa Pasha was compelled to order the galleys to prepare to sail for Constantinople with the small and shattered remnant of his army. Further prosecution of the siege was out of the question, and those of the Turkish army still left alive, struck by a panic, threw away their arms, and fled toward the galleys.

In this hasty and demoralized retreat of the enemy, the Knights saw their chance for an effective dash; so getting a few score of cavalry together, until now inoperative, they fell upon the rear of the fleeing Turks and slaughtered them in large numbers, while many were driven pellmell into the sea, where they were quickly drowned.

While the siege was in active progress, all Europe was anxiously watching the struggle, and when it closed with such decided results, and with the utter discomfiture of the Ottoman power, Europe rejoiced. In Rome (as well as in many other capitals), the ancient city was illumined, and salutes were fired from the fortress of St. Angelo, on the banks of the Tiber, while a thanksgiving mass was celebrated in all the churches. Pope Pius IV., as a special mark of his favor, offered La Vallette a cardinal's hat; but the hero of Malta considered his position far more elevated than that of a cardinal, and graciously declined the honor.

CHAPTER XVI.

Result of the Siege.—Native Women serving as Soldiers.—The Maltese Militia.—The Knights gain World-Wide Applause.— Rage of Sultan Solyman.— Agents of the Grand Master become Incendiaries.—La Vallette, Hero of the Siege.— The Order still Piratical.—The Turks and Knights Affiliate.—Decadence of the Chivalric Brotherhood.—Momentary Revival of the Old Spirit.—Treacherous Surrender.—French Sovereignty.—End of the Order.

Many interesting considerations suggest themselves in connection with this remarkable siege. The lack of discipline which characterizes Oriental soldiery was an element constantly operating against the assailants. Had the siege opened on true engineering and military principles, such an enormous and well-armed number of Turkish fighters must have overwhelmed the Christians at the very outset. This, however, was not the case. The siege seems to have been a series of blunders on the part of the Ottomans from the beginning until the end, or at least until the arrival of Admiral Dragut, who took partial command and gave the operations the benefit of his great military experience. Henceforth something like order and system were evolved from the utter confusion which reigned supreme in the Turkish army.

The vast number of the Ottoman forces, compared with that of the defenders of Malta, only served to emphasize their final and utter defeat. True, there is a great difference between contending parties when one is fighting in the open, while the other is protected by well-constructed walls of stone, but the Turkish commander, though foolhardy, was not blind, and he must have taken that into consideration when he made his opening and reckless attack upon the stronghold of Fort St. Elmo. It is quite possible that excessive numbers may prove an element of disaster, under certain circumstances. This was exactly the case in the first onslaught of the Ottomans, who came to the attack almost in a solid body,—a mere reckless, over-confident mob,— relying upon their numbers rather than upon any appropriate tactics. In after assaults more discipline was adopted and observed. The forces were divided so as to attack various points simultaneously, while a heavy reserve was held well in hand to launch upon the point where any temporary success disclosed a weakness in the defenses. The enemy had learned a bitter lesson by experience; that vain, ill-conceived attack at the opening of the siege having cost them between three and four thousand of their best soldiers. The bodies of these men who were slain before the stout walls of St. Elmo lay unburied for days in the trenches and approaches to the fort, creating a terrible stench, which caused a fever to break out in the Turkish camp, nearly as fatal to them as the missiles and battle-axes of the Knights.

During the progress of the siege the Maltese women not only tended the sick and wounded, but constantly served refreshments to those who could not leave their posts of duty. They also transported the wounded upon stretchers to the hospitals, and brought powder, shot, and rocks, to aid the defenders upon the ramparts. Though many of them were killed and others wounded while thus engaged, they bravely continued their important services to the last. One historian says that twice when the Turkish shot had cut down the red banner of St. John, with its eight-pointed cross of white, it was a Maltese woman who instantly rushed to the exposed point and raised it again over the ramparts, where stout and ready hands once more secured it in position.

It is a notable circumstance that the native population, though so clearly Arabic in their origin, manners, and customs, have never, so far as we know, sympathized with the Mohammedans.

Further details of this memorable siege would but weary the reader. Suffice it to say that the final defeat of the Turks showed them to have lost, since they had landed in Malta, thirty thousand men killed, besides hordes of wounded left unfit for future service. Of the Knights and their auxiliaries, who aggregated, as will be remembered, about nine thousand fighting men, only six hundred remained capable of bearing arms! The Maltese militia, so say contemporary writers, proved to be effective soldiers, numbering about three thousand men at the beginning of the conflict, but they were nearly all destroyed during the protracted siege. They were amphibious fighters, sometimes leaping into the sea, holding their swords in their teeth, and successfully attacking the Turks from this element in which they were so much at home. They aided most materially in the general result, and indeed, but for their gallant services, the Knights could not have held out to the close, when the reinforcements arrived.

This decisive victory gained over the Ottoman power was not alone of great significance to the Order of St. John, but it was of immense importance to all the dwellers in the Mediterranean ports west of the Levant, relieving the several exposed nationalities from the fear of predatory visits of Turkish or Algerine galleys. These notorious corsairs had for centuries made the great inland sea the terror of all honest seamen, seriously crippling its commerce. But at the siege of St. Elmo the most daring leader of the pirates had lost his life, and his followers were no more to be feared, at least for a considerable period. By their brave and successful defense of Malta, the Knights permanently fixed the boundary of the Ottoman power, so far as regarded its possible extension westward. Up to this time, Solyman II., like his father, called the "Magnificent," had his eyes fixed on Europe, the eventual conquest of which they both boldly resolved upon, but the tide of successful warfare in that direction was now stayed. Advance upon the Christian powers was quite impossible, while there remained upon their flank and rear so efficient and implacable an enemy as the Knights of Malta.

The admiration and gratitude of the Christian world at large were manifested by liberal donations from all quarters to swell the depleted treasury of the order, while earnest and able aspirants hastened to join its ranks. The Knights, by their display of indomitable courage and prowess in war, justly won the name of the heroes of Christendom. They were men, as we have seen, of whose morality the less said the better, but who as soldiers merited their unrivaled reputation.

The rage of Sultan Solyman at the complete defeat of his army and the return of his unsuccessful general was terrible. He immediately resolved to gather another army and flotilla, with which to conquer Malta, to lead this expedition himself, and to take with him a hundred thousand soldiers to insure victory. Preparations were accordingly begun in the great arsenal of Constantinople by collecting arms and ammunition for the carrying out of this purpose, especially including the storage of large quantities of gunpowder. When this had progressed for a few months, La Vallette was informed of the object by his well-paid spies in the Turkish capital. The Knights could not withstand another siege. Their ranks had been so thinned as to leave only a skeleton organization, and the outlook for them was indeed desperate. The Grand Master knew that he could no longer hope to oppose force to force successfully, and that other and effective means must be promptly adopted to cripple and discourage the persistent enemy. La Vallette secretly instructed his unscrupulous spies to fire the arsenal of Constantinople, promising a grand premium if success followed the attempt. This was done. Large stores of powder had already been gathered here for the expedition; and its explosion destroyed not only the arsenal itself, with its store of arms and equipments, but also wrecked the entire fleet, which was being equipped close at hand. The instant destruction of human life, as well as of war materials, was enormous, so great, in fact, that the expedition was necessarily abandoned for the time being. The death of the Sultan of Turkey soon followed the blowing up of the arsenal, thus preventing any renewal of the design against the order.

The successful defense of Malta proved to be the last great feat of arms achieved by the Knights of St. John. They had completely broken the Ottoman power, so far as aggressive operations were concerned. There was now no active enemy with whom they were called upon to contend. Rest and recuperation would seem to be absolutely necessary after the terrible strain which had been put upon their endurance; and they had most certainly earned the right to enjoy such a respite. Of the Grand Master, La Vallette, it is recorded that, during the heat of action, when the Turks were storming the walls and his battle-axe was spreading death right and left, his associate Knights besought him not to so expose his life. It was then that he replied: "How can I, at my age of seventy-one years, die more gloriously than in the midst of my brothers, in the service of God, and in defense of our holy religion?" He was the soldier-monk par excellence, possessing grand physical powers, devoutly pious according to his creed, and a grand example of chivalry. It is not too much to say that it was his hand that hurled back the shattered and riven power of the Turks. Age had not withered his ambition or enterprise. He resolved to build at once a new and thoroughly fortified city by the shore, on the promontory of Mount Sceberris, the present site of Valletta, and to remove the capital of the island to the coast. The outcome of this purpose is the beautiful city which we have already described, in the erection and fortification of which the order reached the acme of its defensive purposes. It may be truly said that they were at last fully prepared and able to repulse any force which could possibly be brought against them, and the universal knowledge that this was so prevented any further attempt at molestation.

The galleys of the Knights of St. John still roamed the seas in search of prizes, and woe betide any craft which they encountered sailing under the Turkish flag. It is said that a careful discrimination was not always exercised as to the nationality of the vessels which they attacked. Other craft than Turkish were often seized and pilfered, under some specious pretext, especially if they were Grecian. The galleys of that people, it must be frankly admitted, were mostly of a piratical character.

The rapidity with which the Knights recovered from their late almost hopeless condition was marvelous. A large and thoroughly fortified city seemed to spring into existence as though by magic. To accomplish this, vast sums of money were required, and the principal sovereigns of Europe vied with each other in their gratitude, as to which should most liberally contribute means for the use of the order in Malta. The Valletta of our day, however, was not actually completed until some twenty-five years later.

While Emmanuel Pinto was Grand Master of the order, in 1741, the King of Sicily attempted to establish a claim upon these islands, and sent a select council to preside over its government. These officials, who came hither in great state, were summarily dismissed and sent back to Sicily by the Grand Master. The king in retaliation closed all the ports of Sicily against Maltese vessels. This was a serious matter to the latter, as the group depended upon that country for a large portion of its food supply, especially in grain. To meet this exigency, the Grand Master entered into a treaty with the old foes of the order, namely, the Turks, who gladly accepted a proposal which afforded them a respite from warfare with so active an enemy, and also enabled them, for the time being, to sell supplies to the people of the Maltese group. They joined the Knights also in an offensive marine warfare against the Sicilians, and soon caused the king of that country to regret the step he had taken against the Knights of St. John. After he had lost many vessels to the Knights and Turks combined, he humbly sued for peace, and made such ample reparation as was demanded of him for the needless war which he had caused.

Looking at the current of events from our own standpoint, and through the distance of time, it would seem that the Knights must have found it a rather uncongenial business to fight a so-called Christian power, side by side with their life-long enemies, the infidel Turks. True, it was but a temporary union, the object of which having been accomplished, the old spirit of enmity between the Knights and the Ottomans was resumed, and found expression in an immediate renewal of hostilities.

From this period the glory of the Knights of St. John seems to have gradually waned. Their religious zeal and simplicity of living had long since departed. Is not all growth toward ripeness also toward decay, unless directed heavenward? There was no longer any violent opposition to overcome by energetic action and self-abnegation, no enemy with arms in his hands whom they must conquer. The one power whom they had always antagonized was comparatively exhausted and undemonstrative. True manhood feeds upon—is supported by—antagonism, and opposition is the spur to heroic deeds. The life of constant warfare and the savage use of arms which the

Knights had so long been accustomed to quite over-shadowed their priestly instincts, and as peace now reigned, they sought unholy excitement in various forms, such as were ill-suited to the vows and professions of the order. They now dwelt in sumptuous palaces, lapsing by degrees into utter idleness and libertinism. They had become the richest and most powerful brotherhood in the world. It is true that the outward forms of their religion were observed with more or less regularity, but it was an empty, heartless ceremony. The portraits, still extant, which were painted of them at this period, show that their dress was changed from steel armor and shirt of mail to velvet and gold-wrought fabric, of an effeminate character. Their chivalric impulses had departed. They gave way to the pleasures of the table and to the demoralizing wine-cup. Those who have written of the order understandingly as regards this period tell us that morality was at the lowest ebb with the individual members of the fraternity. In these latter years, joining the organization was the means of providing for a younger brother in titled European families. The order became the resort for libertines who had exhausted all home relations. It was not unusual for men, however dissolute, provided they belonged to the higher ranks, to become Knights of St. John as a final resort, after leading a godless and criminal career.

An instance which occurred so late as 1783 is called to mind, when the Knights, for a brief period, seemed to awaken to the old instincts and professions of their order. It was tidings of the fearfully destructive earthquake in Sicily, happening in that year, which so aroused the fraternity. Manning their galleys, after they had filled them with food, wine, and medicine, they sailed across the sea, and having landed amid widespread desolation, they assumed the rôle of good Samaritans, feeding the hungry, ministering to the sick, and smoothing the pillow of the dying. Thus they once more revived the memory of those grand, unselfish days at Jerusalem, when they were justly renowned and revered as Hospitallers, living up to their vows of poverty, charity, and chastity. This was, however, only the blazing up of dying embers, and the order lapsed once more into luxury and decay.

The final disaster which befell the Knights of St. John, as an organization, came through the medium of treachery, and that, too, of the grossest description, in 1798, when Von Hompesch was the Grand Master. This faithless man, like Bazaine at Metz, proved to be an arch traitor to every trust that had been reposed in him, and won the contempt of all Christendom.

Von Hompesch was a man entirely unfit for such an exigency as then occurred. He was devoid of all firmness or decision of character, and was, indeed, neither priest nor soldier except in name. It seems strange that he should have been chosen to so responsible a situation by his brotherhood, who must have known the man thoroughly. The application of the classic saying is clear: "Whom the gods would destroy, they first make mad." There was evidently considerable discontent under his authority, and rebellious expressions were not wanting. At this distance of time, and with our want of light upon the situation, no satisfactory motive can be adduced for Von Hompesch's treachery and general listlessness. The principal traitors who are known to have been most active in this conspiracy, for conspiracy it was, were the

Knights of the division of Provence, Auvergne, and France, among whom liberal pensions and rewards were freely distributed by the invaders of Malta. It was thus that the French soldiers under Bonaparte obtained ready and easy admittance to the almost impregnable defenses of Valletta, absolute possession being given to them without any real or pretended fighting in their defense. "It was well," said an officer high in command among the invaders, "that some one was within to open the gates for us. We should have found considerable difficulty in entering, if the place had been entirely empty."

French gold and cunning diplomacy, not French valor, opened the way into the well-fortified capital. Three days after the appearance of the French fleet off the harbor, the tricolor was floating over the historic battlements of St. Elmo. The indignation of the native Maltese was so great at this ignominious surrender of the island to the enemy, that the people rose in their anger and assassinated several of the most guilty of the obnoxious members of the Order of St. John.

Bonaparte agreed, by solemn compact duly written and signed, on behalf of his government, with the Grand Master, Von Hompesch, when he gave up the possession of the island to him, that "the inhabitants shall be allowed, as of old, the free exercise of the Roman Catholic religion, their privileges and property shall remain inviolate, and they shall not be subject to any extraordinary tax." This agreement was a mere form on the part of the French, the pledges being all broken within one week from the day on which they were signed.

All Europe was amazed at this blot cast upon the escutcheon of a chivalric brotherhood like that of the Knights, whose record for loyalty to the order and its general purposes had been so gallantly maintained, and at such terrible cost, for so many centuries. To one who recalls the past history of these soldier-priests, such an ending must seem almost incredible. It is impossible not to contrast this shameful surrender with the valorous resistance of the Knights in the terrible siege of 1565, when their blood flowed free as water to sustain the honor of their flag, and to preserve the integrity of their order. The dying of the Knights who formed the forlorn hope of the fort of St. Elmo, one by one fighting at his post until he fell, is one of the grandest and most heroic tableaux known to the annals of history.

The new masters of the Maltese at once banished the traitor Von Hompesch from the island, and perhaps it was necessary in order to save his life, which the native population did not hesitate to threaten openly. He retired to Trieste, after receiving a princely fortune from France. This was in 1799. His death occurred in 1805, at Montpellier, in the sixty-second year of his age. He is dismissed from history, disgraced and forgotten.

The successor of this unknightly leader of the order was the Emperor Paul I., of Russia, who was chosen as a *dernier ressort*. He was solemnly inaugurated, but was never more than nominally Grand Master. His election to the office was so manifestly an incongruous act, that it remained unrecognized. When the French established themselves in Malta, a number of the Knights took refuge in St. Petersburg, and there elected the emperor to the post even before Von Hompesch had formally resigned the office. Paul made several vain attempts to reëstablish the Knights, inviting the nobility of Christendom to enlist in the ranks of the ancient order. Success did not follow his efforts to this end.

The Knights were seen no more in Malta, though up to the arrival of the French they had been sovereign in the islands for two hundred and sixty-eight years. Twenty-eight successive Grand Masters had presided over them here, from L'Isle Adam to Von Hompesch.

The new masters of Malta made themselves odious to the people of the island by their reckless pillage and rapine, so that the French name has ever been held in abhorrence by them. The soldiery invaded the sanctuary of domestic life, and the honor of maid or mother was recklessly sacrificed by brute force to their vile appetite. We have referred in these pages to the faldetta, which is worn by the women of Malta. There is a legend relating to this article of dress which occurs to us in this connection. It is to the effect that after Valletta was seized by the French troops, the women registered a solemn vow that, in memory of the brutal treatment they had received at the hands of the licentious soldiery, they and their descendants should for the period of one hundred years dress in black, whenever they appeared upon the streets, and that all should wear a distinctive hood, which is called the "hood of shame."

The local customs of the Maltese were outraged, and the legal code interfered with, by the French. Among other acts they abolished all titles, altered the laws affecting the tenure of property, and demanded that the sons of rich families should be sent to France for educational purposes. They seemed to try to aggravate the Maltese by petty and needless oppression, until at last, goaded beyond further endurance, especially in matters relating to church affairs, the islanders rose in insurrection, and were joined in their struggle by the English. The fleet of the latter had just arrived at Malta, fresh from the victory of Aboukir, and it heartily seconded the uprising of the Maltese against their oppressors. Without this timely aid they could have made but a feeble struggle for their freedom. The anger of the native population came to a climax when the French soldiery attempted to rifle the old cathedral at Città Vecchia, which was held by them in such special reverence. That ancient temple was to the masses of the islanders what the more modern church of St. John had been to the Knights.

The French invaders were promptly driven within the walls of the fortifications, where they were virtually held as prisoners for the period of two years, submitting to every sort of deprivation, while looking in vain for reinforcements and relief from the government of France. That hoped-for assistance never came. At the close of the second year, the French troops were absolutely starved out, and compelled to surrender to the united English and Maltese. This was effected on honorable terms, the garrison marching out with all the honors of war, the whole force being transported to Marseilles at the expense of the British government. General Vaubois, the soldierly commander whom Bonaparte left in charge of Malta, was a brave and reliable man, and heroically maintained his trust to the very last, when his troops were on the verge of starvation. The English historian says, in relating the circumstances of the surrender: "When the garrison marched out, it was with famine proudly painted on their cheeks."

The siege was raised September 5, 1800, whereupon the English took formal possession of Valletta, together with the entire group, and they have retained it to the present time. They thus became the masters of Malta, but disregarded treaty promises, and refused in 1802, as was duly stipulated, to evacuate, and restore the islands to the Knights of St. John. It was this which occasioned the rupture of the Peace of Amiens. Malta was, however, finally and formally transferred to the possession of England with the approval of the European powers, in 1814, at the treaty of Paris.

Since the year 1798, when the Knights of St. John were expelled from Malta, the ancient order, once so important a factor in the Christian world, has scarcely more than existed in name, though able to point to so proud and warlike a career, extending through a period of seven centuries. Few dynasties of emperors or kings have lasted so long as this famous order of warrior-monks, whose name was once the synonym for loyalty, but whose end was brought about by treachery within its own ranks,—an organization whose members began as paupers, but who ended as sybarites.

# CHAPTER XVII.

Conclusion.—A Picture of Sunrise at Malta.—The Upper Baracca of Valletta.—A Favorite and Sightly Promenade. —Retrospective Flight of Fancy.—Conflict between the Soldiers of the Cross and the Crescent.—A Background Wanting.—Historical and Legendary Malta.—The Secret of Appreciation.—Last View of the Romantic Group.—Farewell.

Travelers in foreign lands learn to rise betimes, stealing from sleep an hour full of intoxicating beauties. There is an interval between the soft mellow light of the breaking day and that of sunrise, so full of promise, of dewy fragrance, and of heavenly incense, that only poets can truly describe it. As one stands upon the upper Baracca of Valletta and faces the east at such a moment, the gradually advancing light seems to melt away the darkness, while angel hands swing wide the golden gates of day. The sky then dons its deepest blue, the encircling sea glows in violet blushes beneath the rosy light of the dawn, while the air, freshened by the dew, is clear and crisp even in this semi-tropical island. At first a dim uncertainty reigns over all things, but slowly the weird and phantom-like forms assume their real shapes. The picturesque town, with its diversified architecture, the tall, isolated lighthouses, the sleeping islands of Gozo and Comino, the delicate tracery formed of the rigging of the ships in the harbor, and even the lonely sentinels upon the battlements come out one by one in bold relief against the background of mingled gold and silver radiance. The heedless world still sleeps, and one cannot but feel half guilty at the selfishness of appropriating alone such an hour of glowing inspiration, while walking hand in hand with Nature.

The Baraccas wore originally roofed, consisting of arches facing the sea, but the wooden coverings were long since removed, and they now form favorite promenades, open to the sky.

Yielding to the fancy of the moment, while standing upon this elevated point, remembering the vivid historical tableaux which had been enacted upon the landscape outspread before us, imagination peopled the scene once more with myriads of grim, warlike, contending forces arrayed against each other. One was closely following the standard of the crescent, the other was ranged beneath the emblem of the cross,—standing breast to breast, ready to meet the fierce onslaught. The clash of arms was heard upon the ramparts, the shrill braying of trumpets sounding the charge, and the steady roll of the drum. In fancy we watched the hordes of frenzied Turks storming the high walls of Fort St. Elmo, hastening up the scaling ladders by scores. We saw them repulsed again and again by the stout arms and flashing weapons of the gallant Knights of St. John; the ditch was piled with the lifeless bodies of the Ottoman foe. The atmosphere trembled with the booming of cannon, the wild shouts of the Mussulmans, the cheering battle-cry of the Christians, and the pitiful groans of the dying, while the surrounding waters were red with human gore. Now clouds of smoke encompass both Turks and Christians. A mine explodes, scattering death among the invaders. Hark! That trumpet sounds the retreat. The Ottoman forces fall sullenly back from before the irresistible power of the Christian arms, leaving half their brethren slain upon the ground. The enemy goes down under the terrible sweeping blows of battle-axe and of mace, like grass before the scythe. Loud rings the shout of victory from the walls of St. Elmo, echoed by forts St. Angelo and St. Michael, while deadly missiles are swiftly launched after the retreating foe.

One was fain to ask, "Is this actually the noise of contending armies, or is it the trick of an overstimulated fancy?" Here, amid such suggestive surroundings, how natural and real it seemed to be!

It is only as regards its great antiquity that one would contrast Malta with our own country. What we are most deficient in is a background in America,—a background to our national scenery, which in itself is hardly equaled, and nowhere excelled. By the word "background" we mean the charm of far-reaching history, legend, classic story, and memories of bygone ages. We have no such special inspiration as is presented in the associations of southern Europe and Asiatic localities,—the Bay of Naples and its surroundings, for instance, or the land of Palestine. America is still in the youth of its civilization, while in this isolated Mediterranean group, so circumscribed in space, we have monuments which may nearly equal the Pyramids in age. These tokens exhibit here a tangible page of Phoenician and there of Punic history, together with ruins of Roman and Grecian temples, besides which there are footprints of many Asiatic tribes. How one's imagination is awakened by the sight of these half-effaced mementos of races dead and buried so long ago! Crumbling ruins are milestones, as it were, on the road of time. What region would not become interesting to an appreciative observer, under such circumstances?

Traveling and sight-seeing, let us remember, are like hospitality, the stranger must freely contribute his share, or the result will surely be naught. "You will find poetry nowhere, unless you bring some with you," says Joubert.

Our last view of the romantic group was under a sky of blue and tranquil loveliness, bathed in a silvery sheen of moonlight, as seen across the azure and limpid waters from the deck of a P. & O. steamship, bound westward to England. We left the harbor of Valletta just at sunset. While the light was fading away, that of the moon and stars was hastening into life. The lofty ramparts overhanging the sea cast purple shadows upon the silent surface of the water. The terraced town stood out in strong relief, here a dome and there a tower overlooking the tall stone warehouses, while the slender tracery of the shipping appeared like spider's webs. The town stood there firm and stately, as though cut out of the solid rock.

Our vessel moved at half-speed until St. Elmo was passed, and before we had fairly laid our course for Gibraltar the clear atmosphere was filled with the floating strains from a military band in St. George's Square. A spirit of rest and peacefulness hung over the picturesque old city of the Knights. Mentally we bade farewell to its curious streets, its palaces and churches, its grim fortifications and teeming population, its beautiful gardens and marvelous antiquities. The cool, delicious fruits and shade of San Antonio lingered in the memory, then Malta, Gozo, and Comino faded into a vignette, until finally the low-lying group dipped into the blue surface of the water and was seen no more.

## BOOKS BY MATURIN M. BALLOU.

**THE STORY OF MALTA**. A New Book. Crown 8vo, $1.50.
A description of the island of Malta, its history, scenery, and inhabitants.

**EQUATORIAL AMERICA**; descriptive of a Visit to St. Thomas, Martinique, Barbadoes, and the Principal Capitals of South America. Crown 8vo, $1.50.

> Nothing worth seeing seems to escape his eye, while all that would delight others to know is portrayed in a rich, graphic style.—*New York Observer.*

**AZTEC LAND**. Crown 8vo, $1.50.

> Mr. Ballou has made an excellent book out of his visit to Mexico. He furnishes what everybody desires to know, and what is not elsewhere accessible in a single volume.—*Boston Herald.*

**ALASKA: THE NEW ELDORADO**. A Summer Journey to Alaska. Crown 8vo, $1.50. *Tourists' Edition.* With 4 Maps. 16mo, $1.00.

> A charming book of travel, full of information concerning our great northwestern territory.—*Boston Budget.*

**DUE WEST**; or, ROUND THE WORLD IN TEN MONTHS. Crown 8vo, $1.50.

> It is a book of books on foreign travel.—*Boston Commonwealth.*

**DUE SOUTH**; or, CUBA PAST AND PRESENT. Crown 8vo, $1.50.

> Full of information concerning the Bahama Islands, the Caribbean Sea, and the island of Cuba.... Mr. Ballou is the

ideal traveler.—*Boston Traveller.*

**DUE NORTH**; or, GLIMPSES OF SCANDINAVIA AND RUSSIA. Crown 8vo, $1.50.

> It is as useful to read him as it is enjoyable to travel with him.—*Journal of Education* (Boston).

**UNDER THE SOUTHERN CROSS**; or, TRAVELS IN AUSTRALASIA. Crown 8vo, $1.50.

> Few persons have traveled so extensively, and no one more profitably, both to himself and the public, than Mr. Ballou.—EDWIN P. WHIPPLE.

## EDITED BY MR. BALLOU.

**A TREASURY OF THOUGHT.** An Encyclopaedia of Quotations from Ancient and Modern Authors. 8vo, full gilt, $3.50; half calf or half morocco, $6.00.

> The most complete and exhaustive volume of the kind with
> which we are acquainted. The literature of all times has
> contributed to it, and the range of reading necessary to its
> compilation is the widest.—*Hartford Courant.*

**NOTABLE THOUGHTS ABOUT WOMEN.** A Literary Mosaic. Crown 8vo, $1.50.

> Full of delicious bits from nearly every writer of any
> celebrity, English, American, French, or German, early and
> modern, it is a fascinating medley. When one takes up the
> book it is difficult to lay it down, for one is led on from
> one brilliant or striking thought to another, in a way that
> is quite absorbing.—*Portland Transcript.*

**PEARLS OF THOUGHT.** Choice Sentences from the Wisest Authors. 16mo, full gilt, $1.25; half morocco, $2.50.

> The first noticeable thing about "Pearls of Thought" is that
> the "pearls" are offered in a jewel-box of printing and
> binding. The selections have the merit of being short and
> sparkling. Authors ancient and modern, and of all nations,
> are represented.—*New York Tribune.*

**EDGE-TOOLS OF SPEECH.** Crown 8vo, $3.50; half calf or half morocco, $6.00.

> A remarkable compilation of brilliant and wise sayings from
> more than a thousand various sources, embracing all the
> notable authors, classic and modern, who have enriched the

pages of history and literature. It might be termed a whole library in one volume.—*Boston Beacon.*

**GENIUS IN SUNSHINE AND SHADOW**. Crown 8vo, $1.50.

Mr. Ballou displays a broad and thorough knowledge of men of genius in all ages, and the comprehensive index makes the volume invaluable as a book of reference, while—a rare thing in reference books—it is thoroughly interesting for consecutive reading.— *The Journalist* (New York).

\*\*\* *For sale by all Booksellers. Sent, post-paid, on receipt of price by the Publishers,*

*HOUGHTON, MIFFLIN AND COMPANY,*
*4 Park St., Boston; 11 East 17th St., New York.*

## GUIDE BOOKS.

**NEW ENGLAND.** A Handbook for Travelers. A Guide to the Chief Cities and Popular Resorts of New England, and to its Scenery and Historic Attractions. With the Western and Northern Borders from New York to Quebec. With 6 Maps and 11 Plans. 13th Edition, revised and enlarged annually. 16mo, $1.50.

> It is a small compact volume, with maps and plans and tours; with history condensed, and such illustrations as make it a constant help and pleasure to the tourist. It is admirably put together, and is a vast labor-saving guide for one who wishes to know what to see and what he is seeing.—Rev. Dr. PRIME, in *New York Observer.*

**THE WHITE MOUNTAINS.** A Handbook for Travelers. A Guide to the Peaks, Passes, and Ravines of the White Mountains of New Hampshire, and to the Adjacent Railroads, Highways, and Villages; with the Lakes and Mountains of Western Maine, also Lake Winnepesaukee and the Upper Connecticut Valley. With 6 Maps and 6 Panoramas, including the new Appalachian Club Map. 12th Edition, revised and enlarged annually. 16mo, $1.50.

> Worthy of rank with the best books of its kind. It is complete and exhaustive, its information is exact, and its maps are voluminous. It is not only a good thing for a satchel, but deserves a place in the library.—*Outing* (New York).

**THE MARITIME PROVINCES.** A Handbook for Travelers. A Guide to the Chief Cities, Coasts, and Islands of the Maritime Provinces of Canada, and to their Scenery and Historic Attractions; with the Gulf and River of St. Lawrence to Quebec and Montreal; also, Newfoundland, and the Labrador Coast. With 4 Maps and 4 Plans. 9th Edition, revised and enlarged annually. 16mo, $1.50.

> By its intrinsic value, copiousness of information, and impartiality it is likely to take the place of all other guides or hand-books of Canada which we know of.—*Quebec Chronicle.*

> You should take a good guide-book (Sweetser's Maritime
> Provinces is by far the best—containing *everything* about
> the various parts of the Provinces).—*British American
> Citizen.*

**DICTIONARY OF BOSTON.** By EDWIN M. BACON. New Edition, revised. With Introduction by GEORGE E. ELLIS, D. D., and Map. 12mo, flexible cloth, $1.50; boards, $1.00.

> One cannot conceive of a more handy book of its kind. For a
> long time just such a compendious volume, with just such
> concisely and authoritatively written articles, has been
> needed.... It is a cyclopaedia of the Boston of to-day,
> interesting and necessary to every Bostonian.—*Boston
> Advertiser.*

**BOSTON ILLUSTRATED.** An Artistic and Pictorial Description of Boston and its Surroundings. Containing full descriptions of the City and its immediate Suburbs, Harbor, and Islands, etc., with numerous Historical Allusions. New Edition, by EDWARD M. BACON, revised to date, and containing additional Illustrations and Map. 12mo, paper, 50 cents.

> The aim has been to present much information in small
> compass; to make a ready reference book as well as a handy
> pocket guide.

**SATCHEL GUIDE.** For the Vacation Tourist in Europe. Annual Edition, revised to date, with additions, and printed from new Plates. A compact Itinerary of the British Isles, Belgium, and Holland, Germany and the Rhine, Switzerland, France, Austria, and Italy. With Maps of Great Britain and Ireland, Continental Europe, Switzerland, Street Plans of London and Paris, Tables of the Comparative Values of United States and European Moneys, a Traveler's Calendar of Ecclesiastical and Popular Festivals, Fairs, etc. 16mo, roan, flexible, $1.50, *net.*

> The book is indeed a model of perspicacity and brevity; all

the advice it gives will be found of immediate service. The "Satchel Guide" tells the reader *how to travel cheaply without a sacrifice of comfort*, and this feature of the book will recommend it to many tourists.—*Pall Mall Gazette.*

No voyager to Europe for the first time should fail to take the "Satchel Guide" with him.... The work stands approved by long experience.—*New York Evening Post.*

It will prove an invaluable companion to any one who wishes to travel quickly, economically, and to the best advantage.—*New York Tribune.*

It is the first book we should put in the hands of one going abroad, with an assurance that it might be implicitly trusted.—*Boston Transcript.*

*HOUGHTON, MIFFLIN AND COMPANY,*
*4 Park St., Boston; 11 East 17th St., New York.*

**Note on the Text:**

Inconsistent hyphenation and spelling in the original document have been preserved.

Minor typographical errors have been corrected without comment.

Lightning Source UK Ltd.
Milton Keynes UK
UKOW021418260911

179305UK00002B/200/P